CASE CONCEPTUALIZATION

A BIBLICAL WELLNESS (B-WELL) APPROACH

DAVID JONES | KEN MILLER | KEVIN HULL

Kendall Hunt
publishing company

Contents

CHAPTER 1

About This Book

David E. Jones

> "The road goes ever on and on down from the door where it began.
> Now far ahead the road has gone, and I must follow, if I can."
>
> — Bilbo Baggins
>
> "Do not forsake wisdom, and she will protect you; love her, and she will
> watch over you. Wisdom is supreme; therefore, get wisdom. Though it
> cost all you have, get understanding."
>
> Proverbs 4:6-7 (NIV)

Book Overview

This book is developed in a stepwise progression for students and counseling practitioners. The book begins by establishing a clear understanding of wellness and then provides an overview of biblical worldview essentials. After offering these two foundations—wellness and biblical perspective—an integrated biblical wellness model is delivered, the **Biblical Wellness (B-Well) model**. Next, case conceptualization (CC) is addressed. It is here that you will gain an understanding of the CC process and how to use the B-Well model in that process. Finally, the last chapters deliver an application of the B-Well model by specific theory by counseling discipline— school counseling, clinical mental health counseling, addiction counseling, pastoral counseling, marriage and family counseling, and special populations—using theories such as solution-focused, cognitive behavioral, acceptance and commitment therapy, Adlerian, psychodynamic, family systems, play therapy, and others.

Who Should Read This Book?

This book is intended for students, counselors, counselor educators, and other helping profession-als who desire to operate from wellness and a Christian worldview when conducting a clinical case conceptualization. This book seeks to offer the student, practitioner, and educator a coherent case conceptualization process by bridging the gap between wellness and a Christian worldview.

Rationale and Purpose of This Book

This book was created to attend to the current clinical "gap" in the field of counseling and bibli-cal counseling, which is a lack of a coherent, integrated case conceptualization (CC) model that joins a wellness-based lens and a Christian worldview. Currently, in Christian counseling training programs, there is a dividing wall between wellness, Christian integration, and the clinical process. At best there is an "ad hoc" process of appending a Christian integration component to the CC process that lacks clear integration of wellness, counseling theory, and a biblical worldview. This leaves students and practitioners in a quandary on how to effectively integrate wellness, much less a biblical worldview, into the process of assessment, diagnosis, case conceptualization, and treatment planning. This, in turn, raises the question of student and practitioners' competencies to ethically operate from wellness and a biblical worldview. We, therefore, offer a path for ethical practice through the B-Well model.

Beyond the perceived "gap," there are several professional standards that call for wellness and religion/spirituality integration in the counseling field. One of the first is the Council for Accreditation of Counseling and Related Educational Programs (CACREP, n.d.a) which is an accrediting body for the field of counseling. We see the following CACREP values aligning with this book's aims: (1) advancing the field of counseling through exemplary preparation for counselors, (2) protecting the public such as our clients, (3) attending to openness towards growth, and (4) addressing client diversity and best practices.

Besides these overarching values, CACREP standards (n.d.b) apply to our work. One of the first is Section 2: Professional Counseling Identity Foundation, B.1., "Reflect current knowledge and projected needs concerning counseling practice in a multicultural and pluralistic society." Our work addresses the wellness/Christian integration gap, and therefore, it attends to this call for multicultural counseling practice. Section 2: Counseling Curriculum, F.2.g, "The impact of spiritual beliefs on clients' and counselors' worldviews," is another relevant section. The B-Well model offers a place for the therapist to adhere to the client's worldview if the client is a "Christian" and to recognize their own spiritual beliefs that influence the case conceptualization process and treatment. We also see our work connecting with 3.i, Human Growth and Development, "Ethical and culturally relevant strategies for promoting resilience and optimum development and wellness across the lifespan." By advancing the understanding and application of wellness, the student and practitioner can use the B-Well model to promote optimal development and recovery in a client. Because the B-Well model uses a holistic view of the client that includes their age, stage of development, contextual factors, and influences over time, it offers an organized approach to address developmental concerns and assets. Finally, standard 5.n under Section 2: Counseling and Helping Relationships, "Processes for aiding students in developing a personal model of counseling," is relevant because the student and the practitioner can develop and apply a coherent model of counseling for those who desire to operate from wellness and a biblical model through the B-Well model.

Besides the CACREP standards (n.d.b), the Association for Spiritual, Ethical, and Religious Values in Counseling (ASERVIC, 2009) calls for the counselor to be able to do the following:

- Recognize the value of a client's belief system as a salutary effect;
- Be able to effectively assess the client's religion and spirituality (R/S);
- Understand and apply the R/S constructs, themes, underlying effects, and influences; and
- Offer client goals that align with the client's R/S factors.

When working with Christian clients, the B-Well model attends to each of these ASERVIC competencies above. It inherently offers a holistic model that values a biblical worldview. It recognizes the salutary effects of wellness and the Christian worldview by using a common biblical framework. Additionally, it provides a communication bridge between the counselor and client that allows for conceptualizing the client's problems and assets to establish collaborative goals that include R/S factors.

There are also counseling ethical codes and standards that support R/S. The American Counseling Association (ACA) has developed a code of ethics for the counseling profession (ACA, 2014). In the first paragraph of the preamble, attention is drawn to the importance of both diversity and wellness. Later in Section C.5 Professional Responsibility: Nondiscrimination, it states counselors do not engage in or allow discriminatory actions in the area of R/S. Further, in Section E.8 Evaluation, Assessment, and Interpretation: Multicultural Issues/Diversity in Assessment, the authors call for counselors to understand the effects of R/S in the area of assessment and the potential bias in process and results. These codes provide evident support for a B-Well model approach to adhere to wellness, a foundation of counseling, and client diversity, which includes Christianity, in all areas of the counseling process.

The Marriage and Family Counseling profession has its own ethical standards established by the American Association for Marriage and Family Therapy (AAMFT, 2015). When reviewing the fourth of their Aspirational Core Values, the MF therapist is directed to "Diversity, equity and excellence in clinical practice, research, education and administration." We perceive the B-Well model offers a path for the MF therapist to advance this call by attending to the "diversity" of Christian clients by offering a holistic model that attends to all aspects of the client—Heart, Mind, Strength, Soul, Neighbor, and Society.

Addiction counselors may follow the ACA code of ethics (2014) but also have the National Association for Alcoholism and Drug Abuse Counselors (NAADAC, 2021) ethical codes. In code I-21, the addiction counselor "shall recognize that each client is entitled to the full extent of physical, social, psychological, spiritual, and emotional care required to meet their [client's] needs." This ethical mandate can be achieved via the B-Well model due to its holistic approach that attends to each of the mentioned facets of a client (e.g., physical, social, psychological, spiritual, and emotional).

The American School Counseling Association (ASCA) ethics standards (2022) also provide support for R/S and wellness. According to the preamble, a student is to be treated with respect and dignity and offered support that is inclusive of all backgrounds, which includes "religious/spiritual identity" (bullet point four). R/S is also noted in A.6.e, Appropriate Collaboration, Advocacy and Referrals for Counseling, regarding respecting a student's R/S. In Section A.5.a, Sustaining Healthy Relationships and Managing Boundaries, the school counselor is called to "foster wellness" with students. In B.3.h, Responsibilities to Self, the school counselor is to attend to their own wellness. The B-Well model, due to its holistic model approach, gives the school counselor a bridge when working with students who adhere to a Christian worldview for attending to both R/S and wellness in a way that offers not only a respectful approach but also one that can be applied in program development.

The national counseling honor society, *Chi Sigma Iota* or CSI, has a strong stance for the use of wellness in counseling. In 2019, CSI delivered a wellness position paper in which the authors stated, "Wellness [is] to be recognized, promoted and practiced as a defining attribute of professional counselor identity" (para. 1). Though this is seen as a foundation of the counseling profession, the authors also state,

> However, the broad recognition of wellness as a defining characteristic of professional counseling and the value of wellness in counseling clinical practice and research are being lost in the absence of a deliberate, articulated plan and advocates for wellness counseling by counselors per se. (para. 1)

Our effort is to advocate for and renew wellness by providing a clear connection of wellness within the case conceptualization process as this is currently lacking in other textbooks available to students, educators, and practitioners.

Finally, it has been reported that counselors do not feel prepared to address spiritual and religious issues (Henriksen et al., 2015). Through our work here, we aim to provide the reader with a biblical wellness framework to assist the counselor in achieving ethical and competent work with their clients.

© David E. Jones

Dr. David "Dj" Jones, EdD, MPH, LPC (OH), NCC is a licensed professional counselor who maintains a private counseling practice and is an Associate Professor in the Department of Counselor Education and Family Studies at Liberty University in Lynchburg, Virginia. Dr. Jones completed his doctorate in counselor education at the University of Cincinnati (UC), his Master of Arts at Cincinnati Christian University (CCU), and his master's in public health at the University of Alabama, Birmingham (UAB). His Master of Arts in counseling provided him with unique training by requiring an additional 30+ hours in seminary where he developed a solid foundation in Christian theology. Before working as a full-time faculty member, Dr. Jones worked with individuals, couples, and families, across the lifespan, and in a variety of settings (K-12, private practice, hospital, community agency, and church). Dr. Jones has published over 15 articles in peer-reviewed journals, newsletters, technical reports, and state guidelines. He has presented over 35 times at the national, regional, state, and local levels. He has developed a teaching specialization in theories and case conceptualization, which he uses across courses such as counseling theories, practicum, internship, human development, and multicultural counseling. Dr. Jones lives near Cincinnati, Ohio with his wife, Kate, their two children, Seth and Cora, and his dog, Percy. When not diving into the world of counseling, Dr. Jones enjoys family time, camping, hiking, reading, and grilling.

© Ken Miller

Dr. Ken Miller, PhD, MDiv, NCC is an Assistant Professor in the Department of Counselor Education and Family Studies at Liberty University. Dr. Miller teaches research and program evaluation, basic counseling skills and techniques, practicum, internship, assessments in counseling, and human sexuality. Before Dr. Miller joined academia, he attended Southwestern Baptist Theological Seminary and then pastored churches for 19 years in Oklahoma, Virginia, and Georgia while developing a keen understanding of pastoral counseling. Dr. Miller's clinical mental health counseling experience spans the suburbs and Fourth Ward of Atlanta. He has served in both pastoral and clinical counseling roles, domestically and internationally. He is currently part of a non-profit counseling agency that focuses on Victims of Crime and Abuse (VOCA) clients. Dr. Miller provides consultation to local government community mental health initiatives and to churches seeking to incorporate biblical wellness into their discipleship process. He conducts guest lectures at state colleges and has presented at state and international conferences. He is a member of the American Counseling Association (ACA) and the American Association of Christian Counselors (AACC). Dr. Miller lives near Atlanta, Georgia, with Michelle, his wife of thirty-five years. They have two grown daughters and two grandsons. He enjoys hiking, fishing, cooking, golfing, and working around the house.

© Kevin B. Hull

Dr. Kevin B. Hull, PhD, LMHC, RPT, CGP owns and operates Hull and Associates, P.A., a private practice in Lakeland, Florida. Dr. Hull is a licensed counselor who has worked with children and adolescents and their families on the Autism spectrum since 2001. He is a Registered Play Therapist and Certified Group Psychotherapist, and he conducts weekly individual and group therapy sessions with children, adolescents, young adults, and families. Dr. Hull has been a professor for 19 years and is currently a core faculty Associate Professor with Liberty University. Dr. Hull has published several books related to his work with play therapy and Autism Spectrum Disorders as well as several chapters for textbooks and journal articles. Dr. Hull specializes in using electronic devices in group and individual play therapy, and his dissertation work examined the use of video/computer games as a play therapy tool with children with emotional difficulties. Dr. Hull enjoys open water endurance swimming in the Gulf of Mexico, playing golf, long walks, biking, and spending time with his wife, Wendy, and their four children.

Contributors

© Deborah Braboy

Dr. Deborah Braboy, PhD, LPC-S, NCC is an Assistant Professor with Liberty University in the Clinical Mental Health Counseling program. She is also a licensed professional counselor/supervisor (LPC-S) in both Arkansas and Oklahoma, a Life Coach, a writer, and most recently, a podcaster. She is a National Board Certified Counselor and an approved supervisor and is certified in EMDR. As a professional counselor at her Anchored Hope Counseling practice, she primarily sees clients with grief and trauma histories. She has worked in community mental health, school-based counseling, and now private practice for the past 16 years. Her training in EMDR helps clients move through and past their trauma. She has been using telehealth to serve clients since 2017. She enjoys her work as a Life Coach with female physicians—"Dr. Deb for Drs"—particularly with assisting this unique group of clients in avoiding burnout and impairment through the global pandemic. Dr. Braboy's clinical interests include trauma, EMDR, grief/loss, wellness, and using the Enneagram to help promote insight and awareness in clients and supervisees. Part of her unique philosophy of care comes from her personal experience and journey of grief as a young widow and also her experience in teaching, mentoring, and supervising counselors in training by using the Enneagram. After years of running her private practice, she now continues to share with others as host and creator of her podcast, "Discovering with Dr. Deb," available anywhere podcasts are available. Dr. Braboy has been married to her husband, Keith, for 23 years, and together they have three adult children and four grandchildren. She enjoys college football, traveling, cooking, spending time with her family, and spoiling her grandchildren.

© Laura Daniel

Dr. Laura Daniel, PhD, LPC (VA) is an Assistant Professor in the Department of Counselor Education and Family Studies at Liberty University. Dr. Daniel's clinical practice has been in educational settings supporting adolescents, young adults, and their families impacted by disability. She is a member of the American Counseling Association (ACA), the American Association of Christian Counselors (AACC), the Virginia Counselors Association (VCA), and the Virginia Association for Counselor Education and Supervision (VACES) where she currently serves on the Board as Secretary. Dr. Daniel lives in Danville, Virginia, with her husband, Stephen, and three daughters, Katherine, Audrey, and Rebecca.

© Karin Dumont

Dr. Karin Dumont, PhD, NCC, LCMHC-S, CCMHC, LCAS, ACS is an Associate Professor and core faculty member in the Department of Counselor Education and Family Studies at Liberty University. She has been a faculty member in the department for 15 years. Dr. Dumont has also taught at Methodist University and Montreat College. She played an instrumental role in the development of the Master of Arts in Addiction Counseling program. She is an active member of the American Counseling Association (ACA), the American Association of Christian Counselors (AACC), the Licensed Professional Counselors Association of North Carolina (LPCANC), and the North Carolina Counseling Association (NCCA). Dr. Dumont practiced for over 20 years in the counseling profession, specializing in addiction counseling, clinical community mental health counseling, and counseling at-risk youth. She has extensive experience in regular outpatient, intensive outpatient, inpatient crisis stabilization, and detoxification services. She also has experience in the area of school counseling. Dr. Dumont has recently taken on the service role of Narrative Writer for the NCMHCE with the National Board of Certified Counselors. She lives near Raleigh, North Carolina, and enjoys spending time with family and friends, weight training, and reading for enjoyment.

© Denise Ebersole

Dr. Denise Ebersole, PhD, LPC (PA), ACS, NCC, NCSC is an Associate Professor in the Department of Counselor Education and Family Studies at Liberty University where she trains future school counselors. In addition to her role in academia, Dr. Ebersole also serves as a solution-focused counselor, career coach, and speaker who specializes in supporting aspiring and current school counselors. Dr. Ebersole is a Licensed Professional Counselor and an Approved Clinical Supervisor, and she is board certified as a Nationally Certified Counselor and a Nationally Certified School Counselor. Dr. Ebersole holds certifications in elementary school counseling (K-6), secondary school counseling (7-12), and as a supervisor of school guidance services (K-12) in Pennsylvania. Previous professional positions include serving as a K-12 school counseling department coordinator, high school counselor, and middle school counselor.

© Courtney Evans

Dr. Courtney Evans, PhD, LCMHC-S, RPT-S, NCC, ACS, BCTMH, CAdPT is a core faculty member in the Department of Counselor Education and Family Studies at Liberty University. In addition to her work in academia, Dr. Evans also maintains a private practice. She specializes in working with children, adolescents, and adults who have experienced trauma. Dr. Evans is a Licensed Clinical Mental Health Supervisor, Registered Play Therapist Supervisor, Nationally Certified Counselor, Approved Clinical Supervisor, and Board Certified Telemental Health Counselor, and she is certified at the Advanced Level in Adlerian Play Therapy. She is active with the League of Extraordinary Play Therapists (LEAPT). Dr. Evans works from an Adlerian theoretical framework while integrating trauma-informed practices and neuroscience into her counseling (e.g., Polyvagal theory, Child and Family Traumatic Stress Intervention [CFTSI], and Eye Movement Desensitization and Reprocessing [EMDR]). She is an active member of the North American Society of Adlerian Psychology and presents locally, nationally, and internationally on Adlerian theory. She has also published many articles in the areas of trauma and Adlerian Play Therapy. In her free time, Dr. Evans enjoys getting outside, going to the beach, hiking, and having lots of fun with her two-and-a-half-year-old twins.

© Dr. Stephanie J.W. Ford

Dr. Stephanie JW Ford, PhD, LPC is a licensed psychologist and Professor at Liberty University in the Department of Counselor Education and Family Studies. Dr. Ford has served as an academician, a department administrator, and a university administrator. She has been employed in departments of counseling and psychology at brick-and-mortar, online, and hybrid-model universities. Dr. Ford has provided clinical mental health services in university, community, hospital, and private practice settings. Her research focuses on diversity in counseling, supervision, and higher education; mental health and marginalized populations; and Christianity and mental health, as well as the impact of neurocognitive disorders on individuals and their families. Dr. Ford presents her research at professional conferences, churches, and community organizations, and she is committed to using her knowledge, skills, and competencies to aid people in achieving wellness, living with hope, and having a tomorrow better than one can imagine.

© LaSonda B. Fuller

Dr. LaShonda Fuller, PhD, LPC, NCC is a Virtual Eagle. She serves as an Associate Professor in the Department of Counselor Education and Family Studies at Liberty University. Prior to training champions for Christ at Liberty, Dr. Fuller served as an Associate Professor of Counseling at Chicago State University and as the advisor of the Chi Sigma Chi chapter of Chi Sigma Iota, an international and professional academic honor society of counseling, for six years. Under her leadership, the organization was awarded by the 2019 Heritage Ball the *Wawa Aba Award* for being an organization that models hardiness and a keen sense of purpose. In 2019, Dr. Fuller was also a recipient of the *Women Who Change the World* leadership award for the non-profit organization, In Her Shoes Foundation. Dr. Fuller has also served as a Faculty Specialist II in the Department of Counselor Education and Counseling Psychology at Western Michigan University, where she earned her doctorate in counselor education and supervision. Dr. Fuller earned her Master of Education degree in guidance and counseling and Bachelor of Science in journalism: TV/radio broadcast from Bowling Green State University. Amongst her many speaking engagements, both nationally and internationally, she is most proud of guest speaking for the NAACP student organization of Bowling Green State University's Annual Women's Conference. Dr. Fuller was awarded the *Ohana Award* by Counselors for Social Justice for affirming diversity and advocating for social justice. She is a Nationally Certified Counselor and Licensed Professional Counselor in Michigan and Texas and has served as a Licensed School Counselor in Michigan and Ohio. Dr. Fuller has enjoyed 10 years as a counselor educator, eight years in clinical practice—more recently serving as a grief consultant—and has worked as a school counselor for two years. Teaching, mentoring, connecting with people through collaborative works with other health professionals within varying communities, serving on task force committees, and presenting research that advocates for wellness, justice, and spiritual peace are her most invested interests. Among her passions are her rest management training retreats, international exploratory voyages, and eating good food among great company.

© Angelica Greiner

Dr. Angelica Greiner, PhD, CDF is an Assistant Professor in the Department of Counselor Education and Family Studies at Liberty University. Dr. Greiner holds certifications in elementary school counseling (K-6) and secondary school counseling (7-12). Before becoming a full-time counselor educator, she was a professional school counselor for 10 years. During her tenure as a school counselor, Dr. Greiner's school counseling program earned the *Recognized ASCA Model Program (RAMP)* award. Dr. Greiner currently serves on ASCA's ethics committee, and she is also an ASCA-certified legal and ethical specialist. She is a member of many professional organizations including the Association of Counselor Education and Supervision (ACES), the Southern Association of Counselor Education and Supervision (SACES), the American School Counselor Association (ASCA), the American Counseling Association (ACA), and the Palmetto State School Counselor Association (PSSCA). Dr. Greiner currently resides in South Carolina with her husband and two daughters.

© Crystal E. Hatton

Dr. Crystal Hatton, PhD, NCC, NCSC, ACS is an Assistant Professor in the Department of Counselor Education and Family Studies at Liberty University. Before joining the faculty at Liberty, Dr. Hatton served as a professional school counselor for 13 years. During her tenure as a school counselor, she also worked as an adjunct professor for counseling students at both Old Dominion University and Arkansas State University. She was fortunate to also serve as a clinical faculty member for the school counseling program at the College of William and Mary where she had the opportunity to supervise and train masters-level practicum and internship students within the school setting. She is a National Certified Counselor, National Certified School Counselor, and an Approved Clinical Supervisor. She is also an ASCA-certified legal and ethical specialist and a cultural competency specialist. Recently, she was selected to receive an award from the National Board of Certified Counselors (NBCC) for extraordinary school counseling efforts that were provided to students during the Covid-19 pandemic. Dr. Hatton and her family currently reside in Virginia. She is passionate about school counseling and is excited to teach and train current and aspiring school counselors.

© Brad Imhoff

Dr. Brad Imhoff, PhD, LPC (OH) earned his doctorate in counselor education and supervision from Ohio University. He currently serves as an Assistant Professor of Counseling in the Department of Education and Family Studies at Liberty University. He is also the Director of the Master of Arts in Addiction Counseling program within the School of Behavioral Sciences at Liberty. His clinical background has largely focused on addiction treatment, specifically related to the opioid epidemic, and working alongside prescribing physicians to provide counseling within a medication-assisted treatment program. Dr. Imhoff enjoys spending time with his wife and young kids and traveling, and he is an avid outdoors person and an accomplished nature photographer.

© John A. King

Dr. John A. King, PhD, MDiv, MA, LPC (PA), NCC is an Assistant Professor of Counseling and core faculty member for Liberty University's CACREP-accredited Clinical Mental Health Counseling program. Dr. King received his doctorate in counselor education and supervision from Regent University, his M.Div. degree from Missio Seminary (Previously Biblical Seminary), and his M.A. in counseling psychology from Kutztown University (PA). He is a Licensed Professional Counselor (LPC) in Pennsylvania and is a National Certified Counselor (NCC). Dr. King is also an ordained pastor in the Brethren in Christ Church (U.S.) and has 27 years of pastoral experience in two different church congregations. Additionally, Dr. King maintains a small private practice for clinical mental health counseling and supervision. Dr. King's clinical interests include marriage and family, pastors and their families, addiction, orphan care issues, and the integration of Christian faith and counseling.

© Bryan Goldberg Photography

Dr. Krista Kirk, PhD, LMHC, NCC, ACS is an Assistant Professor of Counselor Education at Liberty University. She teaches in the CACREP-accredited doctoral Counselor Education and Supervision program and the Clinical Mental Health Counseling program within the Department of Counselor Education and Family Studies. Dr. Kirk continues in clinical practice through the use of telemental health, providing services to under-served populations in the Bronx, New York. She is a licensed mental health counselor in the state of New York, a National Certified Counselor, and an Approved Clinical Supervisor. Dr. Kirk is trained in schema therapy and publishes in the areas of multicultural competence in counselors, gatekeeping in the counseling profession, and the use of psychological safety for counselor development. Dr. Kirk loves all things baseball-related and enjoys chasing after her two little ones while supporting her husband in full-time pastoral Christian ministry in the NYC surrounding areas.

Dr. Charity Anne Kurz, PhD, LPC (OH), LPC Associate (TX), LSC (OH), CSC (TX), NCC is an Associate Professor of Counseling in the Department of Counselor Education and Family Studies at Liberty University. She holds a bachelor's degree in special education, as well as a master's in school counseling. Additionally, Dr. Kurz holds her doctorate in counselor education with an emphasis in mental health from The Pennsylvania State University. Currently, Dr. Kurz is a telemental health counselor for Life by Design Wellness located in Texas. Her theoretical orientation is based on constructivist approaches including cognitive behavioral therapy, solution-focused therapy, and narrative approaches. Dr. Kurz has provided counseling to children, adolescents, and their families in schools and clinical settings. In addition to her work in the United States, Dr. Kurz works in Latin American countries providing consultation and training for professionals working with children and adolescents. Dr. Kurz lives in Ohio with her husband and two adolescent boys. In their free time, they love to play board games and video games and watch movies. Dr. Kurz and her family are actively engaged in the ministry, predominantly focused on cradle-to-career.

Shawn Moore is a student in the Master of Education in School Counseling program at Liberty University, where she is currently an intern completing her graduate fieldwork. She has recently discovered a passion for career readiness at her high school internship site and believes in advocating for equity while collaborating with students, parents, and teachers for student development toward maximum results. Shawn holds a Bachelor of Science degree in biblical and educational studies with a double minor in evangelism and Christian counseling. She has worked as a substitute teacher at a charter school, a kindergarten teaching assistant, and a lead interventionist where she provided educational support to teachers, curriculum coaches, and students needing Tier-2 support. Shawn has been married to her husband, Levi, for 16 years and together they have three children. She has a passion for supporting students' socio-emotional development and believes social and emotional balance is the key to academic success. Shawn seeks a school system where she may apply all her training in a service capacity.

Dr. Robin Switzer, EdD, NCC, LPC is an Assistant Professor in the Department of Counselor Education and Family Studies at Liberty University. In addition to her work in academia, Dr. Switzer develops training materials for local clinical practices, provides clinical supervision, and maintains a private practice specializing in trauma for clients ages three and up. She is a National Board Certified Counselor and a member of the American Counseling Association (ACA), the Association for Counselor Educators (ACE), and the Missouri Counseling Association (MCA). Dr. Switzer is EMDR trained and has worked with traumatized children, adolescents, and adults in hospitalization, residential treatment, day treatment, in-home care, outpatient, and telehealth settings. She has continued her practice across multiple states, becoming a Licensed Professional Counselor in Missouri, Colorado, and Nevada (CPC). Dr. Switzer works from a Psychodynamic theoretical framework utilizing creative activities such as play, sand tray, music, and art to assist all ages in healing expression. Dr. Switzer lives near St. Louis with her husband and enjoys yoga, walking, reading, painting, and continuing to learn the piano.

© Dr. Yulandra Tyre

Dr. Yulanda Tyre, PhD, LPC-S (AL), NCC is an Associate Professor of Counseling in Liberty University's CACREP-accredited Clinical Mental Health Counseling program. Dr. Tyre received her doctorate in counselor education and supervision from Auburn University. She has over 20 years of experience as a counselor, counselor educator, author, and higher-education leader. She has extensive experience in student affairs and served as Assistant Vice Chancellor for Student Affairs, providing direct oversite to a university counseling center, career center, and disability services. She is an active part of her professional community—recently serving as the 2021-2022 President of the Alabama Counseling Association—and is a current Executive Board member for Alabama Mental Health Authority. Her research interests include counselor wellness and self-care, compassion fatigue, and issues surrounding college counseling and supervision. She has been married for 27 years, is a mother of two adult daughters, and is a grandmother.

© Gina Childress, Picture This Photography

Dr. Shannon Warden, PhD, LCMHCS (NC) is an Associate Professor and core faculty member in Liberty University's Department of Counselor Education and Family Studies. She has more than 25 years of experience counseling families, couples, adults, and children. Dr. Warden co-authored two parenting books with Dr. Gary Chapman (author of the acclaimed *5 Love Languages* books) and contributed to the development of several of the *5 Love Languages* quizzes. She is a member of the American Counseling Association (ACA), the American Association of Christian Counselors (AACC), the Association of Counselor Education and Supervision (ACES), the International Association of Marriage and Family Counselors (IAMFC), the North Carolina Counseling Association (NCCA), the North Carolina Association of Counselor Education and Supervision (NCACES), and the Licensed Professional Counselors Association of North Carolina (LPCANC). Dr. Warden earned her doctorate in counseling and counselor education from the University of North Carolina at Greensboro, her master's in counseling from Wake Forest University, and her bachelor's in journalism from Elon College. She and her husband, Stephen, and their three children (Avery, Carson, and Presley) live in Winston-Salem, North Carolina. Among their favorite family activities are serving in their church community, rooting for their favorite NASCAR racers, having family movie nights, and taking trips to the beach.

© Jacqueline Wirth

Dr. Jacqueline L. Wirth, PhD, EdS, NCC, NCSC is an Associate Professor at Liberty University. She is a faculty member for the Master of Education in School Counseling program. Dr. Wirth worked for 27 years as a school counselor in Florida, Louisiana, and Maryland, in elementary, middle, and high school settings. Dr. Wirth has supervised counseling practicum and internship students for several Florida universities. She served as an Adjunct Professor for Florida Atlantic University in Boca Raton, Florida, and as an alcohol and drug prevention/intervention specialist in the East Baton Rouge Parish School Board in Baton Rouge, Louisiana. In addition to her degrees, Dr. Wirth is a Clinical Educator for the state of Florida and holds a Florida Professional Educator Certificate as a school counselor (Pre-K-12) and as an elementary educator. Dr. Wirth is a National Board Certified Counselor and a National Board Certified School Counselor. She is a member of many professional organizations including the Association of Counselor Education and Supervision (ACES), the Southern Association of Counselor Education and Supervision (SACES), the American Association of Christian Counselors (AACC), the American School Counselor Association (ASCA), the American Counseling Association (ACA), the Florida School Counseling Association (FSCA), the Virginia School Counseling Association (VSCA), and the Lone Star State School Counseling Association (LSSSCA) in Texas. She enjoys her family, time in prayer, travel, beach walks, and hiking.

References

American Association for Marriage and Family Therapists (AAMFT). (2015). *Code of ethics.* https://aamft.org/Legal_Ethics/Code_of_Ethics.aspx

American Counseling Association (ACA). (2014). *2014 ACA code of ethics* https://www.counseling.org/knowledge-center

American School Counseling Association (ASCA). (2022). *ASCA ethical standards for school counselors.* https://www.schoolcounselor.org/About-School-Counseling/Ethical-Legal-Responsibilities/ASCA-Ethical-Standards-for-School-Counselors-(1)

Association for Spiritual, Ethical and Religious Values in Counseling (ASERVIC). (2009). *Competencies for addressing spiritual and religious issues in counseling.* https://www.counseling.org/docs/default-source/competencies/competencies-for-addressing-spiritual-and-religious-issues-in-counseling.pdf?sfvrsn=aad7c2c_8

Chi Sigma Iota. (2019). *Wellness position paper.* https://www.csi-net.org/members/group_content_view.asp?group=162835&id=854566

Council for Accreditation of Counseling and Related Educational Programs (CACREP). (n.d.a). *About CACREP.* https://www.cacrep.org/about-cacrep/

Council for Accreditation of Counseling and Related Educational Programs (CACREP). (n.d.b). *2016 CACREP standards.* https://www.cacrep.org/for-programs/2016-cacrep-standards/

Henriksen Jr., R. C., Polonyi, M. A., Bornsheuer-Boswell, J. N., Greger, R. G., & Watts, R. E. (2015). Counseling students' perceptions of religious/spiritual counseling training: A qualitative study. *Journal of Counseling & Development, 93,* 59–69. https://doi.org/10.1002/j.1556-6676.2015.00181.x

National Association for Alcoholism and Drug Abuse Counselors (NAADAC) & The National Certification Commission for Addiction Professionals (NCC AP). (2021). *Code of ethics.* https://www.naadac.org/assets/2416/naadac_code_of_ethics_112021.pdf

New International Bible. (2011). The NIV Bible. https://www.thenivbible.com (Original work published 1978)

Tolkien, J. R. R. (1954). *The fellowship of the ring.* George Allen and Unwin.

Wellness

Ken D. Miller, Jacqueline L. Wirth, & David E. Jones

> "He answered, 'Love the Lord your God with all your heart and with all your soul and with all your strength and with all your mind' and, 'Love your neighbor as yourself.'"
>
> — Luke 10:27 (NIV)

History of Wellness

The concept of health has significantly changed throughout the centuries. Greek mythology shaped the earliest concepts of health and wellness. Apollo, the god of healing, had a son named Aesculapius, the god of medicine. Aesculapius had several children from which many medical terms used throughout the world have evolved: *Iaso*—medicine; *Aceso*—healing: *Aglea-Egle*—healthy glow; *Panacea*—universal remedy; and *Hygeia* from which "hygiene" is derived (Morford & Lenardon, 1995). The efforts of *Hygeia,* promoting hygiene, are at the roots of the wellness approach to healing (Myers & Sweeney, 2005, 2007). Aristotle wrote that a state of happiness or flourishing is the ultimate expression of the ability to live and fare well. He addressed the philosophy of *Eudemonia,* which literally translated means "nothing in excess." Descartes in his writings linked the health of body and mind. He saw body and mind as two separate entities working together in a mechanistic manner (Morford & Lenardon, 1995). The biblical writer of Proverbs viewed a cheerful heart as good medicine and a crushed spirit as drying up the bones (*New International Bible*, 1978/2011, Proverbs 17:22).

The concept of health continued to evolve through the eighteenth and nineteenth centuries by being defined as an absence of disease or infirmity. This transformation of health continued into the twentieth century. The World Health Organization's (WHO) 1947 definition of health was physical, mental, and social well-being, not merely the absence of disease or infirmity. The WHO (1964) held this definition until 1964. In 1964, health was a state of *complete* physical, mental, and social well-being.

The modern wellness movement began in the early 1960s and 1970s. Halbert L. Dunn (1959a), the architect of modern wellness, was the chief of the National Office of Vital Statistics. He suggested new terminology to express the positive aspects of health that people could achieve, beyond simply avoiding sickness. In the late 1950s, Dunn (1961) outlined a dynamic process in direct contrast to the WHO's static state of wellness. His concept of "high-level wellness" perceived wellness as an integrated method of functioning oriented toward maximizing the potential of the individual and what they are capable of and maintaining a continuum of balance and purposeful direction within their environment. Halbert L. Dunn published the concept of high-level wellness in 1961 in his book titled, *High-Level Wellness: A Collection of Twenty-Nine Short Talks on Different Aspects of the Theme "High-level Wellness for Man and Society."* The book is regarded as a classic in the wellness field and is the basis for many current wellness practices.

In 1975, John W. Travis, at his California Wellness Resource Center, used Dunn's concepts of wellness. He promoted self-directed visualization, improvement in fitness and nutrition, self-assessment, and relaxation approaches (Travis, 1984; Travis & Ryan, 2004). In 1976, Donald Ardell published an article in *Prevention* magazine profiling Travis's California Wellness Resource Center. This article was at the beginning of national recognition of the wellness concept. Ardell and Travis separately and together published wellness definitions and developed models that promoted the advancement of wellness.

William Hettler was inspired by and impressed with Travis and Ardell's work (Zimmer, 2010). At the University of Wisconsin, Hettler, along with colleagues Dennis Elsenrath and Fred Leafgren, held wellness symposiums in 1975 and 1976 (NWI, 2020). Hettler developed The Six Dimensions of Wellness model which presents wellness through a physical health lens. Hettler defined wellness as an active process through which people become aware of and make choices toward a more successful existence (Hettler, 1984).

In 1977, the University of Wisconsin colleagues established The Institute of Lifestyle Improvement at the University of Wisconsin-Steven Point Foundation (UWSP). A name change occurred in 1985 and The Institute of Lifestyle Improvement became the National Wellness Institute (NWI). The National Wellness Institute continues to provide a platform for wellness by holding an annual conference, maintaining a speaker's bureau, and providing resources for wellness.

Models of Wellness in Transition

Several wellness models have been established and adopted by the NWI since it's inception in 1977 (Crose et al., 1992; Depken, 1994; Durlak, 2000; Greenberg, 1985; Hettler, 1984; Lafferty, 1979; Leafgren, 1990; Renger et al., 2000). Three of the nine wellness models (Crose et al., 1992; Hettler, 1984; Leafgren, 1990) use the same dimensions in their model (social, emotional, physical, intellectual, spiritual, and occupational) (Roscoe, 2009), but it is Hettler's Six Dimensions of Wellness model (1984) that is recognized as foundational for modern wellness models (Myers & Sweeney, 2008; Roscoe, 2009). The six dimensions of Hettler's wellness model are seminal for those who have sought to develop psychological wellness models (Myers & Sweeney, 2008; Oliver et al., 2019).

The Social dimension of Hettler's model encapsulates the interdependence and interconnectedness of one to nature and their community and the extent of their contribution to their well-being (Hettler, 1980). The Emotional dimension measures the awareness, acceptance, and regulation of one's emotions. Managing diet and exercise, with an emphasis on cardiovascular strength and flexibility, is measured by the Physical dimension. A person's ability to gain knowledge, share their acquired knowledge with their community/society, and engage in stimulating and creative thinking is evaluated by the Intellectual dimension. The Spiritual dimension measures the existential matters of human existence. Work satisfaction and vocational satisfaction are measured by the Occupational dimension. These six constructs directly contribute to subsequent wellness models.

Like the Crose et al. (1992), Hettler (1984), and Leafgren (1990) models, The Wheel of Wellness (Myers et al., 2000) maps Hettler's six dimensions of wellness with slight differences. While the Crose et al. (1992), Hettler (1984), and Leafgren (1990) models regard the six dimensions through a multidimensional and systemic lens, Hettler hints at a holistic approach to wellness by explaining the six dimensions through a continuum of wellness-to-premature death (1984, p. 79). The Hettler model encompasses the lifespan but falls short of promoting a model that is holistic. We look to Myers et al. (2000) Wheel of Wellness model as one of the first wellness models in counseling that maps to the six dimensions and promotes a holistic view of wellness.

Models of Wellness in Counseling

Sweeney and Witmer (1991) were the first to present a theoretical model of wellness based on a counseling theory. This integrated model of wellness, referred to as The Wheel of Wellness or WOW (Myers et al., 2000), contains all the constructs from Hettler's Six Dimensions of Wellness model (1984), directly mapping to the first, third, and fourth factors (innermost, third, and fourth concentric circles in Figure 1) of The Wheel of Wellness known as *life tasks* (Myers et al., 2000).

At the center hub of the wheel is the life task of Spirituality. Spirituality is widely considered essential to subjective well-being, functioning as the epicenter of mental and physical health and ultimately life satisfaction (Myers et al., 2000; Seaward, 1995; Sweeney & Whitmer, 1991; Waite et al., 1999). Self-direction, the second life task, emanates from a healthy spirituality. Twelve subtasks comprise the self-direction task: sense of worth, sense of control, realistic beliefs, emotional awareness and coping, problem-solving and creativity, sense of humor, nutrition, exercise, self-care, stress management, gender identity, and cultural identity (Figure 1). When the twelve subtasks are actively pursued, the result is cognitive and emotional self-regulation, which supports the remaining Adlerian (Adler, 1954) life tasks of Work and Leisure, Friendship, and Love (Sweeney & Witmer, 1991). They contended that people who consistently self-regulate their thoughts, feelings, and actions exhibit the characteristics of holistic health and well-being.

Seeing the need to move the Wheel of Wellness from theory into the counseling office, Myers et al. (2000) developed a four-phase process that included 1) Wheel of Wellness psychoeducation, 2) informal and formal assessment, 3) interventions using the Wheel of Wellness self-direction subtasks, and

FIGURE 1 The Wheel of Wellness—Myers et al. (2000)

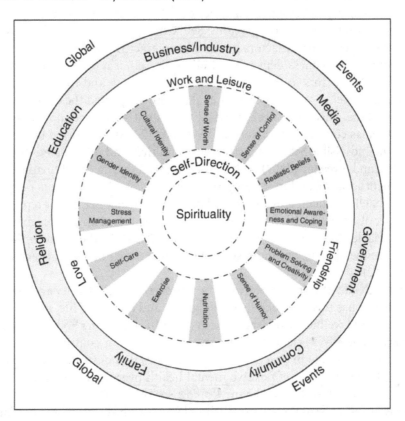

4) reevaluation and revisiting of phases two through four as needed (p. 257) (Wirth & Villares, 2015, Wirth: 2012). This four-phase process has since been used in populations ranging from middle school-aged students to older adults in clinical, academic, and cross-disciplinary settings (Myers et al., 2000). This led the Myers team to a definition of wellness from a counseling perspective:

Wellness is a way of life oriented toward optimal health and well-being, in which body, mind and spirit are integrated by the individual to live life more fully within the human and natural community. Ideally, it is the optimum state of health and well-being that each individual is capable of achieving. (p. 252)

The characteristics or "life tasks" associated with healthy people living longer and reporting higher levels of life satisfaction paved the way for the development of The Indivisible Self Model of Wellness (Myers & Sweeny, 2005). The life tasks used in the Indivisible Self-Model serve a foundational role in the development of wellness models.

The Indivisible Self—An Evidence-Based Model

After twelve years of study, Myers, Sweeney and colleagues' (2004) exploratory factor analysis enhanced and refined The Wheel of Wellness model into The Indivisible Self Model of Wellness (IS-Wel). The IS-Wel model provides an alternative perspective for viewing wellness across the lifespan. The IS-Wel model, grounded in Adlerian theory of holism, emphasizes the whole of a person rather than the parts. Adler's theory suggests an individual's wellness is based on healthy interactions between environmental (immediate surroundings) and ecological factors (the outside world). Adler (2019) contended that heredity and environment alone do not shape one's attitude toward life. Rather, it is how the individual interprets genetic and epigenetic influences and uses them to interact with their ecosystem (Adler, 2019; Jones et al., 2021; Myers & Sweeney, 2004). Individual wellness includes life tasks and subtasks that permit interaction with the environment to promote and develop a healthy lifestyle. The IS-Wel model consists of a wheel representing this empirical interaction. The self as indivisible is at the center surrounded by five interacting second-order factors: Creative Self, Coping Self, Social Self, Essential Self, and Physical Self. Each of these second-order factors has its own interacting factors, totaling seventeen (Figure 2).

The IS-Wel model of wellness depicts the Indivisible Self as a higher-order indivisible factor that interacts with the other factors in the broader context of society and the lifespan (Myers & Sweeney, 2004). The original Wheel of Wellness (Myers et al., 2000) supported the conceptualization of spirituality at the center of the wheel. However, spirituality was not supported, nor were the third-order factors with each other, as conceived by Myers and Sweeney (2008). Supported by research, changing the Spiritual Self to the Indivisible Self demonstrated the multiple and interrelated dimensions of wellness. In addition, Myers and Sweeney (2004) revised their understanding of contextual life forces that shape the individual, incorporating and modifying some of the ecological concepts originally purported by Bronfenbrenner (1999). As stated previously, the holistic Indivisible Self factor represents the interaction of the higher-order of wellness with five second-order factors (consisting of seventeen components) and the contextual variables found in life (Myers & Sweeney, 2004). In the words of Myers and colleagues (2000), "Ideally, [wellness] is the optimum state of health and well-being that each individual is capable of achieving" (p. 252).

The Essential Self consists of one's spirituality, self-care, gender identity and cultural identity. Spirituality, not religiosity, has positive benefits for longevity and quality of life, and it was viewed by Adler as central to holism and wellness (Mansager & Gold, 2000). A person's Social Self consists of two components: friendship and love. Friendship and love can exist on a continuum and, as a consequence, are not clearly distinguishable in practice. Multiple studies demonstrate that Social Support remains the strongest identified predictor of positive mental health over the lifespan (Stalnaker-Shofner et al., 2022). Sweeney and Myers (2004) describe the Coping Self as having realistic beliefs, the ability to manage stress, having a healthy sense of self-worth, and being involved in leisure activities. These elements

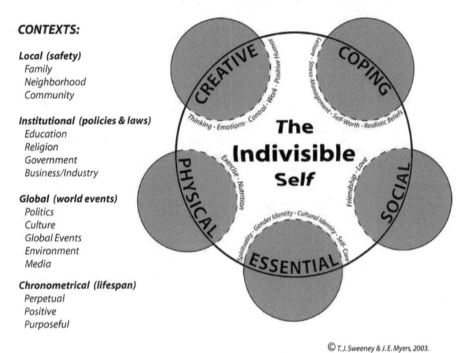

THE INDIVISIBLE SELF:
An Evidence-Based Model Of Wellness

CONTEXTS:

Local (safety)
 Family
 Neighborhood
 Community

Institutional (policies & laws)
 Education
 Religion
 Government
 Business/Industry

Global (world events)
 Politics
 Culture
 Global Events
 Environment
 Media

Chronometrical (lifespan)
 Perpetual
 Positive
 Purposeful

© *T. J. Sweeney & J. E. Myers, 2003.*

regulate responses to life events and provide a means for transcending any negative feelings. A healthy Creative Self thinks clearly, has an internal locus of control, engages in positive humor, and has a balanced work life. Positive expectations influence emotions, behavior, and anticipated outcomes. Positive humor is known to have a pervasive influence on physical as well as mental functioning. Enriching one's ability to think clearly, perceive accurately, and respond appropriately can decrease stress and enhance the humor response, which medical research has shown affects the immune system positively. People exhibit a healthy Physical Self through exercise and healthy eating. These two factors, Creative Self and Physical Self, are widely promoted and sometimes over-emphasized, which may lead to neglect of the other factors. For a more detailed definition of the five second-order factors and seventeen supporting subfactors, see Figure 3.

The Pursuit of Wellness in Context

The IS-Wel model views wellness as both holistic and global. Clients that pursue wellness begin to see themselves as well only when the Indivisible Self and the second-order factors are consistently assessed and adjusted according to their individual wellness plan. Individual wellness assessment and adjustment happen in four ecological contexts and sixteen sub-contexts, and within the primary, first, and second-order factors of the IS-Wel model (see Figure 2, Myers & Sweeney, 2004). In the termination and follow-up of the counseling process, the counselor works with the client to address potential hindrances and stressors that the client's four ecological contexts may present.

FIGURE 3 Abbreviated Definitions of Components of The Indivisible Self Model of Wellness—Myers and Sweeney (2008)

Abbreviated Definitions of Components of the Indivisible Self Model

Wellness Factor	Definition
Total Wellness	The sum of all items on the 5F-Wel; a measure of one's general well-being or total wellness
Creative Self	The combination of attributes that each of us forms to make a unique place among others in our social interactions and to positively interpret our world
Thinking	Being mentally active, open-minded; having the ability to be creative and experimental; having a sense of curiosity, a need to know and to learn; the ability to solve problems
Emotions	Being aware of or in touch with one's feelings; being able to experience and express one's feelings appropriately, both positive and negative
Control	Belief that one can usually achieve the goals one sets for oneself; having a sense of planfulness in life; being able to be assertive in expressing one's needs
Work	Being satisfied with one's work; having adequate financial security; feeling that one's skills are used appropriately; the ability to cope with workplace stress
Positive Humor	Being able to laugh at one's own mistakes and the unexpected things that happen; the ability to use humor to accomplish even serious tasks
Coping Self	The combination of elements that regulate one's responses to life events and provide a means to transcend the negative effects of these events
Leisure	Activities done in one's free time; satisfaction with one's leisure activities; having at least one activity in which "I lose myself and time stands still"
Stress Management	General perception of one's own self-management or self-regulation; seeing change as an opportunity for growth; ongoing self-monitoring and assessment of one's coping resources
Self-Worth	Accepting who and what one is, positive qualities along with imperfections; valuing oneself as a unique individual
Realistic Beliefs	Understanding that perfection and being loved by everyone are impossible goals, and having the courage to be imperfect
Social Self	Social support through connections with others in friendships and intimate relationships, including family ties
Friendship	Social relationships that involve a connection with others individually or in community, but that do not have a marital, sexual, or familial commitment; having friends in whom one can trust and who can provide emotional, material, or informational support when needed
Love	The ability to be intimate, trusting, and self-disclosing with another person; having a family or family-like support system characterized by shared spiritual values, the ability to solve conflict in a mutually respectful way, healthy communication styles, and mutual appreciation
Essential Self	Essential meaning-making processes in relation to life, self, and others
Spirituality	Personal beliefs and behaviors that are practiced as part of the recognition that a person is more than the material aspects of mind and body
Gender Identity	Satisfaction with one's gender; feeling supported in one's gender; transcendence of gender identity (i.e., ability to be androgynous)
Cultural Identity	Satisfaction with one's cultural identity; feeling supported in one's cultural identity; transcendence of one's cultural identity
Self-Care	Taking responsibility for one's wellness through self-care and safety habits that are preventive in nature; minimizing the harmful effects of pollution in one's environment
Physical Self	The biological and physiological processes that compose the physical aspects of a person's development and functioning
Exercise	Engaging in sufficient physical activity to keep in good physical condition; maintaining flexibility through stretching
Nutrition	Eating a nutritionally balanced diet, maintaining a normal weight (i.e., within 15% of the ideal), and avoiding overeating
Contexts	
Local context	Systems in which one lives most often—families, neighborhoods, and communities—and one's perceptions of safety in these systems
Institutional context	Social and political systems that affect one's daily functioning and serve to empower or limit development in obvious and subtle ways, including education, religion, government, and the media
Global context	Factors such as politics, culture, global events, and the environment that connect one to others around the world
Chronometrical context	Growth, movement, and change in the time dimension that are perpetual, of necessity positive, and purposeful

Note. 5F-Wel = Five Factor Wellness Inventory.

From *Journal of Counseling and Development, Vol. 86, Issue 4, Fall 2008* by Jane E. Myers and Thomas J. Sweeney. Copyright © 2008 American Counseling Association. Reprinted by permission.

Four Ecological Contexts

© pics five/shutterstock.com

A person's family, neighborhood, and community are key elements of the *local* context. This first of the four contexts is where the client seeks safety, even though influences may be unhealthy and negative (Myers & Sweeney, 2004). For instance, the client may have wellness deficits in their second-order factors of Self-Worth, Nutrition, and Exercise that must be addressed in a local context where food is viewed as a coping mechanism as part of a strict cultural patriarchy. The client may need to adjust parts of the Social

Self and Physical Self that also intersect with the cultural identity of their Essential Self. The policies and laws that directly and indirectly affect the client are administrated through the *institutional* contexts of education, religion, government, and business/industry. The educational context of the client can affect multiple second-order factor components like Thinking, Friendship, Cultural Identity, and Work. Second-order factor strengths or deficits in Spirituality, Gender Identity, Thinking, Work, and Leisure may affect how the client interacts vocationally with religious and business/industry contexts.

The milieu of global events, politics, culture, environment, media consumption, and community comprise the *global* context of the IS-Wel model (Myers & Sweeney, 2004). A client's wellness interacts with the rapidly changing world that presents them with a multitude of stressors and hindrances to their wellness. Wellness counselors assist clients in developing a wellness plan that helps the client develop strategies to manage not only their local contexts but also inva-

VLADGRIN/shutterstock.com

sive global contexts like media. Management of media intake may be one of the most important intervention strategies with which a wellness counselor assists their clients across the lifespan.

As the wellness counselor conceptualizes an individual's wellness plan, it is essential they account for the *chronometrical* context—the context of time and space. That means the interdimensional and indivisible first- and second-order factors of one's life interact with local, institutional, and global contexts across the lifespan. The chronometrical context helps the wellness counselor work with the client to appraise the acute and chronic effects of their lifestyle choices on their wellness across the lifespan (Myers & Sweeney, 2004).

Assessing Wellness

5F-Wel. The WOW and the IS-Wel model have been measured through several instruments. Building on the Wellness Evaluation of Lifestyle (WEL) inventory developed by Myers and colleagues (1996), the Five Factor Wellness Inventory (5F-Wel) was developed to provide researchers with a shorter and more reliable instrument (Myers et al., 2004). Myers and colleagues (2004) saw the need to refine both the IS-Wel model and the 5F-Wel instrument to provide future researchers with a more statistically sound means of assessing wellness. Their work resulted in significant refining of the 5F-Wel, producing five factors of wellness.

4F-Wel. The 4F-Wel was developed out of the authors' scientific dissatisfaction with both the WEL and the 5F-Wel. Beginning with the WEL instrument that resulted in the Wheel of Wellness model, Myers et al. (2004) determined there were four reasons for improving their work. First, researchers using the WEL had difficulty consistently verifying correlations among the instrument's 17 sub-factors. Second, the statistical evolution from the WEL to 5F-Wel and subsequent research using the 5F-Wel indicated greater correlations than originally calculated in the 5F-Wel. Third, continued research revealed less-than-robust reliability of the 5F-Wel. Fourth, the authors understood the need for instrument parsimony. Since the research pointed to a shorter version of their model, Myers and colleagues embarked on a further revision of their previous work.

Over a four-year period, Myers and Sweeney (2004) administered the 5F-Wel to 3,993 participants. Their intercorrelation and reliability study exhibited an acceptable statistical fit and a subsequent confirmatory factor analysis (CFA) resulting in four new constructs that were found to be both valid and reliable. The authors identified the four constructs as the Cognitive-Emotional Wellness (CEW), Physical Wellness (PW), Spiritual Wellness (SW), and Relational Wellness (RW) factors. The CFA also provided a more parsimonious instrument, reducing the number of items from 74 to 56.

The four factors are not only more statistically sound, but they also provide researchers and clinicians with more concise and congruent constructs for assessment and case conceptualization in the dimension of wellness (Myers et al., 2004). The first three factors map directly to the established mind-body-spirit paradigm found in both secular and religious literature. The CEW factor was originally conceived as assessing coping strategies; they are instead presented as preventative strategies to assist the client in developing healthy cognitions that lead to wellness in affect and emotions (Myers & Sweeney, 2004). The PW factor incorporates all things physical, including exercise, diet, nutrition, and general physical health. The SW factor encompasses all spiritual and religious beliefs and their related values system. In contrast to the Wheel of Wellness model that posited the SW factor as central and the most important of all factors.

The SW is statistically equal in importance with the other factors. RW, the fourth factor, is broader in its conception compared to the authors' earlier models and constructs. Rather than being inward-focused, the RW factor reflects a person as "self-in-relation" to their contexts. The evolution and development of wellness models used in assessment and clinical interventions has assisted with a comprehensive definition including spiritual wellness.

© Polarpx/shutterstock.com

Definition of Wellness

Today, those subscribing to the concept of wellness understand that wellness is multidimensional and synergistic in nature, offering a holistic balance within each person as they operate in both inner and global contexts. Wellness promotes a "whole person" approach, integrating methods of functioning (Dunn, 1959b) within a continuum dependent on self-responsibility and motivation (Myers & Sweeney, 2005; Myers et al., 2000; Sweeney & Witmer, 1991; Witmer & Sweeney, 1992). The Whole Person approach emphasizes personal choice and responsibility and how wellness choices are self-empowering for immediate and long-term lifestyle choices (Myers et al., 2011). Wellness is more than the absence of illness and it is not an end state (Roscoe, 2009). Rather, wellness maximizes one's potential capabilities within the intra/inter and global contexts in which the individual functions (Dunn, 1959b). Wellness, then, is "a way of life oriented toward optimal health and well-being, in which body, mind, and spirit are integrated by the individual to live life more fully within the human and natural community" (Myers et al., 2000, p. 252).

Summary

The concept of wellness in the literature began with a term from Greek mythology, Hygeia, that connoted on the need to maintain one's health (Myers & Sweeney, 2005, 2007). The concept of wellness evolved from Aristotle's view that a state of flourishing should include a practice of nothing in excess in one's life. Descartes introduced a body/mind interaction of wellness congruent with a biblical view. Little was accomplished in wellness thought from the Renaissance period until the World Health Organization defined wellness as not just the absence of physical disease, but rather physical, mental, and social well-being.

The seminal work of Halbert L. Dunn began what is now known as the wellness movement. Although Dunn's work was grounded in physical health, he introduced the concept of wellness as one's potential of functioning at the highest level. From there, wellness as a concept continued to develop through the work of Crose et al. (1992) and Leafgren (1990). It was Bill Hettler's introduction of the emotional and intellectual constructs to current wellness that influenced wellness theories and research most significantly. Hettler's work (Hettler, 1980, 1984; Hettler et al., 1980), along with that of Alfred Adler (1930), influenced Myers and colleagues to develop the Wheel of Wellness.

Based on their initial development of the WEL inventory and the resulting Wheel of Wellness model (Myers et al., 2000), Jane Myers and her colleagues created the Indivisible Self Model of Wellness and its accompanying Five Factor Wellness Inventory (5F-Wel). After the successful application of both the WEL and 5F-Wel in numerous research studies, the authors saw the need to refine and seek a more statistically sound instrument. The result the 4F-Wel to encourage the examination of influences, both internal and external to the individuals' self in their planning processes.

References

Adler, A. (1930). *Individual psychology.* In C. Murchison (Ed.), *Psychologies of 1930* (pp. 395–405). Clark University Press. https://doi.org/10.1037/11017-021

Adler, A. (1954). *Understanding human nature.* Fawcett. (Original work published 1927)

Adler, A. (2019). The fundamental views of individual psychology. *The Journal of Individual Psychology, 75*(3), 185-187. https://doi.org/10.1353/jip.2019.0023

Ardell, D. B. (1976). *Prevention magazine. April, Side Bar.*

Bronfenbrenner, U. (1999). Environments in developmental perspective: Theoretical and operational models. In S. L. Friedman & T. D. Wachs (Eds.), *Measuring environment across the life span: Emerging methods and concepts* (pp. 3–28). American Psychological Association. https://doi.org/10.1037/10317-0

Crose, R., Nicholas, D. R., Gobble, D. C., & Frank, B. (1992). Gender and wellness: A multidimensional systems model for counseling. *Journal of Counseling & Development, 71*(2), 149-156. https://doi.org/10.1002/j.1556-6676.1992.tb02190.x

Depken, D. (1994). Wellness through the lens of gender: A paradigm shift. *Wellness Perspectives, 10*(2), 54-69.

Dunn, H. L. (1959a). High-level wellness for man and society. *American Journal of Public Health, 49*, 786-792.

Dunn, H. L. (1959b). What high-level wellness means. *Canadian Journal of Public Health, 50*(11), 447-457.

Dunn, H. L. (1961). *High-level wellness: A collection of twenty-nine short talks on different aspects of the theme "High-level wellness for man and society."* R. W. Beatty, Ltd.

Durlak, J. A. (2000). Health promotion as a strategy in primary prevention. In D. Cicchetti, J. Rappaport, I. Sandler, & R. P. Weissberg (Eds.), *The promotion of wellness in children and adolescents* (pp. 221-241). CWLA Press.

Greenberg, J. S. (1985). Health and wellness: A conceptual differentiation. *Journal of School Health, 55*(10), 403-406. https://doi.org/10.1111/j.1746-1561.1985.tb01164.x

Hettler, B. (1980). Wellness promotion on a university campus. *Family and Community Health*, *3*(1), 77–95. https://doi.org/10.1097/00003727-198005000-00008

Hettler, B. (1984). Wellness: Encouraging a lifetime pursuit of excellence. *Health Values: Achieving High-Level Wellness*, *8*, 13-17.

Hettler, B., Weston, C., Carini, J., & Amundson, J. (1980). Wellness promotion on a university campus. *Family and Community Health*, *3*(1), 77-95.

Jones, D. E., Park, J. S., Gamby, K., Bigelow, T. M., Mersha, T. B., & Folger, A. T. (2021). Mental health epigenetics: A primer with implications for counselors. *Professional Counselor*, *11*(1), 102-121. https://doi.org/10.15241/dej.11.1.102

Lafferty, J. (1979). A credo for wellness. *Health Education, 10*, 10-11. https://doi.org/10.1080/00970050.1979.10619163

Leafgren, F. (1990). Being a man can be hazardous to your health: Life-style issues. In D. Moore & F. Leafgren (Eds.), *Problem solving strategies and interventions for men in conflict (pp. 265–311).* American Association for and Development.

Mansager, E., & Gold, L. (2000). Three life tasks or five? *Individual Psychology*, *56*(2), 155.

Morford, M. P. O., & Lenardon, R. J. (1995). *Classical mythology* (5th ed.). Longman.

Myers, J. E., & Sweeney, T. J. (2004). The indivisible self: An evidence-based model of wellness. *Journal of Individual Psychology, 60*, 234-244.

Myers, J. E., & Sweeney, T. J. (2005). *Counseling for wellness: Theory, research, and practice.* American Counseling Association.

Myers, J. E., & Sweeney, T. J. (2007). Wellness in counseling: An overview. *Professional Counseling Digest, ACAPCD-09.* American Counseling Association.

Myers, J. E., & Sweeney, T. J. (2008). Wellness counseling: The evidence base for practice. *Journal of Counseling & Development, 86*(4), 482-493. https://doi.org/10.1002/j.1556-6678.2008.tb00536.x

Myers, J. E., Luecht, R. M., & Sweeney, T. J. (2004). The factor structure of wellness: Reexamining theoretical and empirical models underlying the wellness evaluation of lifestyle (WEL) and the five-factor wel. *Measurement and Evaluation in Counseling and Development, 36*(4), 194-208. https://doi.org/10.1080/07481756.2004.11909742

Myers, J. E., Sweeney, T. J., & Witmer, J. M. (1996). *The wellness evaluation of lifestyle.* Mindgarden.

Myers, J. E., Sweeney, T. J., & Witmer, J. M. (2000). The Wheel of Wellness counseling for wellness: A holistic model for treatment planning. *Journal of Counseling and Development, 78*, 251-266. https://doi.org/10.1002/j.1556-6676.2000.tb01906.x

Myers, J. E., Willse, J. T, & Villalba, J. A. (2011). Promoting self-esteem in adolescents: The influence of wellness factors. *Journal of Counseling & Development, 89*(1), 28-36. https://doi.org/10.1002/j.1556-6678.2011.tb00058.x

New International Bible. (2011). The NIV Bible. https://www.thenivbible.com (Original work published 1978)

National Wellness Institute (NWI). (2022). https://nationalwellness.org/about-nwi/

Oliver, M. D., Baldwin, D. R., & Datta, S. (2019). Health to wellness: A review of wellness models and transitioning back to health. *International Journal of Health, Wellness & Society, 9*(1), 41–56. https://doi.org/10.18848/2156-8960/CGP/v09i01/41-56

Renger, R. F., Midyett, S. J., Soto Mas, F. G., Erin, T. D., McDermott, H. M., Papenfuss, R. L., Eichling, P. S., Baker, D.H., Johnson, K. A., & Hewitt, M. J. (2000). Optimal Living Profile: An inventory to assess health and wellness. *American Journal of Health Behavior, 24*(6), 403-412. https://doi.org/10.5993/AJHB.24.6.1

Roscoe, L. J. (2009). Wellness: A review of theory and measurement for counselors. *Journal of Counseling & Development, 87*(2), 216-226. https://doi.org/10.1002/j.1556-6678.2009.tb00570.x

Seaward, B. L. (1995). Reflections on human spirituality for the worksite. *American Journal of Health Promotion, 9*(3), 165-168.

Stalnaker-Shofner, D. M., Lyness, K., & Keck, S. (2022). The influence of race/ethnicity, gender, age, social support, religion/spirituality, and occupational history on the total wellness of counseling practicum graduate students: A pilot study. *Journal of Counselor Preparation and Supervision, 15*(2).

Sweeney, T. J., & Witmer, J. M. (1991). Beyond social interest: Striving toward optimum health and wellness. *Individual Psychology: Journal of Adlerian Theory, Research & Practice, 47*(4), 527–540.

Travis, J. W. (1984). The relationship of wellness education and holistic health. In J. S. Gordon, D. Jaffe, T. Bresler, and E. David (Eds.), *Mind, body and health, toward an integral medicine* (pp. 188-198). Human Sciences Press.

Travis, J. W., & Ryan, R. S. (2004). *Wellness workbook: How to achieve enduring health and vitality.* Random House Digital, Inc.

Waite, P. J., Hawks, S. R., & Gast, J. A. (1999). The correlation between spiritual well-being and health behaviors. *American Journal of Health Promotion, 13*(3), 159-162. https://doi.org/10.4278/0890-1171-13.3.159

Wirth, J. (2012). The effect of a classroom intervention on adolescent wellness, success skills academic performance (Doctoral dissertation)

Wirth, J. & Villares, E. (2015). Examining adolescent wellness, success skills and academic performance: A classroom intervention approach. The Journal of Happiness and Well-Being, 3(2), 204-217

Witmer, J. M., & Sweeney, T. J. (1992). A holistic model for wellness and prevention over the life span. *Journal of Counseling & Development, 71*(2), 140-148. https://doi.org/10.1002/j.1556-6676.1992.tb02189.x

World Health Organization (WHO). (1947). Constitution of the World Health Organization. *Chronicle of the World Health Organization, 1,* 29-43.

World Health Organization (WHO). (1964). *Basic documents.* Geneva, Switzerland: Author.

Zimmer, B. (2010). Wellness. *The New York Times, 123*(2000), 11.

Biblical Essentials

David E. Jones, Ken D. Miller, & Kevin B. Hull

> "Your word is a lamp for my feet, a light on my path."
>
> — Psalm 119:105 (NIV)
>
> "For the word of God is alive and active. Sharper than any double-edged sword, it penetrates even to dividing soul and spirit, joints and marrow; it judges the thoughts and attitudes of the heart."
>
> Hebrews 4:12 (NIV)

In the field of counseling, many, if not all, case conceptualization books are secular. By working through a secular lens, there is a fundamental assumption of materialism (naturalism), meaning, a human is only composed of substance. This is an implicit assumption that the reader may not recognize. Counseling textbooks, generally, inadequately address religion and spirituality (R/S), the non-matter aspects of self, or the integration of the whole person (material + spiritual). For example, Cashwell and Giordano (2018) provide an overview of the major world religions, including about a page on a Christian worldview. Sue and Sue (2016) offer only a two-page response to the "Dangers and Benefits" of spirituality within their chapter on non-western healing practices. Neither of these counseling textbooks provides an understanding or application of R/S to the field of counseling.

The CACREP 2016 standards (n.d.), Section 2: Counseling Curriculum, F.2.g, has religion and spirituality (R/S) in the multicultural standard, but it is limited in application. There is a current debate, as of the time this book was written, about the removal of the R/S language in the 2023 CACREP standards. Other counseling professions offer some guidance towards R/S in counseling but are limited, as reviewed in Chapter 1: About This Book.

With the limited scope or lack of addressing R/S by CACREP and other counseling professions, a potential dilemma is developed. How does the counselor competently use an R/S lens in assessment, diagnosis, case conceptualization, and treatment (the golden thread) with a client who is spiritually-religiously centered and requests this in their treatment? More specifically, how would a counselor effectively work as a "Christian counselor"?

To begin to address these concerns, we believe each student and practitioner must have a foundational understanding of a biblical worldview. We will provide a foundational biblical worldview for the Christian counselor and student. We will offer what we believe are essential aspects of the Christian worldview. Later in the book (Chapter 4), this Christian foundation will be integrated into a counseling wellness model, the Biblical Wellness (B-Well) model, for the student and practitioner to operate from. This chapter establishes a foundation for engaging in R/S from a Christian worldview that informs the student and counseling practitioner across the treatment process. To achieve this, we will deliver an understanding of being human (anthropology), the influence of sin, the work of grace, the process of sanctification, and the intersection of faith and reason.

Christian Anthropology

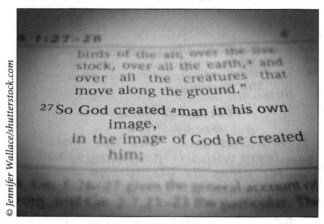

Our starting place will be a clear understanding of Christian anthropology, the study of what it means to be human. The place to gain this Christian understanding of personhood is scripture, which is God's special revelation through Christ and the work of the Holy Spirit in the lives of apostles, prophets, etc. (*New International Bible*, 1978/2011, 2 Timothy 3:16) ... versus general revelation, which is where God offers evidence of his character and moral law through creation (Romans 1:20). Let's look at several foundational scriptures. We offer italics for key areas to focus your attention.

In Genesis 1:26, God said:

> Let us make man [humankind] in o*ur image*, after our likeness, and let them *rule over* the fish of the sea and the birds of the air, over the livestock, over all the earth, and over all the creatures that move along the ground. (*New International Bible*, 1978/2011)

Again, this was affirmed in Genesis 1:27, "... in the *image of God* he created him; male and female he created them." In Genesis 1:28, God commanded them (Adam and Eve) to, "Be fruitful and increase in number; fill the earth and *subdue it. Rule over* the fish of the sea, and the birds of the air and over every living creature that moves on the ground." Finally, in Genesis 2:7, "The Lord God formed the man from the dust of the *ground* and *breathed* into his nostrils the breath of life, and the man became a living being." There are several insights to gain here on Christian anthropology. Let's unpack them.

One of the first insights is a counter to the materialism that pervades the current secular case conceptualization books. We see a connection between the material (ground) and God (breathed). The ground or "dust" points to the origins of humankind in the material, but we also see evidence of God's breath vitalizing the person to life. As Mathews (1996) notes, "Man does not possess a *nepeš* [breath] but rather is a *nepeš* (individual person) ... a transcendent life force in man" (p. 197). Therefore, the breath of God energized the dormant body, which became a "living person." In Job 33:4 (*New International Bible*, 1978/2011), we see this evidenced as well: "The Spirit of God has made me, and the breath of the Almighty gives me life." God created humankind from both material and breath—humans are body and soul, as stated by Grudem (1994). In other terms, humans are "as truly natural as supernatural" (Kidner, 1967, p. 65). Current case conceptualization textbooks lack the component of "breath" in the case conceptualization process, only operating from a materialistic worldview. It is not that any of the authors deny the importance of or do not accept R/S into their personal worldview, but they may not see it as relevant in a case conceptualization process as we do.

The second implication is that humans are made in God's image or likeness. Humans have a unique and special place in the created order; we are not just another animal. God gave humans special rights by giving them domain (i.e., to rule; subdue) over creation or God's regent. Theologians call this the Functional view (Cottrell, 2004; Grudem, 1994). This is the foundation for our view of *imago Dei* (image of

God), but out of this Functional view flows two other relevant views: the Substantive and the Relational. The Substantive view is about qualities humans possess because we are made in His image. You can see evidence of this in humans' ability to develop complex languages, to reason, and to create, in addition to their awareness of the past, present, and future and having morals associated with anger and rage toward injustice. The Relational view focuses on our capacity for relationships with God and others (vertical and horizontal). Ultimately, we are made in the image of God, and out of these three views, we have the command to rule as regents over creation, the capacity for deeply meaningful relationships with other humans and creation, and the ability to engage in our innate intellect, creativity, volition, morality, and emotions with God, other humans, and creation to seek change and achieve the commands as a regent.

The final implication is that we possess a body and a soul (Grudem, 1994). The concept of soul is derived from the Hebrew word *nephesh*. It is not a separation of body and soul [*nephesh*], but it is a single unit. People are unified entities. As Schultz (1996) states, "... in the Old Testament a mortal is a living soul rather than having a soul" (par. 8). From a Jewish perspective (Cottrell, 2004; Grudem, 1994; Mathews, 1996), we live an embodied life that is indivisible, both material and soul in a unified whole. This counters the limited view of personhood in current case conceptualization textbooks that have a singular focus via materialism.

We see several scriptures that support this position that humans are an indivisible whole—body and spirit—not body or spirit or body only. Note we see the use of soul and spirit as synonymous or a dualism view of being human (see Cottrell, 2004 for more insight). Isaiah 58:10 (*New International Bible*, 1978/2011) states, "Satisfy the desire [*nephesh*] of the afflicted;" and Psalm 69:1 includes, "The waters have come up to my neck [*nephesh*]." The spirit (*nephesh*) is found in Genesis 35:18 also, "... as her [Rachel's] soul [*nephesh*] was departing." In 1 Kings 17:21 (*English Standard Bible*, 2001), Elijah prayed that a dead child's *nephesh* would "come back into him again." The Lord listened to Elijah and "the *nephesh* (life) of the child came into him again and he revived" (v. 22). From these passages in the Old Testament (OT),

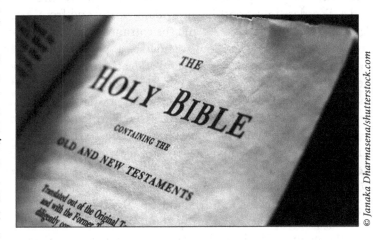

we have a picture of an indivisible self, a unity. But what is found in the New Testament?

In the New Testament (NT), the soul and body are both part of an indivisible self (Cottrell, 2004; Grudem, 1994; Reese, 2018). There is a clear distinction between body and soul, but this distinction is part of the whole—the body and soul come together to be a unity of personhood. Moreover, the separation of body and soul was not the original intent but a consequence of the fall (Cottrell, 2004). Several NT scriptures support this view. For example, in 2 Corinthians 7:1 (*English Standard Bible*, 2001), Paul references both the body (*sarx*, "flesh") and soul (*pneuma*, "spirit") and a call to holiness. This holiness is not only the body or the spirit but the entire person, the body and spirit. We also see this call to holiness of the body and soul in 1 Corinthians 7:34, thus adding further support to body and soul unity; it includes "how to be holy in body and spirit [soul]." Other scriptures support this view, such as Matthew 10:28, "And do not fear those who kill the body but cannot kill the soul. Rather fear him [God] who can destroy both soul and body in hell." We also find a reference in 1 Peter 2:11, "Beloved, I urge you ... to abstain from the passions of the flesh, which wage war against your soul."

© Pictrider/shutterstock.com

Sin

Sin can be defined as, "Lawlessness, disobedience, impiety, unbelief, distrust, darkness as opposed to light, a falling away as opposed to standing firm, weakness not strength. It is unrighteousness, faithlessness" (Doriani, 1996, p. 737). In Genesis 3:1-24 (*New International Bible*, 1978/2011), the fall of Adam and Eve came about because of their sin, disobedience to God. The serpent, the devil, lured Eve to a place of temptation by choosing to eat the fruit from the tree of knowledge of good and evil, which God had forbidden (Genesis 2:16). Eve, along with Adam, ate this forbidden fruit of their free will, which is an aspect of *imago Dei*. From this free will act, coerced by the serpent, the fall happened. Sin has marred the image of God but has not destroyed it (Cottrell, 2004).

From this disobedience, we see several consequences. The first is "shame" when Adam and Eve noted they were naked (*New International Bible*, 1978/2011, Genesis 3:7). Adam and Eve avoided each other and God because of the disruption in their understanding of self because of their sinful act. The result was a marred, broken view of self and how it related to God and others. Beyond shame is interpersonal disruption, The blaming of others for our actions. Adam blames Eve, who then blames the serpent for their predicament (Genesis 3:12-13). Additionally, God set forth new conditions due to the deception of the serpent and the disobedience of Adam and Eve (Genesis 3:14-19). The serpent is transformed into a slithering being and will have hostility with Eve. Eve will have increased pains during childbirth and a disordered relationship with Adam (v. 16), and from Adam's action, we see a global curse on the "ground" (v. 17; Romans 8:22) and the entrance of death into humanity (v. 19; Romans 5:12). Finally, in connecting with body and soul, we now see a split that did not exist previously. Once death entered, the unified whole became fractured, and at death, the soul survives but the body returns to dust (v. 3:19). Before the fall, it is important to note that God said creation was good (heavens, land, sky, plants, animals, etc.; Genesis 1:1-25) and that creation of Adam and Eve was "very good" (Genesis 1:31). So, from the fall, this "goodness" has been corrupted by sin and is evident to this day.

How is this evident in mental health? Due to the fall, humanity is sinful by nature and in a corrupt state where individuals experience fear, anxiety, isolation, depression, and many other disruptions to mind, body, and spirit. Eric Johnson offers in Matthew Stanford's (2010) book, *The Biology of Sin*, "Sin doesn't occur in a vacuum. We sin by choice, but our choices are often guided by inclinations that we often don't understand" (p. 2). This becomes obvious when we look at the world around us. We see selfish acts that bring about neglect in vulnerable clinical populations such as children and the elderly. There is physical, emotional, and spiritual abuse between couples and parents to their children. There are also "sins of the father" where heredity is corrupt and disorders propensity is passed on from one generation to another, such as substance abuse, schizophrenia, and bipolar. There is also systematic corruption of humankind with overt and implicit bias against groups of people, such as racism, ableism, and sexism across the world, creating unequal outcomes in health. We see this marred state in neuroscience—the activation of the sympathetic nervous system (fight/flight/freeze) puts people in states of reactivity, with no grounding (Porges, 2011) and thus "wise in their own eyes" which leads to disaster. There is evidence of this coaction between the individual and mental health outcomes even at the cellular level. There is genetic and epigenetic level evidence indicating how the interaction between a client and their environment modifies the likelihood of a poor condition (e.g., increased risk of depression, disordered eating, addiction) (Jones et al., 2021).

Grace

Through God's mercy, death is conquered, and He has provided an avenue for escape from the consequences of sin (*New International Bible*, 1978/2011, Acts 15:11; Ephesians 2:8-9; Hebrews 2:9; Romans 3:24; Titus 2:11). This life path is grace. Grace in Greek is *charis*, which can be defined as unearned favor or mercy. In the OT, two terms are evident, *ḥesed* and *ḥēn*, meaning mercy and favor, respectively (Shogren, 1992). By God's grace (unmerited favor, mercy) the sinner is saved through faith in Jesus Christ. Believing in the death and resurrection of Jesus Christ for the sins of the world (John 3:16) allows for God's mercy to flow into the individual and move them from death in sin to life in Christ, which is called regeneration or where a client is born again (Grudem, 1994). An

individual who believes in Jesus Christ as their Lord and Savior is also made right or righteous before God, or the declaring of our sins forgiven: justification. Additionally, the believer becomes more like Christ through sanctification, which will be elaborated on below.

Beyond this special grace (redemptive grace) for salvation, there is also common grace (McMinn, 2008). Common grace is God's unmerited favor that falls upon all creation, the believer as well as the unbeliever. Scripture supports this view through verses such as Matthew 6:26 (*New International Bible*, 1978/2011) which states, "Look at the birds of the air; they do not sow or reap or store away in barns, and yet your heavenly Father feeds them. Are you not much more valuable than they?" and Matthew 5:45, "He causes his sun to rise on the evil and the good, and sends rain on the righteous and the unrighteous." This is the preservation of His creation. Through this preservation, we see the "needs" of the righteous and unrighteous being met by God through His creation. McMinn (2008) believes common grace works in all counseling relationships, which can include positive regard, compassion, active listening, and engaging in positive non-verbals such as SOLER (sitting square, open posture, leaning forward, eye contact, relaxed body state). There is also the preservation of order at the universe level noted in the keeping of earth, sun, and planets in place and order. For a greater understanding, see *Why the Universe Is the Way It Is* by Hugh Ross (2010).

Through common grace, God subdues sin and provides a moral compass for all humans via their conscience. When looking at God's moral law, He has placed it in all humans based on *imago Dei*. According to Romans 2:14-15,

> Indeed, when Gentiles, who do not have the law, do by nature things required by the law, they are a law for themselves, even though they do not have the law. They show that the

requirements of the law are written on their hearts, their consciences bearing witness, and their thoughts sometimes accusing them and at other times even defending them. (*New International Bible*, 1978/2011)

Another way God subdues sin is by His providential work through governmental bodies. Romans 13:1 supports this: "Everyone must submit himself to the governing authorities, for there is no authority except that which God has established."

Sanctification

Because the Christian (by special grace) can choose to have faith in Christ and from faith in Christ is made righteous before God (justified), this enables sanctification. Note there are differences in views on how grace and how freewill operate, see *Justification: Five Views* edited by Beilby and Eddy (2011). Once a believer puts on the robes of righteousness, or is justified (*New International Bible*, 1978/2011, Isaiah 61:10), the believer receives the indwelling of the Holy Spirit (Acts 2:38). The process of sanctification is the work of the Holy Spirit in the life of the believer. As the believer listens to and obeys the Holy Spirit, they will grow, becoming more like Christ (Romans 8:1-17; 1 Thessalonians 5:23). Through this "growing" in Christ, a Christian will bear the fruit of the Spirit—"love, joy, peace, patience, kindness, goodness, faithfulness, gentleness, [and] self-control" (*English Standard Bible*, 2001, Galatians 5:22-23). Because the Christian is a new creation (2 Corinthians 5:15-17), they can bear the fruit through the work of the Holy Spirit when working with a client.

THE FRUIT OF THE SPIRIT IS

LOVE

joy

PEACE

patience

KINDNESS

goodness

FAITHFULNESS

gentleness

SELF-CONTROL

GALATIANS 5: 22-23

© Max9545/shutterstock.com

As Christian counselors grow in Christ, we "bear" more of the fruit of the Spirit. As we advance in our ability to offer love, joy, peace, patience, kindness, goodness, faithfulness, gentleness, and self-control to our clients, it assists in building rapport, valuing our clients as image-bearers, being patient with tough clients, offering gentleness to a broken client, and engaging in self-control to avoid countertransference, to name a few.

As Christians, we also have earthly and special wisdom. Earthly wisdom is wisdom that all humans possess based on being created in the image of God. Special wisdom comes from God as revealed in Christ (Kynes, 2021). As James notes in 3:15-17,

> This is not the wisdom that comes down from above, but is earthly, unspiritual, demonic. For where jealousy and selfish ambition exist, there will be disorder and every vile practice. But the wisdom *from above* is first pure, then peaceable, gentle, open to reason, full of mercy and good fruits, impartial and sincere. (*English Standard Bible*, 2001)

This special wisdom may come from the Holy Spirit and His work in our lives. As we grow in Christ, we also grow in heavenly wisdom (e.g., truths found in scripture, such as the fear of the Lord and righteous actions), which allows a Christian counselor to serve their clients uniquely and profoundly ... by engaging in both the divine wisdom given to us through the Holy Spirit and the earthly wisdom based on our *imago Dei*.

Faith and Reason

A final acknowledgment is the intersection of faith and reason. Pope John Paul II's encyclical "On Faith and Reason" (1998) stated, "There can never be a true divergence between faith and reason since the same God who reveals the mysteries and bestows the gift of faith has also placed in the human spirit the light of reason" (p. 31). As you think about Christian counseling and integration of a Christian worldview, we advocate for the application of faith, a biblical worldview, and the Godly reasoning we all have as God's regents. There are several views of Christian counseling integration (Entwistle, 2015; Hawkins & Clinton, 2015; Johnson, 2010; Tan, 2011), and we advocate for the middle path, a more balanced approach. One view seeks reason (science) only, and the other side advocates for the Bible only when conducting Christian counseling. Our integrated wellness model is first filtered through a biblical worldview and then infused with wellness. We then offer a path to apply your chosen secular theory, e.g., person-centered, psychodynamic, cognitive-behavioral, narrative, etc. within the biblical-wellness framework. We will offer more detail on this integration approach in Chapter 4.

Summary

This chapter provides a Christian foundation of what we perceive as the biblical essentials for counseling students and practitioners. From this chapter, you will now have an understanding of how God has created humanity as unique image-bearers and regents of creation. As a regent, our client has a capacity for reasoning, creativity, volition, and action in solving their clinical problems. Yet, the image is marred by sin. Sin has infiltrated the ranks of humanity, bringing about trouble, strife, and pain. Yet, we have succor through Christ our Lord and Savior. Through faith in Christ, we are redeemed and moved from death (sin) to life. In this new life, there is the regeneration of our mind, body, and soul that engenders the capacity to become more like Christ (e.g., evidencing the fruit of the Spirit). As a counselor, we can bear fruit of the Spirit towards our clients and assist the client, if Christian, in bearing their fruit of the Spirit. Finally, we will offer the Biblical Wellness model for assisting you to bridge the gap between secular and sacred.

References

Beilby, J. K., & Eddy, P. R. (2011). *Justification: Five views.* IVP Press.

CACREP. (n.d.). *2016 CACREP standards.* https://www.cacrep.org/for-programs/2016-cacrep-standards/

Cashwell, C. S., & Giordano, A. L. (2018). Spiritual diversity. In D. G. Hays & D. T. Erford (Eds.), *Developing multicultural counseling competence: A systems approach* (3rd ed., pp. 503-532). Pearson.

Cottrell, J. (2004). *The faith once for all: Bible doctrine for today* (3rd ed.). College Press.

Doriani, D. (1996). Sin. In W. A. Elwell (Ed.), *Evangelical dictionary of biblical theology* (electronic ed., pp. 737). Baker Book House.

English Standard Bible. (2001). ESV Online. https://esv.literalword.com/

Entwistle, D. N. (2015). *Integrative approaches to psychology and Christianity: An introduction to worldview issues, philosophical foundations, and models of integration* (3rd ed.). Cascade Books.

Grudem, W. (1994). *Systematic theology: An introduction to biblical doctrine.* Zondervan.

Hawkins, R., & Clinton, T. (2015). *The new Christian counselor: A fresh biblical & transformational approach.* Harvest House.

Johnson, E. L. (Ed.). (2010). *Psychology and Christianity: Five views* (2nd ed.). IVP Academic.

Jones, D. E., Park, J. A., Gamby, K., Bigelow, T. M., Mersha, T., & Folger, T. (2021). Epigenetics primer with implications for counselors. *The Professional Counselor, 1*(11), 116–135. https://doi.org/10.15241/dej.11.1.116

Kidner, D. (1967). *Genesis: An introduction and commentary* (Vol. 1, p. 65). InterVarsity Press.

Kynes, W. (2021). *The Oxford handbook of wisdom and the Bible.* Oxford University Press.

Mathews, K. A. (1996). *Genesis 1-11:26* (Vol. 1A, p. 197). Broadman & Holman Publishers.

McMinn, M. R. (2008). *Sin and grace in Christian counseling: An integrative paradigm.* IVP Academic.

New International Bible. (2011). The NIV Bible. https://www.thenivbible.com (Original work published 1978)

Paul II, J. (1998). *Encyclical letter fides et ratio of the supreme pontiff John Paul II, to the bishops of the catholic church, on the relationship between faith and reason.* https://www.vatican.va/content/john-paul-ii/en/encyclicals/documents/hf_jp-ii_enc_14091998_fides-et-ratio.pdf

Porges, S. W. (2011). *The polyvagal theory: Neurophysiological foundations of emotions, attachment, communication, and self-regulation.* (1st ed.). W. W. Norton.

Reese, N. N. (2018). The doctrine of humanity: Human nature. In B. Ellis and M. Ward (Eds.), *Lexham survey of theology.* Lexham Press.

Ross, H. (2010). *Why the universe is the way it is (reasons to believe).* Baker Books.

Schultz, C. (1996). Soul. In W. A. Elwell (Ed.), *Evangelical dictionary of biblical theology.* Baker Book House.

Shogren, G. S. (1992). Grace: New Testament. In D. N. Freedman (Ed.), *The anchor Yale Bible dictionary* (Vol. 2, pp. 1086–1087). Doubleday.

Stanford, M. S. (2010). *The biology of sin: Grace, hope, and healing for those who feel trapped.* InterVarsity Press.

Sue, D. W., & Sue, D. (2016). *Counseling the culturally diverse: Theory and practice.* Wiley.

Tan, S. Y. (2011). *Counseling and psychotherapy: A Christian perspective.* Baker Academic.

Biblical Wellness (B-Well) Model

David E. Jones & Ken D. Miller

> "Can you bind the chains of the Pleiades? Can you loosen Orion's belt?
> Can you bring forth the constellations in their seasons or lead out the
> Bear with its cubs?
> Do you know the laws of the heavens? Can you set up God's dominion
> over the earth?"
>
> — Job 38:31-33 (NIV)
>
> "He has told you, O man, what is good; and what does the Lord require
> of you but to do justice, and to love kindness, and to walk humbly with
> your God?"
>
> — Micah 6:8 (ESV)

In 1989, wellness was reaffirmed as a foundational value by the American Counseling Association (Myers, 1992). Through this textbook, we also affirm wellness defined as "a way of life oriented toward optimal health and well-being, in which body, mind, and spirit are integrated by the individual to live life more fully within the human and natural community" (Myers et al., 2000 p. 252). The primary reasons for supporting the wellness model over other models are (1) it integrates the multifaceted self (e.g., mind, body, and spirit); (2) it adds a positive lens of health; and (3) it is versatile-transtheoretical, meaning that our individual counseling theories (e.g., cognitive-behavioral, psychodynamic, solution-focused, person-centered) can be integrated within the wellness framework (Ohrt et al., 2019). Finally, in our wellness affirming pursuit, we have adopted the IS-Wel model, a counseling evidence-based model of wellness, and in particular, the factors found in the 4F-Wel instrument (Myers et al., 2004) within our biblical wellness model.

The theoretical foundation for the development and interpretation of the IS-Wel model is Adler's individual psychology (IP). We first offer an evaluation of IP theory from a biblical worldview (found in Chapter 3: Biblical Essentials), including the incompatibilities and alignments to a biblical worldview.

A Biblical Critique of IP

As you may recall from Chapter 2: Wellness, Alfred Adler developed the construct of life tasks (Dreikurs & Mosak, 1966, 1967; Mosak & Dreikurs, 1967). Life tasks are areas to be mastered over a lifetime. Initially, Adler offered three life tasks—love, friendship, and work. Later, Mosak and Dreikurs added the "self" and the "spirituality" life tasks after a careful analysis of Adler's work. Adler upheld a unique clinical view at that time, one of wholeness. The client was conceptualized as a whole, an indivisible self of mind, body, and spirit. Moreover, Adler's individual psychology offered that a client's basic motivations are to belong (connectedness), to contribute socially (Sperry & Sperry, 2012), and to overcome inferiority.

© Prazis Images/shutterstock.com

Through our deconstruction of individual psychology (IP) from a biblical worldview, we identified constructs (i.e., philosophical underpinnings) that we perceive to be contrary to a biblical worldview. The first contrary construct to a biblical worldview is the view of self, others, and the world through the lens of constructivism (Murdock, 2017). Watts (2003) suggested that Adlerian theory operates from relational constructivism. This form of constructivism adheres to both social and cognitive constructivism, which "accounts for both the social-embedded nature of human knowledge and the personal agency of creative and self-reflective individuals within relationships" (p. 139). Constructivism is problematic from a biblical worldview in that it removes objective truths. Constructivism is a client's individual interpretation or understanding of the self, others, and the world—a social construction of reality. A constructivist view opens the door to relativism or the "belief of no absolute right or wrong" (Grudem, 2018, p. 41). Yet, from a Christian lens, we have a transcendent, unchanging God (*New International Bible*, 1978/2011, Isaiah 40:28; Malachi 3:6) who is the author of "truth" (Titus 1:2). From this transcended truth, we find what is just or right (Deuteronomy 32:3-4) as well as what is good (Exodus 34:6). These truths come from God's unchanging moral character. Though our society changes and the perceptions of right or wrong may vary (i.e., healthy or hurtful can be a moving target according to cultural norms), God remains holy, truthful, just, righteous, and good. These truths are evident because they come from God who is independent of creation. We know these truths via general revelation as well as special revelation (i.e., scripture) as defined in Chapter 3. We, all humans, are also held accountable to God's truths (Romans 1:20-21). These truths are not bound by the internal client world (cognitive constructivism) or the embeddedness of the client (social constructivism) in the establishment of their "reality." They are transcending truths of "reality" from God.

Another critique of IP is Adler's view of spirituality, his fifth life task. Mosak and Dreikurs (1967) discovered that Adler upheld a more general definition of spirituality. It aligned with Adler's constructivist lens, which was not bound by any religion or worldview. This is problematic because it may

© Colored Lights/shutterstock.com

engender a syncretic (i.e., a fused) worldview of spirituality and religion. It can become an incoherent spirituality that holds to logical fallacies, or incongruences. Evidence of this can be found in Adler's essay (1987) to Ernst Jahn. Adler believed, "Each individual forms an image of the functioning and shape of the supreme being which differs from that of the next man" (p. 523). He also had a particular interest in the supremacy of social interest and inferiority: "Whether the highest effective goal is called God or Socialism or, as we call it, the pure idea of social interest ... the goal of overcoming [inferiority]" (p. 524). Yet, at other times he invoked Christian concepts and terms: "The sacred uniting of man with the goal-setting God ... he accomplished his unification with God as the redemption from all evil" (p. 524). From one lens, Adler supported Karl Marx (an atheist) and Nietzsche (rejected a Christian God); and yet invoked a biblical worldview by pointing to the sacred relationship between God and humans. From this, you can see evidence of a potential syncretic view that mixes belief systems.

A final criticism of IP is the focus on inferiority and striving toward superiority. As Tan (2011) draws attention, Adler's view that the "human tendency ... [for] strength and mastery in oneself" (p. 77) is key to overcoming inferiority. This alludes to a humanistic or a Rogerian lens of self-actualization; due to a client's striving, there is a sense of overcoming inferiority and moving toward superiority by one's efforts. This view falls short in several ways from a biblical worldview. First, it does not consider the fall and the sinful nature of humans. Biblically, all our efforts of striving will fall short and are sinful (*New International Bible*, 1978/2011, Genesis 3:1-24; Romans 3:23). A sense of inferiority is a characteristic of the fall. Humans are in a broken state due to sin (Romans 5:12).

The second issue, the efficacy of the client's efforts to overcome, is found primarily within the individual's power. Adler believed that through our strivings each person can overcome their environment and their heredity by constructing their reality, the constructivism/phenomenological view of self (Adler, 1913/1956). This bears faulty reasoning biblically. It ignores the reality of the fallen nature of humans—the limits of striving. Scripture demonstrates that humanity is made in the image of God (*New International Bible*, 1978/2011, Genesis 1:26-27) and has the capacity to strive (Acts 26:14; Genesis 32:24-28; 2 Samuel 19:9), but this is limited by the marred state, the sinful condition (Genesis 3). Moreover, social sin oppresses by bringing about racism, classism, sexism, poverty, etc. Everyone's sinful choices have consequences, and these consequences can limit the individual's autonomy of striving based on their context.

Yet, later in Adler's work, he moved to a more realistic view of superiority. Lazarsfeld (1966) noted that Adler believed there is a "normal" striving for perfection while knowing that it will never be fully met, and there is also a maladaptive approach to seeking the perfect without the realization of its unattainability. She differentiated the "normal" individual who strives for perfection while knowing the limitations from the maladaptive person who tries to be perfect. This is a more realistic alignment with a biblical worldview in that we will always fall short of this ideal state. Yet, it still holds a hyper-focus on the individual and their striving, without the clear, biblical understanding of the work of the Holy Spirit (e.g., justification, regeneration, and sanctification) in the life of believers and non-believers (i.e., limits of striving due to sin and operating through general revelation and not special revelation).

Christian Worldview and IP Alignment

Now that we have evaluated the potential concerns with IP through a biblical worldview, we offer how IP may align with a biblical worldview. We hold that IP aligns with a biblical worldview in the following ways: spirituality, social interest, personal choice-responsibility, and wholeness. We will examine each one below.

As Adler included "spirituality" into his theory, it was a radical move then and now. When Mosak and Dreikurs (1967) reviewed Adler's "life tasks," there were initially three: problems of behavior toward others, problems of occupation, and problems of love. However, Mosak and Dreikurs discovered that

Adler alluded to another life task of spirituality. Adler, unlike his contemporaries, viewed religion/ spirituality positively. Spirituality was a path for the client's efforts moving towards, or attempting to move towards, success or "perfection." Adler even considered IP as "rediscovering" the lost aspects of Christian counseling, perceiving God as a model of success or perfection, and through this model, overcoming inferiority.

Adler's social interest is evidenced in the Trinity (God, Son, and Holy Spirit). God, the Son, and the Holy Spirit are in an eternal relationship, a forever-loving, holy, and perfect relationship (Barry et al., 2016). In Mark 1:11 (*English Standard Bible*, 2001), after John baptizes Jesus, God the "father" declares, "You are my Son, the Beloved, with you I am well pleased." The father-son relationship is also documented in the transfiguration of Jesus in Luke 9:35, "This is my Son, my Chosen One; listen to him." Furthermore, social connection is evident during Jesus' baptism with the Holy Spirit, empowering Jesus for his earthly mission. Another example supporting this interconnecting relationship is in the book of Acts. After Jesus ascended into heaven (glorification), Jesus sent the Holy Spirit as seen in the outpouring of the Spirit on Pentecost (Acts 2:32-33). Finally, there is 1 Peter 1:2 (*New International Bible*, 1978/2011) which references, "[Those] who have been chosen according to the foreknowledge of God the Father, through the sanctifying work of the Spirit, to be obedient to Jesus Christ and sprinkled with his blood."

God also created humans for relationships, both vertical (humans and God) and horizontal (human-to-human) relationships. Therefore, it is easy to conclude that relationships are an essential aspect of being human because we are made in God's image—or likeness, and the Trinity has been in a relationship with one another eternally (*New International Bible*, 1978/2011, Isaiah 44:6; Genesis 1:2; John 1:1; Revelation 22:13). The creation of humankind was bound in the desire for a relationship with one another and with God. This connects well with IP in that Adler supported this foundation of belonging or social interest. For Adler, social embeddedness was a key aspect of the client. The client's relationship to the self, others, the physical world, and the spiritual world (e.g., God, god, religion, spirituality, etc.) was critical to understand. The client's sense of belonging and how they viewed this belonging (e.g., phenomenologically) was important for how they functioned and therefore, how to treat the client. Moreover, Adler supported collectively working toward the common good of society as a healthy approach to life.

A biblical worldview also connects with Alder's view on personal choice-responsibility. As you recall from Chapter 3: Biblical Essentials, we are created in the image of God, and in that image, we are both body and soul. From this soulfulness, we have the capacity for self-direction, but we also have God working in and around our individual lives supporting us and attempting to influence us to come to a saving relationship through Christ and, if a Christian, to fulfill the Great Commandment (*New International Bible*, 1978/2011, Matthew 22:36-40; 28:19-20). Though self-direction (free will) is limited by a sinful, fallen world, everyone has an agency (choice), even if limited by their social class, race, gender, etc. Even with these limitations, the Holy Spirit influences the client's personal choice as well as those around the client. As McMinn (1996) notes, "God continually redeems people from poverty, isolation, loneliness, emptiness, depression, alienation, and sin ... we see God working through circumstances and other people" (p. 248). The Holy Spirit can work in the world through common grace and special grace (McMinn, 2008). Through the work of the Holy Spirit and the client's obedience to God, they can move toward wellness. For a believer, this is the manifestation of the fruit of the Spirit: "Love, joy, peace, forbearance, kindness, goodness, faithfulness, gentleness, and self-control" (Galatians 5:22-23). A non-believer can move toward the fruit of the Spirit as well, but they are limited without the indwelling of the Holy Spirit. We offer more on this below and through the B-Well model continuum.

Another positive aspect of IP is the wholeness of the client. Adler moved away from the reductionist approaches and called for the counselor to attend to the entire person within their context. This is the natural connection with the Jewish worldview of soul (*nephesh*) and the foundation of our biblical wellness model. The client's *nephesh* is understood as a unified self (body and soul), our understanding of personhood (see Chapter 3, p. ??). It is seen as a unified whole, not the demarcation of body and soul. The person is not a separate entity, but in the language of wellness, it is an indivisible whole. This connects to the biblical view of *nephesh* as a unified entity of body—the material self—is conjoined with the spiritual.

The Biblical Wellness (B-Well) Model

The B-Well model does not view the client from a fractured lens but conceptualizes the person as a whole, or the sum is greater than the parts. This whole-person view is important in that the client's problems and solutions (interventions) are not isolated from each other but are interrelated. It is the coaction of the individual's whole self (body and soul) and their embeddedness in the environment that brings about problematic outcomes (e.g., depression, anxiety, addiction). Yet, there is also the promise of bringing about changes through a comprehensive treatment of the embedded whole self—interventions that attend to body and soul within the client's context, incorporating the individual and community assets.

But the fruit of the Spirit is Love, Joy, Peace, Forbearance, Kindness, Goodness, Faithfulness, Gentleness and Self-control. Against such things there is no law.

Galatians 5:22-23

© PicSOl/shutterstock.com

Though the foundation of our approach to wellness is based on the 4F-Wel instrument factors (Cognitive-Emotional Wellness, Physical Wellness, Spiritual Wellness, and Relational Wellness), we reoriented the 4F-Wel terms from a secular worldview to a biblical worldview. Cognitive and emotional wellness is Mind and Heart; physical wellness moves to Strength; spiritual wellness moves to Soul; and relational wellness is now Neighbor. We also added a Society facet based on the IS-Wel model "contexts" components of local, institutional, global, and chronometrical.

The new "labels" have a foundation in the biblical call from Jesus to love God and love our neighbor. In Matthew 22:37-40, Jesus replied:

'Love the Lord your God with all your heart and with all your soul and with all your mind.' This is the first and greatest commandment. And the second is like it: 'Love your neighbor as yourself.' All the Law and the Prophets hang on these two commandments. (*New International Bible*, 1978/2011)

In Luke 10:27, "[Jesus] answered, 'Love the Lord your God with all your heart and with all your soul and with all your strength and with all your mind' and, 'Love your neighbor as yourself.'" The foundation of the B-Well model is built on these verses.

LOVE
THE LORD
YOUR GOD
with all your
HEART
soul
MIND

Matthew 22:37

© lukpedclub/shutterstock.com

In the B-Well model, the Soul encapsulates the cognitive, emotional, and physical aspects of a human being created in the image of God. This symbiosis is found in 1 Thessalonians 5:23 (*New International Bible*, 1978/2011), "Now may the God of peace himself sanctify you completely and may your *whole* spirit and soul and body be kept blameless at the coming of our Lord Jesus Christ." Additionally, the understanding of *nephesh* explained in Chapter 3, as well as the human capacity for change based on the *imago Dei* explained in Chapter 3, contribute. These beliefs undergird the B-Well model with a theoretical foundation for the soul's indivisibility, provide a direction of wellness (order of salvation), and define the spaces within the soul where wellness is developed (see Figure 1).

The relational construct of the B-Well model is grounded in humanity's innate interconnectedness with each other (i.e., Great Commandment; *New International Bible*, 1978/2011, Luke 10:27; Matthew 22:37) and the exhortation of Jesus to love other human beings as we are loved by God (John 15:12-13). Loving others is evidenced by bearing fruit in one's life (Galatians 5:22-23; John 15:16). The capability of fruit-bearing is given by the Spirit, but producing the fruit of "love, joy, peace, forbearance, kindness, goodness, faithfulness, gentleness and self-control" (Galatians 5:22-23) requires the active involvement of the client and a desire to pursue wellness (striving). Yet, it is important to note that, throughout Galatians, salvation is not based on works or striving. Striving is the response to what God has done for us through his Son, Jesus Christ, and the working of the Holy Spirit in our life.

The arrow moving through the Soul from the Heart to one's Neighbor (see Figure 1) represents the progression of intrapsychic wellness of the individual that flows from the innermost parts of the individual to the interpersonal, one's neighbors. Wellness born of the Spirit emanates from one's innermost being and refreshes others (*New International Bible*, 1978/2011, John 7:37-38). James 1:27 states, "Religion that God our Father accepts as pure and faultless is this: to look after orphans and widows in their distress and to keep oneself from being polluted by the world." James, no doubt, was recalling the exhortation of Jesus to his followers that living by the Spirit is to feed the hungry, clothe the naked, and care for the sick (Matthew 26:35-40). Another evidence of biblical wellness is showing love by serving one's neighbors and those in the broader social context. This clearly connects to Alder's focus on the common good of society but is defined through a more intrapersonal lens.

Romans 8:19-21 is also a theological foundation for the wellness continuum of the B-Well model (see Figure 1).

> For the creation waits in eager expectation for the children of God to be revealed. For the creation was subjected to frustration, not by its own choice, but by the will of the one who subjected it, in hope that the creation itself will be liberated from its bondage to decay and brought into the freedom and glory of the children of God. (*New International Bible*, 1978/2011)

FIGURE 1 The theoretical foundation of the B-Well model

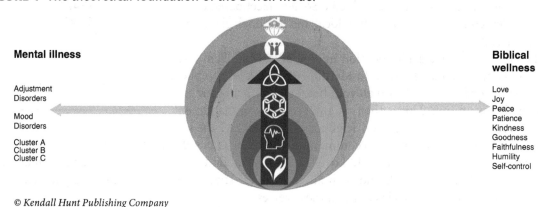

© *Kendall Hunt Publishing Company*

The Fall in Genesis 3 permeated all of creation, including the mental health of human beings. The account of Adam and Eve provides insight into the interpersonal, intrapsychic, and religious struggles of damaged relationships. Adam expressed fear, shame, isolation, and blame as maladaptive responses to those closest to him. Throughout history, mental illness has been observed and recorded and is now categorized in the *Diagnostic and Statistical Manual-5*

(*DSM-5*; APA, 2013). The B-Well model represents the spectrum of wellness that spans from broad categories of mental illness (*DSM-5* mental health categories) to the constructs of biblical wellness. The idea of conceptualizing emotions or mental illnesses on a continuum is not a new one. Psychotic symptoms and affect continuums are numerous in the literature (Nuevo et al., 2012; Siddaway et al., 2018; Tebeka et al., 2021; Van Os et al., 2009). We, therefore, contend that a biblical wellness spectrum is well within theoretical feasibility. The model depicts the individual "soul's" movement on the biblical wellness spectrum to the degree that they choose to engage in the pursuit of wellness.

The Biblical Wellness Facets

We agree with the 4F-Wel that heart-minds are not separate but work together. We perceive that heart-mind-strength is a unified concept found within the soul. This is inherent in the foundation of the soul and the indivisible self. Yet, a therapist isolates these constructs when assessing, conceptualizing, and treating, addressing various thoughts, feelings, and behaviors based on one's primary counseling theory (e.g., person-centered, emotion-focused, cognitive-behavioral). We then offer each facet as a heuristic for assessment, case conceptualization, and treatment planning. We separate the facets below as a process of practice but know in reality their separation is a fabrication, and there are many interactions across facets such as the mind-heart-strength.

Heart

The Heart is our place for the client's emotions. The client's emotions can range across the wellness continuum with their onset, duration, frequency, and severity. For example, a client who is in a manic state has an elevated mood that can be elated, ebullient, giddy, and rapturous but also angry and raging. The emotional states can be more maladaptive, moving toward dysfunction on the wellness spectrum, or adaptive, based on the context. We can also have clients who experience depression. We all feel sorrowful or gloomy at times but when the duration is long-lasting and increases dysfunction, this can move to disorder. The client may feel morose, forlorn, or woeful daily for weeks on end, affecting their ability to function normally. Yet, from our model, we understand there are assets of the Heart as well. These assets may include the ability to regulate emotional arousal, the ability to identify and label emotional states in self and others, and the ability to experience life, generally, in a happy state.

Mind

We can conceptualize the Mind as the seat of cognition—the client's thought life of the self, others, and the world. Borrowing from cognitive behavioral therapy, you can understand these thoughts as surface-level thoughts (automatic thoughts) as well as deeper thoughts (beliefs). The client's thought world influences emotions and behaviors. However, it is not unidirectional; emotions influence a client's thinking. Some of the client's thoughts are maladaptive and others are helpful in the pursuit of wellness. A maladaptive thought can support an addiction, for example. The client can rationalize that they "need" the drug and that they have a faulty core belief, such as "I am helpless," driving the addiction. The other side of the coin is those helpful or friendly thoughts about self, others, and the world. This could include a healthy sense of self and associated thought life on self-efficacy, abilities, view of others in a positive light, and perceiving a place in the world with purpose.

 ## Strength

Strength includes the physical, physiological, and behavioral aspects of the client. Clinically, this is on a spectrum as well. An unwell client may be experiencing nightmares and may be having trouble falling asleep and staying asleep. A client may exhibit tics, stereotypic movements (e.g., rocking, head bobbing, hair-pulling), rigidity in movement, and purging-binge eating. These may point toward disorders. There also may be problems of impulsivity, avoidance, hyperventilation, self-injury, and suicide attempts. On the other side of the wellness continuum, you will find prosocial and effective behaviors based on the circumstances. This would be the opposite of the listed maladaptive behaviors. The client may offer purposeful movements, eat a well-balanced meal, handle anxiety with effective coping (i.e., no panic attacks, avoiding others or situations), have healthy sleep patterns, and engage with others in a prosocial manner.

 ## Soul

The Soul is the place of connection between the physical and the spiritual world. We know from scripture (*New International Bible*, 1978/2011, Genesis 2:7) that God created humans from the ground and breathed His spiritual life into them. From this, we gain evidence of this material and spiritual connection in humans. Beyond this physical-spiritual dyad, it is through the soul that we have a direct connection to God. This is especially true for believers in Christ who have the indwelling of the Holy Spirit. The Holy Spirit works through believers via their consciousness (McMinn, 2008). Moreover, if we are created in the image of God (Genesis 1:26-27) and we are a unified whole—body and spirit—it then has implications when incorporating "soul" in counseling. Jones and Butman (2011) offered the following implications from a biblical worldview of the client: (1) We are a created being, not only materialistic in origin; (2) we have intrinsic value being made in the image of God; (3) each human has meaning and purpose; and (4) we are separate from God but rely on God and others. It is through the Soul facet a counselor intentionally attends to the client's spiritual and religious faith.

Through the Soul facet, the counselor may recognize the influence of the spiritual. As Paul states in Ephesians 6:12 (*New International Bible*, 1978/2011), "For our struggle is not against flesh and blood, but against the rulers, against the authorities, against the powers of this dark world and against the spiritual forces of evil in the heavenly realms." The counselor may observe, based on the continuum of the B-Well model, negative and/or positive spiritual influences upon the client. Some negative examples are toxic faith, such as works-based salvation beliefs that may increase the likelihood of false guilt or the influence of legalism upon the client, which may engender perfectionism and increased anxiety. Though difficult to discern, the false guilt and anxiety may be influenced by the "spiritual forces of evil." For example, think about *The Screwtape Letters* by C. S. Lewis. Yet, there are also positive influences, such as the work of the Holy Spirit within a believer's life that engenders the fruit of the Spirit—joy, peace, patience, self-control (*English Standard Bible*, 2001, Galatians 5:22-23) and the influence of God's word to correct the lies of the world ... "the renewing of your mind" (*New International Bible*, 1978/2011, Romans 12:2).

🏺 Neighbor

Neighbor is how the client engages, connects, and relates with others. This may include healthy relationships with a spouse, parents, siblings, friends, colleagues, and others and those outside the immediate client system. This may be a service to the church but also aid the community. This is the place where the client directly engages with others to support and love the community - the call by Christ to serve others (*New International Bible*, 1978/2011, Mark 10:43-45).

Yet, noting the influence of the B-Well model continuum, there is a downside to "neighbors." This is evidenced by neglectful or abusive parenting, unhealthy marital relationships, and dysfunctional family systems (e.g., diffuse, enmeshed, toxic). The client may be directly impacted by family or friends who experience addiction or other mental health disorders, or direct or indirect discrimination based on age, race, ethnicity, gender, disability, etc.

Society

Though we most often directly work with a client in the areas of Mind, Heart, Strength, Soul, and Neighbor, we cannot forgo the contextual factors (Society) that influence the client. The embedded client is bound within their contextual framework from gestation to death, experiencing both Neighbor (direct) and Society (indirect) influences. Society offers the clinician the opportunity to examine the indirect contextual factors for threats as well as resources for recovery and prevention. This Society construct is based on the IS-Wel model and the ecological systems theory - later called the bioecological model (Bronfenbrenner & Ceci, 1994) - where the client has concentric rings of influence that are direct (microsystem or Neighbor) to indirect (mesosystem, exosystem, macrosystem or Society) as you move further away from the client, as well as the time element, or chronosystem. The Society facet captures those indirect effects that may engender poor or healthy outcomes. Society can encompass local, state, regional, national, and international indirect impacts on the client (e.g., the COVID-19 pandemic). There may be positive influences, such as safe housing and communities and local and state safety nets for those in need. There may also be deleterious influences, such as policies at local, state, regional, or national levels that may increase the likelihood of limited, needed resources (i.e., Maslow's hierarchy of needs). These could include underfunded school systems, entrenched poverty, segregation, mass media, workplace policies, etc.

Summary

The B-Well model is biblically integrated with the evidence-based IS-Wel, particularly the four factors of the 4F-Wel. The B-Well model is our approach to attend to the whole person (mind, body, and spirit) that not only examines the problem areas but also calls for a positive lens, or the assets, of the client. The B-Well model functions within a continuum of poor mental health to biblical wellness. To engender a holistic lens, the model offers six facets—Heart, Mind, Strength, Soul, Neighbor, and Society. Each facet attends to a different aspect of the client and their context, seeking out deficits and assets within each facet to bring about a holistic assessment and case conceptualization, which leads to a robust treatment plan with stronger outcomes. The B-Well model expands beyond the current case conceptualization approaches by offering a framework where your personal counseling theory can be incorporated. In the following chapter, you will learn how to apply the B-Well model to "explain" the client's situation, using the six facets, which will assist you in the development of goals, recommendations, and interventions.

References

Adler, A. (1913/1956). *The individual psychology of Alfred Adler*. (H. L. Ansbacher & R. R. Ansbacher, Eds.), Harper Torchbooks. (Original work published in 1913)

Adler, A. (1987). Religion and individual psychology. *Individual Psychology, 43*(4), 522-526.

American Psychiatric Association (APA). (2013). *Diagnostic and statistical manual of mental disorders* (5th ed.). https://doi.org/10.1176/appi.books.9780890425596

Barry, J. D., Bomar, D., Brown, D. R., Klippenstein, R., Mangum, D., Sinclair Wolcott, C., Lazarus, W., Widder, W. (Eds.). (2016). *The Lexham Bible Dictionary*. Lexham Press.

Bronfenbrenner, U. (1979). *The ecology of human development: Experiments by nature and design*. Harvard University Press.

Bronfenbrenner, U., & Ceci, S. J. (1994). Nature-nurture reconceptualized: A bio-ecological model. *Psychological Review, 101*(4), 568–586. https://doi.org/10.1037/0033-295X.101.4.568

Dreikurs, R., & Mosak, H. H. (1966). The tasks of life I: Adler's three tasks. *Individual Psychologist, 4*, 18-22.

Dreikurs, R., & Mosak, H. H. (1967). The tasks of life II: The fourth life task. *Individual Psychologist, 4*, 51-55.

English Standard Bible. (2001). ESV Online. https://esv.literalword.com/

Grudem, W. (2018). *Christian ethics: An introduction to biblical moral reasoning*. Crossway.

Jones, L. J., & Butman, R. E. (2011). *Modern psychotherapies: A comprehensive Christian appraisal*. IVP Academic.

Lazarsfeld, S. (1966). The courage for imperfection. *Journal of Individual Psychology, 22*(2), 93-96.

McMinn, M. R. (1996). *Psychology, theology, and spirituality in Christian counseling*. Tyndale House Publishers.

McMinn, M. R. (2008). *Sin and grace in Christian counseling: An integrative paradigm*. IVP Academic.

Mosak, H. H., & Dreikurs, R. (1967). The life tasks III: The fifth life task. *Individual Psychology, 5* (1). 18-22.

Murdock, N. L. (2017). *Theories of counseling and psychotherapy: A case approach*. Pearson.

Myers, J. E. (1992). Wellness, prevention, development: The cornerstone of the profession. *Journal of Counseling & Development, 71*(2), 136–139. https://doi-org.ezproxy.liberty.edu/10.1002/j.1556-6676.1992.tb02188.x

Myers, J. E., Luecht, R. M., & Sweeney, T. J. (2004). The factor structure of wellness: Reexamining theoretical and empirical models underlying the wellness evaluation of lifestyle (WEL) and the five-factor wel. *Measurement and Evaluation in Counseling and Development, 36*(4), 194-208. https://doi.org/10.1080/07481756.2004.11909742

Myers, J. E., Sweeney, T. J., & Witmer, J. M. (2000). The Wheel of Wellness counseling for wellness: A holistic model for treatment planning. *Journal of Counseling & Development, 78*, 251–266. https://doi.org/10.1002/j.1556-6676.2000.tb01906.x

New International Bible. (2011). The NIV Bible. https://www.thenivbible.com (Original work published 1978)

Nuevo, R., Chatterji, S., Verdes, E., Naidoo, N., Arango, C., & Ayuso-Mateos, J. L. (2012). The continuum of psychotic symptoms in the general population: A cross-national study. *Schizophrenia Bulletin, 38*, 475–485. https://doi.org/10.1093/schbul/sbq099

Ohrt, J. H., Clarke, P. B., & Conley, A. H. (2019). *Wellness counseling: A holistic approach to prevention and intervention.* American Counseling Association.

Siddaway, A. P., Taylor, P. J., & Wood, A. M. (2018). Reconceptualizing anxiety as a continuum that ranges from high calmness to high anxiety: The joint importance of reducing distress and increasing well-being. *Journal of Personality and Social Psychology, 114*(2), e1-e11. https://doi.org/10.1037/pspp0000128

Sperry, L. S., & Sperry, J. S. (2012). *Case conceptualization: Mastering this competency with ease and confidence.* Routledge.

Tan, S. Y. (2011). *Counseling and psychotherapy: A Christian perspective.* Baker.

Tebeka, S., Geoffroy, P. A., Dubertret, C., & Le Strat, Y. (2021). Sadness and the continuum from well-being to depressive disorder: Findings from a representative U.S. population sample. *Journal of Psychiatric Research, 132,* 50-54. https://doi.org/10.1016/j.jpsychires.2020.10.004

Van Os, J., Linscott, R. J., Myin-Germeys, I., Delespaul, P., & Krabbendam, L. J. P. M. (2009). A systematic review and meta-analysis of the psychosis continuum: Evidence for a psychosis proneness-persistence-impairment model of psychotic disorder. *Psychological Medicine, 39*(2), 179-195. https://doi.org/10.1017/S0033291708003814

Watts, R. E. (2003). Adlerian therapy as a relational constructivist approach. *The Family Journal, 11*(2), 139-147. https://doi.org/10.1177/1066480702250169

CHAPTER 5

Case Conceptualization (CC) and Treatment Planning

David E. Jones, Angelica A. Greiner, & Crystal Hatton

"We believe that case conceptualization is the most important counseling competency besides developing a strong therapeutic alliance."

— Jon and Len Sperry

"The discerning person acquires knowledge, and the wise person seeks knowledge."

— Proverbs 18:15 (NET)

What is case conceptualization (CC), also called case formulation? It can be defined as "a tool for improving [clinical, pastoral] practice by helping describe and explain clients' [students, parishioners, family] presentations in ways that are theoretically informed, coherent, meaningful and lead to effective interventions" (Kuyken et al., 2008, p. 759). For some counseling professionals (e.g., clinical mental health, addiction, marriage and family), it is helpful to discriminate between a diagnosis and a case conceptualization. For others, such as school counselors and pastoral counselors, it has less relevance, but we will provide a brief overview for clarity.

A diagnosis is an atheoretical categorizing of signs and symptoms (*DSM-5*; American Psychiatric Association [APA], 2013). Diagnosis is the process of "describing" the client's presentation by labeling the predominant symptoms and other factors into a grouping such as major depressive disorder or generalized anxiety disorder (Schwitzer & Rubin, 2015). For example, when examining the client's presentation, you may see evidence of symptoms around a social anxiety disorder (e.g., anxiety about specific social situations such as school, home, and/or church; avoidance of anxiety-producing social situations that is excessive for the event; and the anxiety impairs daily functioning).

Contrary to diagnosis, case conceptualization is a process of "understanding," not labeling the symptoms. Through the analysis of the collected client data, the counselor can generate a theoretical understanding of the potential causes and contributing factors of the presenting problem and other problems. For example, using CBT, a client diagnosed with social anxiety disorder can be conceptualized as a client who has

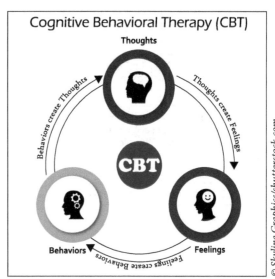

Cognitive Behavioral Therapy (CBT)

Thoughts

Behaviors create Thoughts

Thoughts create Feelings

CBT

Behaviors

Feelings

Feelings create Behaviors

an excessive fear of negative evaluations driven by a potential maladaptive core belief of "helplessness." Behaviorally, the client will encounter cues from their surroundings, such as a business trip and airplane travel, which elicit a specific phobia of flying. The client then engages in avoidant behaviors, such as driving long distances or canceling the business trip, as maladaptive coping approaches. By using CBT in the case conceptualization process, the counselor can understand the cognitive and behavioral processes that are maintaining the dysfunction. Identifying these factors then provides a pathway to tailor CBT interventions for the treatment of social anxiety disorder around these cognitive and behavioral dysfunctions.

Now that we have a clearer demarcation between diagnosis and case conceptualization, let us move into how to apply the B-Well model in case conceptualization. As a visual aid, we first offer a decision tree in Figure 1 as a stepwise approach to engaging in case conceptualization, and then we will walk you through the process. You will note there are two paths. The one on the right is for those who require a diagnosis. The path on the left does not apply the *DSM-5* to the case conceptualization process.

As found in Figure 1, assessment and data collection are the first steps. There are a variety of ways of assessing a client. In the clinical setting, a common approach is using a semi-structured interview (SSI) along with formal assessments as needed. The SSI would include an oral interview on a variety of domains (e.g., demographics, presenting problem, signs and symptoms, family, work, school, physical and mental history, cultural factors, military, trauma history, self-harm, harm to others, strengths/resources, and barriers to treatment) depending on the client profile and treatment approach (e.g., adults, child, couple, family). We believe it is during assessment and data collection that the B-Well model can first be applied. During the intake and assessment, the clinician views the client as a whole.

Conceptually, using the B-Well model, the presenting problem is a window to the coaction of the individual's whole self and their embeddedness in the environment. To evaluate the client as a whole,

FIGURE 1 Flow Diagram for Case Conceptualization

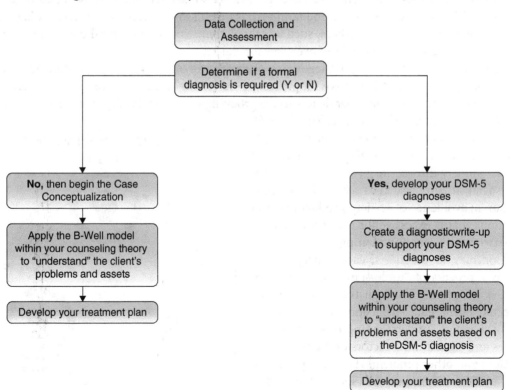

we will need to assess the Mind, Heart, Strength, Soul, Neighbor, and Society. As exampled above, a semi-structured interviewing process has the potential to cover most of the B-Well facets. Let's say you are examining the presenting problem using a semi-structured interview. At the minimum, it may include a symptom checklist and the mental status exam (MSE), allowing insight into the Mind, Heart, Strength, and Neighbor facets by retrieving cognitive concerns, affect/mood problems, physical ailments, and disorders in sleep, eating, and intrapersonal. Moreover, some semi-structured interview processes examine the Soul by investigating the religious and spiritual aspects of the client as required by a number of ethical codes noted in Chapter 1. Additionally, as you gather data on the problem areas by facet, it is important to glean the client's assets. This can be accomplished by asking specific open and closed questions as well as listening to the client's narrative to find the client's resources in the areas of Mind, Heart, Strength, Soul, Neighbor, and Society. For example, a client may speak about his problems at home with his child, and during this narrative, he discloses his sound relationship with his wife; or the client may remark on his daily reading of scripture. In these areas, you could ask clarifying questions to get a fuller, deeper understanding of the relationship with his wife and the spiritual disciplines in which he may engage, and how they help him cope.

If you do not work in a clinical setting, a simple process can be to write down the six facets on paper, or a computer, as an aid when asking the client about the problem. This ensures you capture both problems and assets in each of the relevant facets. Here again, the key is wisdom in asking open and closed questions to guide the client in the six facets, as well as employing essential counseling skills (i.e., active listening, reflection, paraphrasing, summarizing) as you listen to the client's narratives.

After data collection and assessment, you then organize your data by clinical concerns. This organization by themes can be done in a variety of ways—theoretically (e.g., CBT with maladaptive thinking, maladaptive behaviors), in areas of dysfunction based on the signs and symptoms (e.g., severity in anxiety, depression, avoidant behaviors), or *DSM-5* classifications (major depressive disorder, generalized anxiety disorder, opioid use disorder). Yet, we advocate for the use of the B-Well model's facets to organize both problems and assets—a holistic approach.

As you recall, the B-Well model has six facets—Heart, Mind, Strength, Soul, Neighbor, and Society. Heart offers a place to understand the dysfunction of mood and affect. We can understand the client to have elevated sadness or anger that is frequent, durable, and impairs the client's functioning. Mind offers a lens for the cognitive process. The client may be impaired by obsessive thinking, worry, tangential thought processes, or distractibility that harms their functioning. Strength offers a connection to the physical. A client may suffer from a chronic illness, panic attacks, disordered eating, and difficulty falling asleep. Soul can be a place for spiritual warfare, struggles that are not of this world but the spirit. This can be the influence of the devil or a place of intergenerational sin, but it also can be the inherent sinful choices we all make that disrupt healthy functioning. Neighbor points toward areas of disconnection or dysfunction within the family system, peers, and work that may interact across contexts. For example, a child may have few friends and struggle with understanding social cues. A wife may have poor communication with her husband, or a client may experience discrimination at work (e.g., glass ceiling). Finally, Society is the indirectly influencing systems around the client. The client may experience poverty, live in poor-quality housing, have an impoverished school system, have poor access to healthcare, or live in a food desert.

The B-Well model evaluates the client for assets alongside problem areas, identifying what aspects of the Heart, Mind, Strength, Soul, Neighbor, and Society can be helpful during treatment. The client may have the Heart advantage of a rich emotional vocabulary. Barrett (2017) suggests that emotional granularity is a powerful tool in emotion regulation. The client has the ability to adjust their emotional evaluation from a global "terrible" to a more accurate, "tense." A Mind asset is the ability to reframe a situation or identify unhealthy thoughts. A Strength could be physical health ... not having chronic ailments. The Soul facet points to a healthy spiritual identity, using Christian spiritual disciplines such as prayer, meditation, reading scripture to grow and cope, and a healthy view of God. The Neighbor facet may be a healthy family system and other healthy social connections such as friends. Socially, the client may have an advantage culturally. The client could be a White male who has implicit strengths based on social norms. The client could have a college education and a career that is in demand. Overall, during the assessment, the applications of both open and closed questions elicit client assets and difficulties in the six B-Well facets to gain a comprehensive understanding of the client and context.

© Maksym Drozd/shutterstock.com

The next step in moving forward in a case conceptualization is to determine if a *DSM-5* diagnosis is necessary. Several factors may determine if a formal diagnosis is required. If the client is using insurance, the client's insurance company may require a *DSM-5* diagnosis to indicate medical necessity. Your place of employment may require a diagnosis; the organization may bill for insurance (e.g., Medicare, Medicaid, Humana, Anthem, etc.). A diagnosis may also be required based on the diagnosis and your ethical and legal requirements. If a diagnosis is required, then develop your diagnosis, the diagnostic rationale, and then the case conceptualization using the B-Well model.

In contrast, if a diagnosis is not mandated by your organization or for insurance billing purposes, then your role may dictate otherwise. For example, if you are a marriage and family counselor and not billing insurance in your private practice, the use of the *DSM-5* may contraindicate based on your theoretical orientation, which is likely to view the client as part of a system. Another example is that as a school counselor or a pastor, diagnosis is not a part of your professional role. If a diagnosis is not required, then you can move directly to the B-Well case conceptualization.

Conducting a Case Conceptualization

We have now arrived at the case conceptualization (CC) process. We define case conceptualization as the process of *understanding* and *explaining* the clinical problems and assets. Let's start with a "problems" lens. If you did not need or desire to create a *DSM-5* diagnosis, then you can begin to explain the clinical problems through the B-Well's six facets (Mind, Heart, Strength, Soul, Neighbor, and Society). Which of these facets is used will depend on the assessment data collected and the problems identified. A thorough assessment will highlight which of the six facets are relevant for the client. After conducting an assessment, the clinical themes by facets may be excessive worry (Mind), fear orientation (Heart), avoidant/isolation behaviors (Strength), existential anxiety in the existence of God (Soul), difficulty in obtaining and maintaining social ties (Neighbor), and systematic discrimination (Society).

The therapist who developed the B-Well problem themes and a *DSM-5* diagnosis can approach the CC process in one of two ways. They can develop a CC based on the B-Well clinical problem themes (e.g., Heart, Mind, Strength, Soul, Neighbor, Society) only or they can integrate the *DSM-5* diagnosis and the clinical problem facet themes, explaining the diagnosis through the lens of the six facets. Let us offer an example.

A counselor has diagnosed a client with major depressive disorder (MDD) and a z-code of problems related to employment and unemployment. The client has experienced sadness for the past two months after losing his job. During these two months, the client has had difficulties falling asleep, loss of appetite, and troubled concentration. The client experienced a layoff due to cutbacks and economic contextual factors from the COVID-19 epidemic. When looking at the MDD diagnosis, an effective connection is between Heart and sadness. The Mind facet highlights difficulties with concentration. Strengths are discovered through physiological concerns—difficulties falling asleep and loss of appetite. Unemployment can be associated with the Society facet, with being laid off and other contextual factors (e.g., COVID-19) bringing about the unemployment.

With a holistic approach, it is also important to conceptualize the client's resources and assets. The Mind may offer a resiliency that the client exhibits during his job loss. A client may experience few or no physical ailments (Strength) that could exacerbate the major depressive disorder. An asset of the Soul facet that a Christian client may have would be a sound biblical view of suffering in which the client seeks God as succor during the trial and has hope in the here and now as well as an eschatological hope of Heaven and Christ's return. The client may have a Neighbor asset by being a member of a church where he has a sense of belonging and serves others.

Treatment and Intervention Planning

Clinical Mental Health, Addiction, and Marriage and Family Counseling

After the establishment of the case conceptualization, you then move to the final step of treatment planning. A variety of treatment planning approaches exists and is dependent on your clinical organization and the electronic health record system. For example, if working from a private practice, you may use an online program such as TherapyNotes, Theranest, or Simplepractice. Each of these has treatment plans organized around goals, objectives, and interventions. The goals are broad treatment outcomes. The objectives are written as what the client will do during the treatment process, and the interventions are what the counselors will do to help the client reach the objectives and the collaborative goals. If you work for a hospital, they may use an electronic health record system such as Epic. A hospital may tailor its Epic interface, but the treatment plan may follow the same format of goal, objective, and intervention. What is important from our perspective is that the golden thread of assessment, diagnosis, and case conceptualization drives the treatment plan's goals, objectives, and interventions. A disconnect does not exist between the diagnosis and/or conceptualization of the client and your treatment plan outcomes. Let's offer a case for clarity using the B-Well model.

When developing a treatment plan through the lens of the B-Well model, the first step is to recall that it is a holistic model that attends to both assets and deficiencies when using the six facets. For this example, we will work from an explicit Christian integration that was requested and consented by the client. This request is documented in progress notes to operate ethically. The goals may or may not be driven by your specific clinical theory (e.g., psychodynamic, Adlerian, CBT, marriage and family), but the B-Well model may influence the goals by applying the facets as the potential end of treatment outcomes. For example, for our client above experiencing major depressive disorder, a Heart goal is to replace depressive symptoms with joy and gladness; a Strength goal is reestablished homeostasis (e.g., elimination of sleep and appetite disturbances, improved concentration); and a Society goal would be re-established employment.

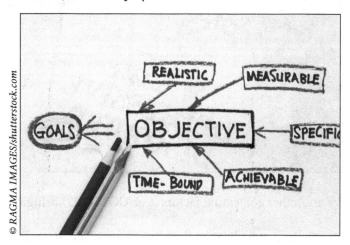

The next step in a treatment plan, based on our approach, is the development of objectives and interventions for each goal. As noted above, an objective is what the client will do. The first goal above is a Heart goal—to replace depressive symptoms with joy and gladness. Here you can integrate your theory lens and the B-Well model. I, the first author, generally work from a cognitive behavioral lens. From an integrated CBT lens, an objective can be, "The client will replace perceived unlovability with an accurate biblical understanding of self." As an aside, depending on organizational requirements, the objective can be modified using more secular language: "The client will replace perceived unlovability with an accurate understanding of self." To accomplish this objective, the therapist can use both biblical and CBT interventions as ethically appropriate. For example, a clinician may have a client engage in a thought log, replacing automatic thoughts with a scriptural understanding of self. A Strength objective can be, "The client will attend service once per week at church" as a way to engage in behavioral activation. The counselor may use activity scheduling to assist the client in behavioral activation. To reach employment (the Society goal), the client can generate an updated resume and develop a cover letter. In addition to problem-solving based on the COVID-19 systematic influences on employment, the counselor may provide psychoeducation on current best practices for resumes and cover letters and connect the client to job-seeking services within his community.

Of course, the objectives' interventions will need to be client-specific and adhere to ethical and legal codes. As noted above, the client was a Christian and desired to use his Christian worldview in treatment. When working with a secular client, the goals, objectives, and interventions would be modified. Yet, the therapist can still apply the B-Well model in generating a holistic treatment plan based on the six facets that would have been used in assessing and conceptualizing the client.

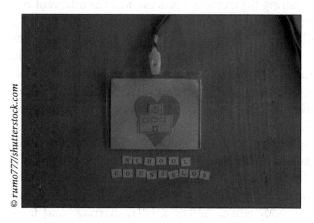

School Counseling

School counselors have an ethical obligation "to address PreK-12 students' academic, career, and social/emotional development needs" (American School Counselor Association [ASCA], 2016, p. 1), and this includes serving all students with various cultural characteristics. Furthermore, Kimbel and Schellenberg (2013), suggest that school counselors have an ethical obligation to address the whole child, which includes students' religious and spiritual needs. When school

FIGURE 1 The Microskills Hierarchy: A Pyramid for Building Cultural Intentionality

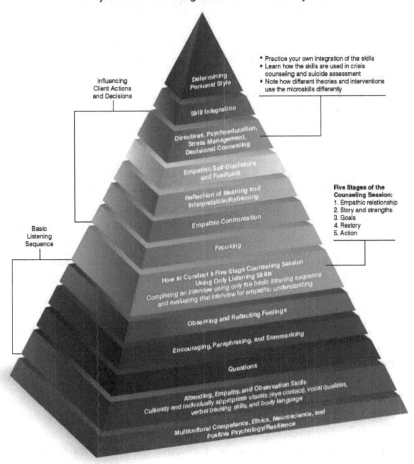

The Microskills Hierarchy
A Pyramid for Building Cultural Intentionality

From *Intentional Interviewing and Counseling: Facilitating Client Development in a Multicultural Society* by Allen E. Ivey, Mary Bradford Ivey, Carlos P. Zalaquett. Copyright © 2017 Cengage Learning. Reprinted by permission.

counselors adhere to the profession's ethical standards and exemplify a biblical worldview, they can demonstrate unconditional love, compassion, and grace to effectively meet the holistic needs of students.

Accordingly, a key role of school counselors is to work collaboratively with their students to help them navigate a variety of issues. As school counselors support their students, they must provide them with the necessary tools to solve their issues, rather than giving them advice or solving their problems for them. School counselors can use their counseling skills and theory of preference (e.g., person-centered, solution-focused brief therapy, Adlerian) to guide their work with students.

Ivey and colleagues (2017) provide a hierarchy of counseling skills that school counselors can integrate into their sessions with students (see Figure 1). At the base of the hierarchy are the following counseling skills: multicultural competence, attending skills, and empathy skills. The school counselor must establish rapport before discussing a student's issue. Once rapport has been established, school counselors will use their active listening skills (e.g., open and closed questions, encouraging, paraphrasing, summarizing, and reflecting feelings) to conduct a school counseling session. Specifically, school counselors will use their active listening skills to draw out their students' stories and assets, including the six facets of the B-Well model (e.g., Heart, Mind, Strength, Soul, Neighbor, and Society). Once school counselors conceptualize the students' stories and assets, they will want to collaboratively brainstorm goals and potential alternatives to address the issue. After the school counselor and student jointly determine agreed-upon goals, they will develop an action plan. The action plan consists of specific interventions that are taken to assist students in achieving their goal(s). The interventions must be tailored to each student's specific goal(s). The action plan can include the following: discussing natural and logical consequences, providing directives, psychoeducation, and/or theoretical interventions. For this textbook, we are going to apply the B-Well model to theories that are commonly used by school counselors and provide recommended goals and interventions for each theory.

Pastoral Counseling

Pastors, generally, do not develop treatment plans but will establish interventions based on the client's needs via a plan of care. Best practices are to write a plan of care for each client. The spiritual care assessment and case conceptualization are the baseline for the "treatment" of spiritual concerns. Based on a sound assessment and case conceptualization, collaborative goals and associated interventions are developed. Many times, the focus is on "spiritual" and "emotional" concerns.

A plan of care is dependent on the client's reported problems. If the client is in hospice care experiencing elevated anxiety, the pastor develops a goal(s) to relieve the suffering with the perceived problem of death and associated fear. The goal(s) could be (1) to fully express fear associated with death, (2) to develop acceptance of the process of death, or (3) to cognitively, emotionally, and/or physically recognize and accept the love of God or the divine. The goals will be achieved through interventions such as providing unconditional positive regard, assisting in the expression of associated fear, understanding the client's religious beliefs associated with God or the divine, and facilitating the scriptural hope of Heaven, etc.

To enhance the current process, the pastor can utilize the six facets during the assessment and conceptualization phases, which then allows the pastor to filter the goals and interventions through the six facets. The pastor can reflect on each facet to see if the problem needs to be expanded beyond anxiety (Heart) to other aspects of the client (e.g., Mind, Strength, Soul, Neighbor, Society). As the pastor listens to the client's narrative, they may discover that the physical ailments (Strength) are increasing the client's worry. They may also hear unsound beliefs about who God is (Soul). Additional goals and interventions can be added to the plan of care to assist the client with a holistic approach (mind, body, and spirit) to bring comfort to the client.

Summary

Historically, case conceptualization or case formulation is the process of "explaining" a client's concerns through a theory. We advanced this process by applying the B-Well model and its six facets to the case conceptualization process. Using the B-Well model moves beyond a single theoretical orientation by engaging in a holistic lens that attends to not only the clinical problems but also the client's assets.

As the counselor assesses the client, they will determine if a diagnosis is required or not. Based on this knowledge and their professional needs, the counselor will engage in a case conceptualization process that assists in the explanation of the problems that lead to a treatment plan, action plan, or plan of care. This plan of care is a holistic approach that is driven by assessment and case conceptualization. The ideal plan offers holistic goals and interventions, attends to the identified problems, and engages the client's assets to bring about relief and healing.

The case conceptualization process and planning will be further elaborated within the subsequent chapters. The following chapters are separated by discipline—school counselor, clinical mental health counselor, addiction counselor, pastoral counseling, marriage and family counseling, and special populations (e.g., children and late adulthood). Each chapter (i.e., school, clinical mental health, etc.) will offer the use of a specific theory within the B-Well model to conceptualize a case study and offer an associated treatment plan.

References

American School Counselor Association (ASCA). (2016). *ASCA ethical standards for school counselors.* https://www.schoolcounselor.org/About-School-Counseling/Ethical-Legal-Responsibilities/ASCA-Ethical-Standards-for-School-Counselors-(1)

American Psychiatric Association (APA). (2013). *Diagnostic and statistical manual of mental disorders* (5th ed.). https://doi.org/10.1176/appi.books.9780890425596

Barrett, L. F. (2017). *How emotions are made: The secret life of the brain.* Harper Paperbacks.

Ivey, A. E., Ivey, M. B., & Zalaquett, C. P. (2017). *Intentional interviewing and counseling: Facilitating client development in a multicultural society* (9th ed.). Cengage Learning.

Kimbel, T. M., & Schellenberg, R. (2013). Meeting the holistic needs of students: A proposal for spiritual and religious competencies for school counselors. *Professional School Counseling, 17*(1), 76-85. https://doi.org/10.1177/2156759X0001700110

Kuyken, W., Padesky, C. A., & Dudley, R. (2008). Process issues: The science and practice of case conceptualization. *Behavioural and Cognitive Psychotherapy, 36*(6), 757–768. https://doi.org/10.1017/S1352465808004815

New English Translation. (2020). The NET Bible. https://netbible.org/ (Original work published in 2001)

Schwitzer, A. M., & Rubin, L. C. (2015). *Diagnosis & treatment planning skills* (2nd ed.). Sage.

Sperry, J., & Sperry, L. (December 7, 2020). *Case conceptualization: Key to highly effective counseling.* https://ct.counseling.org/2020/12/case-conceptualization-key-to-highly-effective-counseling/#comments.

B-Well Model in School Counseling Using Solution-Focused Brief Therapy

Denise B. Ebersole and Charity A. Kurz

> "Finally, brothers and sisters, whatever is true, whatever is noble, whatever is right, whatever is pure, whatever is lovely, whatever is admirable—if anything is excellent or praiseworthy—think about such things. Whatever you have learned or received or heard from me or seen in me—put it into practice. And the God of peace will be with you."
>
> — Philippians 4:8-9 (NIV)

This chapter will focus on the application of the B-Well model in school counseling using solution-focused brief therapy (SFBT). In this chapter, we will share a brief summary of SFBT and the application of SFBT in the school counseling role. Additionally, we will include a Christian integration approach and application to the case study of Joey, applying the B-Well model to the case study and including specific SFBT interventions. For the purpose of the current chapter, the authors will use the term *therapy* rather than counseling and *complaint* rather than problem to be consistent with the origins of the SFBT approach. The term *student* will be used instead of client as the authors are writing specifically about the integration of SFBT and B-Well with students in the school setting. Finally, the term *counselors* used throughout refers to school counselors.

Background of Solution-Focused Brief Therapy (SFBT)

SFBT has become more commonly utilized in school settings. It has been found to be impactful in schools and effective while working with children (Sklare, 2014). In their initial study, Mostert and colleagues (1997) found that training school counselors in the solution-focused brief counseling model was both "feasible and practical" (p. 23) and that it was an appropriate fit for the school setting due to the brief nature of the approach. More recently, Sabella (2020) described the solution-focused approach as a "forerunner for counseling approaches that are becoming more integrative" (p. 23). The solution-focused approach is now viewed as a best practice within schools and encompasses individual and group counseling as well as when integrated into a comprehensive school counseling program. Finally, regarding the brief nature of SFBT and the number of recommended sessions, de Shazer (1985) described the goal as being "as few as possible" (p. 4) as the intent of SFBT is to help resolve the problem as quickly as possible. LaFountain and Garner (1998) also affirmed the importance of utilizing a brief approach in a school setting as has Sklare (2014) who asserted that focusing on solutions results in briefer counseling sessions.

Origins

Solution-focused brief therapy (SFBT) is a solution and future-focused constructive approach. In applying SFBT, counselors use interventions to help individuals shift their focus toward the future, effectively use their strengths, and make necessary changes toward potential solutions (Molnar & de Shazer, 1987; Murdock, 2017). After noticing that the majority of therapists focused on "problems," de Shazer (1985) became intent to change the direction of counseling. More specifically, de Shazer believed

that an emphasis on problems and problem solving might not be as effective as focusing on the solution, the process of the solution, and utilizing simple solution-focused tasks to "promote satisfying change" (p. xv). de Shazer's contributions challenged the traditional methods of identifying the problems and root cause(s). Instead of focusing on problems, or "locks," where things are not working, de Shazer emphasized solutions and interventions describing them as "keys" or more specifically, skeleton keys, that could unlock many different doors. Grounded in this newer approach, clients could benefit from a less complicated method by shifting away from the problem focus while noticing that "complaints" could be more easily addressed by creating a more satisfactory future or vision for themselves.

In more recent years, solution-focused therapists and counselors have continued to expand the original intent of SFBT and have applied it across diverse settings. Now, instead of taking an in-depth approach to understanding problems, the solution-focused approach shifts toward solutions and necessary action and is applicable in the school setting (Sklare, 2014). Counselors grounded in the SFBT approach guide individuals toward identifying what is already going well and that which could be going better, or a preferred future, as if the complaint no longer exists.

View of Human Nature

The overall view of human nature according to the SFBT approach is helping individuals understand what they already have within them that they can use to "make a satisfactory life" (de Shazer, 1985, p.6) without focusing on underlying problems that need to be corrected. Instead, from the SFBT perspective, individuals are viewed to have tried everything that they can to address their complaints yet still feel stuck regardless of their effort (de Shazer, 1985). Rather than continue to focus on the complaints, the SFBT counselor is grounded in searching for solutions and implementing interventions designed to help the individual identify possible solutions, thereby identifying a new vision for their preferred or satisfactory future. Instead of analyzing the past or trying to fully understand every detail, an SFBT counselor helps the individual construct a solution that will prompt change (Sabella, 2020). Focusing on the cooperative nature between the school counselor and the individual is also important as the SFBT counselor views the individual as being capable of making change occur.

View of Change

The view of change from the SFBT approach is for counselors to help individuals start to see how they could do something different, which could then prompt them toward making necessary and positive changes (de Shazer, 1985). Unlike other approaches, SFBT counselors do not attempt to fully understand a complaint before considering interventions; rather, they intentionally start to shift the focus of the session toward creating opportunities for small, measurable, and immediate change (Sabella, 2020). Additionally, SFBT counselors aim to help individuals shift their focus from the past to the present and, ultimately, to the future to help them identify that which is already going well so they can build upon those strengths (de Shazer, 1985). SFBT counselors also strengthen and propel the collaborative relationship by helping the student identify past successes and what they did that resulted in that success to help them work toward a preferred future (Sabella, 2020). Additionally, effective goal setting is a structured approach in that goals for change need to be detailed, within the student's control,

and involve action to help avoid feeling stuck (Sabella, 2020). Within the school setting, SFBT is an excellent approach to use as the school schedule and other time constraints would inhibit more traditional approaches that are not brief in nature (LaFountain & Garner, 1998). In summary, the SFBT counselor views change as being within the client's control, possible, and necessary to help individuals get "unstuck" so they can move toward their preferred future.

SFBT school counselors aim to help their students better understand, identify, and reframe their language (LaFountain & Garner, 1998). More specifically, by helping students replace more negative language, such as labels or absolutes, counselors can teach students to use more accurate words to describe themselves or their situations. By using SFBT interventions in a collaborative relationship, counselors can teach students how to identify and apply their innate strengths to make small, measurable, and immediate changes in other areas of their lives. Useful SFBT tools and interventions include but are not limited to the Crystal Ball Technique or Miracle Question, reframing, identifying strengths, goal setting, and scaling. These are just a few of the incredibly useful and effective tools that SFBT counselors can use to help clients make progress and get unstuck (Sabella, 2020).

Christian Integration Perspective

Regarding Christian integration, the authors want to distinguish two important aspects of integration including the experience of Christians employed as school counselors in secular settings and the integration of the SFBT approach within the Christian faith. It is helpful to reflect upon Jones and Butman's (2011) ideal scenario for Christian integration in that both faith and scholarship should "naturally mix" (p. 19). Although it would be ideal to easily integrate, or naturally mix, faith and scholarship, it can be difficult at times. Entwistle (2015) presents four integration models counselors could consider when trying to rectify spiritual beliefs and their work. It is important to note that incongruency can and will occur without having a solid integrative approach. For example, SFBT and Christian integration, at the forefront, might appear to be an oxymoron, because SFBT is labeled as a constructivist approach. Constructivism, at its core, teaches that there is no right or wrong and emphasizes autonomy in how the student constructs their reality. Therefore, it is important to acknowledge the theory itself relies on the student's interpretation and construction of their reality.

From a biblical standpoint, all people are limited in their autonomy to reach perfection. However, the Bible does address strengths as God-given and the responsibility of the Christian to work toward sanctification, which includes participating in Godly thoughts and behaviors. According to Philippians 4:8-9, Paul, in his letter to the church at Philippi, says,

> Finally, brothers and sisters, whatever is true, whatever is noble, whatever is right, whatever is pure, whatever is lovely, whatever is admirable—if anything is excellent or praiseworthy— think about such things. Whatever you have learned or received or heard from me, or seen in me—put it into practice. And the God of peace will be with you. (*New International Bible*, 1978/2011)

Notice that Paul starts the passage by talking about how to think and ends by reminding the Philippians to "put it into practice," which suggests a shift in thinking and behavior change.

School counselors who are Christians often face challenging situations and circumstances that make it difficult to integrate their faith or at least know how to respond in a way that is congruent with their faith. For example, how should a school counselor who is a Christian respond in a scenario at school when they are expected to affirm something that they perceive as being inconsistent with their faith? How should they respond when their professional school counseling association expects them to believe and ultimately act upon the association's position that all school counselors must act, think, and/or behave in a way that is in direct violation of their faith? Many school counselors, including the authors, have unfortunately faced these and other similar situations where it has resulted in significant concerns and difficult decisions for Christians, especially when employed in public school settings.

However, school counselors who are Christians know full well that they are to avoid "imposing their values on students, especially when the school counselor's values are discriminatory in nature" (ASCA, 2016, A.6.e.) and adhere to training standards (CACREP, 2016). While Christians do not view their faith-based beliefs as discriminatory, and instead view their school counseling role as an extension of their ability to serve and love others even with differences, it can be challenging to confidently serve as school counselors with a biblical worldview. The authors have experienced incongruent thoughts and feelings while trying to integrate faith and counseling. As culture, legislatures, and the general norms of society continue to deviate farther away from traditional Christian values and beliefs, school counselors will increasingly be in situations where their faith and professional roles do not easily mix. As a result, the authors recommend that Christians engage in spiritual disciplines, familiarize themselves with the models presented by Entwistle (2015), adhere to professional and ethical standards, and make intentional decisions about how they will respond in a way that is consistent with those expectations without negating their faith.

A Case Study: Joey

© BearFotos/shutterstock.com

Joey is an 8-year-old, Caucasian male who lives with his birth parents and two younger siblings in rural Pennsylvania. Both of his parents are at home, mom as a homemaker and dad as a farmer, and struggle financially to make ends meet. Joey began third grade three months ago in the local public school. Prior to this academic year, Joey was attending a private, K-12 Christian college-prep school with small group instruction. Because of financial concerns, his parents could no longer afford this option. The family is heavily involved in church, participating in Sunday school, Sunday morning service, and Wednesday night classes.

Recently, mom received a phone call from Joey's school counselor. The school counselor reported that she, as well as his classroom teacher, were concerned because Joey has appeared to be distracted during class time. She stated that Joey interacts appropriately with peers, but he is not meeting the academic standards for third grade. The school counselor reported that she observed Joey "dancing" around the classroom during work time. Teachers reported he rarely finishes his class work, and Joey must be continuously redirected. His behavior is disruptive to the other students and appears to be increasing in frequency. In addition, the school counselor shared concerns from his teacher about his lack of effort in completing assignments. She stated that he makes careless mistakes in his work. She reported it appears he is not listening to her when she speaks even though he makes appropriate eye contact.

Mom began to ponder Joey's behavior in the home. She realized he appears off-task and distracted when trying to complete basic chores such as picking up his toys and struggles to regulate his energy. When Joey is asked to clean his room, his mom must tell him exactly what to do. Additionally, mom claims that Joey appears to have difficulty in beginning and completing the task. Mom recalled a time when Joey was running circles around the outside perimeter of the home just before bed. When confronted, Joey reported, "My body is tired, but I have so much energy." Mom reported that he loves to be outside, working with his hands, and building. He also enjoys helping  on the family farm and hopes to work full-time on the farm after high school. Mom also recalled Joey recently sharing that he was having difficulty paying attention at school. He stated that he wished that he could pay attention to his teacher.

When the school counselor asked Joey about his inattentiveness at school, Joey reported that he "hates being stuck inside" and desires to be outside. Joey shared that, "School is stupid and a waste of time." He described this school as a "prison" that keeps him from doing what he wants to do. He reported that he gets frustrated when he must do schoolwork. He said that he becomes frustrated mainly in reading and writing, but he loves his P.E. and art classes. Joey reported that he also enjoys outdoor soccer and basketball but is unsure if he will be able to continue due to the financial concerns at home. When asked about the differences between his old school and his new school, he reported that he liked learning in a small group and that the school talked about God. He reported that he wishes that he was at his old school so that he could talk about God. When asked about his relationships at school, he reported that he enjoys building forts after school with his friend Stephen, who is in his class. He also reported that he enjoys talking to his P.E. teacher since they share similar interests in sports.

Applying the B-Well Model Using SFBT

As mentioned in a previous chapter, the B-Well model was designed using a biblical worldview lens and is grounded in wellness. Examining the facets of the B-Well model and how they apply to this case using an SFBT approach is the primary objective of this section. It is important to note the authors advocate for counseling in schools with a biblical worldview while adhering to the ACA Code of Ethics (2014) which prohibits counselors from "imposing-their own values, attitudes, beliefs, and behaviors" (A.4.b.) and ASCA Ethical Standards for School Counselors which prohibits "imposing personal beliefs or values rooted in one's religion, culture or ethnicity" (A.1.f.). In the application of the B-Well model and SFBT, both the model and theory look at student complaints and interventions holistically, based on student strengths. The goal of SFBT is to help the student move toward change and embrace management while using a solution focus as opposed to a problem focus (Sabella, 2020).

Heart

From the perspective of the Heart in the B-Well model, it is vital to address Joey's overall wellness, including his emotional state and presenting complaints. Joey's complaints of frustration are centered around his inability to be active, yet the onset of his negative emotions began when he moved to a new school which triggered feelings of grief/loss. Changes in friendships, faith-based school, and community produced feelings of instability and significantly affected his emotional state. The school counselor will not be able to change Joey's desire, but instead can help Joey understand his emotions and the language he uses, as well as identify healthy coping strategies to better manage his strong emotions.

Mind

Joey's Mind is fixated on being actively kinesthetic and his desire to be outside. His surface-level thought compares school to a "prison," which insinuates that Joey believes he is trapped and being held captive. Joey's worldview influences his feelings because he believes, as an 8-year-old, that he should be allowed to be outside. This ineffective thought influences his ability to complete his assignments and engage in the school setting. The thought in and of itself is not wrong, but it has become excessive in nature. He does not see the need for schooling, as evidenced by his calling school "stupid" and a "waste of time." Additionally, he may believe that he is not competent to complete the work and thus avoids it.

Strength

Strength is a core tenant of SFBT as well as a facet of the B-Well model. According to the B-Well model, wellness is a continuum that includes both effective and ineffective physical and behavioral choices. It is apparent that Joey has developed maladaptive behaviors, such as inattention and increased hyperactivity, to cope with grief/loss. Joey is a strong kinesthetic learner, who has demonstrated excellent motor memory. The teachers report that he engages in prosocial behavior, yet the hyperactivity appears to impact his academic performance. Dancing in the classroom is purposeful in meeting his sensory needs, but again, impacts his ability to be academically successful.

Soul

Regarding the Soul, Joey is uncomfortable in his current setting as he perceives he is limited in his expression of his faith in God. He has stated several times that he misses the opportunity to freely share his faith in God. It is evident that he has an unmet spiritual need of being able to engage in spiritual conversations. Additionally, he is not able to express his intrinsic value associated with being made in the image of God, as the focus is primarily on him as a student. Unification of the spiritual and physical connection is missing, thus producing this spiritual gap.

Neighbor

From the Neighbor facet, Joey appears to be socially connected to peers but disconnected from his previous community. Prior to starting at this new school, he felt spiritually connected to teachers and students within his school community. While he still feels connected to his mother, it is important to note that he may not feel a connection to his father. Within his local community, Joey is appropriately engaged with peers as he participates in school and on a soccer team. Additionally, he relates well to the P.E. teacher.

Society

Overall, Joey's Society facet and contextual factors, including proximal relationships, have affected him. His current relationships are impacting his feeling of being stuck, which in turn, is causing him to feel emotionally lethargic. For example, Joey identifies as Christian and has expressed his desire to discuss God in his public school, but he is unable to spiritually connect with peers and adults in this setting. Additionally, Joey described school as a "prison," which signifies that he sees this system as a barrier to his success. The concentric rings of influence, including his place of residence, socioeconomic status, and educational demands, as well as peer influence, are incongruent with his family expectations and his own sense of self.

Recommended Goals and Interventions

When considering a wellness approach, the American School Counselor Association Ethical Standards (ASCA, 2016) emphasize the need for school counselors to incorporate a wellness model in their work with students. It is important to note that wellness includes spirituality (Hettler, 1976). Additionally, in the case of Joey, his spirituality is an important aspect of himself. Failing to address the spirituality piece with Joey in the action plan and interventions would be considered unethical (ASERVIC, 2009; Kimbell & Schellenberg, 2014).

The authors recognize that the B-Well model and SFBT look holistically at the student when conceptualizing complaints and implementing interventions. Student complaints and interventions are not separated but rather are interconnected and amendable. A sample intervention plan for Joey is presented below (Table 1). It is important to note the SFBT interventions presented do not have to be implemented in a particular order but rather are interchangeable and pliable. Additionally, goal setting is a common intervention used in SFBT to help students address complaints (Sabella, 2020). It is recommended that school counselors use SMART goals in creating comprehensive school counseling programs, including individual counseling, group counseling, and classroom lessons (ASCA, 2019).

The initial intervention, not outlined in the plan, is rapport building with an emphasis on hearing the student's story and listening for language that signifies absolutes, labels, and the student's willingness to change. It is important that Joey's willingness to change be assessed prior to developing a plan of action. The school counselor may ask questions such as, "What is going well? What do you want to change or do differently? What has worked for you in the past?" As the student shares their story, the counselor will identify how to incorporate the various interventions presented in the plan below. The overarching goal for working with Joey would be to help him get unstuck and start using his strengths more proactively in the present with a view to the future in regard to Heart, Mind, Strength, Soul, Neighbor, and Society.

Complaint (Mind and Soul)

It is evident that Joey does not like school. He mentioned his thoughts about how he perceives school as a "prison." It would be important to help reframe Joey's thinking about the purpose of school. In counseling from a future-focused lens, the counselor may include a discussion about the connection between school and Joey's desire to work as a farmer. From an SFBT approach, it will be important for the school counselor to help Joey identify what has worked for him in the past to complete his assignments and tasks. The counselor may also elicit academic strategies that have helped Joey meet academic demands before coming to the new school. If Joey believed that he was competent to complete the work, Joey may be more motivated and experience success, which, in turn, could impact his view of school. The school counselor should assess his commitment to change as part of the counseling process as well. His commitment level could also be a strength.

The school counselor would work with Joey to develop a plan to meet the academic standards. Joey would also benefit from a friendship group to build connections at school and to school. Additionally, if the school offers a Bible study club before or after school, this may be an opportunity for Joey to exercise the religious and spiritual side of himself. Research has consistently outlined the need for children to experience a sense of belonging (Davis & Davis, 2007; Metcalf, 2021). This sense of belonging would hopefully increase Joey's success at school.

Complaint (Strength)

An area of growth, from an SFBT perspective, includes improving the completion of assignments and incomplete tasks. Although the presented case does not identify past achievements, it will be important for the school counselor to help Joey recognize his previous successes and apply them to his current strengths. Based on teacher and parent reports, Joey appears to be having difficulty staying on task at home and at school. He is not completing assignments, which is causing him to not meet grade-level standards. The school counselor can use scaling with Joey to determine the baseline and the potential goal. Additionally, the school counselor can help Joey use scaling to determine his time on task and his level of work completion. It is recommended that both the teacher and Joey use the scaling questions so that Joey can compare his scores to the teacher's scores to determine growth. Scaling conceptualizes student complaints and progress on a continuum, which mirrors the B-Well model because the model is viewed as a continuum of wellness (see Chapter 4).

It will be important for the school counselor to help Joey identify additional resources and opportunities, outside of soccer, that help meet his desires to be kinesthetically active. It is recommended that Joey receives mentorship from an adult within the school building. Because of his positive relationship with the P.E. teacher, it is suggested that this relationship be used to mentor Joey both educationally and kinesthetically. This connection to an adult at the school would also impact Joey's wellness from the Neighbor facet of the B-Well model.

Complaint (Neighbor)

Joey has expressed his own desire to be outside more often during the day. Although this may be limited while at school, it may be feasible after school. The school counselor should work collaboratively with Joey and his parents to help Joey articulate his need to be outside and working on the farm. Based on the action plan, it is recommended that Joey increase his time outside to shadow his father on the farm and to potentially join a club such as 4-H. This will allow Joey experience in farm work prior to graduation, but it will also allow him to meet his sensory needs that are not able to be met at the level he needs within the school building.

TABLE 1 Recommended Goals and Interventions Using SFBT

Complaint	Goal	Intervention #1	Intervention #2
Joey does not like school because he is unable to talk about his faith, and he is unable to be active with peers.	In two months, Joey will increase his desire to come to school by 2 on a Likert scale from 1 (no desire) to 10 (extremely desirable). [Mind, Soul]	Reframing purpose of school and its value/connection to his future work on the farm	Participating in a friendship group to build connection, as well as recommend the Bible study on campus before/afterschool

Complaint	Goal	Intervention #1	Intervention #2
Joey is often off-task and does not complete his work.	In two months, Joey will complete his classwork in the allotted time identified by the teacher, 80% of the time. [Strength]	Scaling to determine time on task and verbal praise and amplification	Mentorship with P.E. teacher to create educational opportunities (i.e., tutoring) and kinesthetic opportunities (i.e., afterschool sports)
Joey wants to be outside more often with his dad and peers.	Over the next two weeks, Joey will go outside for at least 10 minutes per day most days. [Neighbor]	Shadowing his dad on the farm	Connecting Joey with a 4-H program

Summary

As mentioned, school counselors who are Christians can find it difficult to integrate their theoretical approach and their own spirituality. We hope that the readers had the opportunity to conceptualize the application of the B-Well model in school counseling using solution-focused brief therapy (SFBT). Our intent was for school counselors who are Christians to become more familiar with SFBT, the application of SFBT in the school counseling role, and the importance of Christian integration, and to consider the application of SFBT and the B-Well model. One of the foundational pillars of counseling is using a wellness lens to conceptualize presenting concerns. Using the B-Well model along with SFBT will allow school counselors to not only address wellness from a spiritual perspective but also help school counselors implement SFBT interventions to minimize student complaints and help them reach their goals.

References

American Counseling Association (ACA). (2014). *2014 ACA code of ethics.*

http://www.counseling.org/Resources/aca-code-of-ethics.pdf

American School Counselor Association (ASCA). (2016). *ASCA ethical standards for school counselors.* https://schoolcounselor.org/About-School-Counseling/Ethical-Legal-Responsibilities/ASCA-Ethical-Standards-for-School-Counselors-(1)

American School Counselor Association (ASCA). (2019). *The ASCA national model: A framework for school counseling programs* (4th ed.). Author.

Association for Spiritual, Ethical, and Religious Values in Counseling (ASERVIC). (2009). *Competencies for addressing spiritual and religious issues in counseling.* https://aservic.org/wp-content/uploads/2021/04/ASERVIC-Spiritual-Competencies_FINAL.pdf

Council of the Accreditation of Counseling and Related Educational Programs (CACREP). (2016). *2016 standards for accreditation.* https://www.cacrep.org/for-programs/2016-cacrep-standards/

Davis, S., & Davis, J. (2007). *Schools where everyone belongs: Practical strategies for reducing bullying.* Research Press.

de Shazer, S. (1985). *Keys to solutions in brief therapy.* W. W. Norton and Company.

Entwistle, D. N. (2015*). Integrative approaches to psychology and Christianity: An introduction to worldview issues, philosophical foundations, and models of integration* (3rd ed.). Wipf and Stock Publishers.

Hettler, B. (1976). *The six dimensions of wellness model.* http://www.NationalWellness.org

Jones, L. J., & Butman, R. E. (2011). *Modern psychotherapies: A comprehensive Christian appraisal.* InterVarsity Press.

Kimbel, T., & Schellenberg, R. (2014). Meeting the holistic needs of students: A proposal for spiritual and religious competencies for school counselors. *Professional School Counseling 17*(1), 76-85. https://doi.org/10.1177/2156759X0001700110

LaFountain, R. M., & Garner, N. E. (1998). *A school with solutions: Implementing a solution-focused/Adlerian based comprehensive school counseling program.* American School Counselor Association.

Metcalf, L. (2021). *Counseling toward solutions: A practical, solution-focused program for working with students, teachers, and parents.* Routledge.

Molnar, A., & de Shazer, S. (1987). Solution-focused therapy: Toward the identification of therapeutic tasks. *Journal of Marital and Family Therapy, 13*(4), 349-358. https://doi.org/10.1111/j.1752-0606.1987.tb00716.x

Mostert, D. L., Johnson, E., & Mostert, M. P. (1997). The utility of solution-focused, brief counseling in schools: Potential from an initial study. *Professional School Counseling, 1*(1), 21-24. https://www.jstor.org/stable/42731885

Murdock, N. (2017). *Theories of counseling and psychotherapy.* (4th ed.). Pearson.

New International Bible. (2011). The NIV Bible. https://www.thenivbible.com (Original work published 1978)

Sabella, R. A. (2020). *Solution-focused school counseling: The missing manual.* Sabella & Associates, LLC.

Sklare, G. B. (2014). *Brief counseling that works: A solution-focused therapy approach for school counselors and other mental health professionals* (3rd ed.). Corwin Press.

CHAPTER 7

B-Well Model in School Counseling Using Existential Therapy

LaShonda B. Fuller and Shawn Latrice Moore

"The more the words, the less the meaning, and how does that profit anyone?"

— Ecclesiastes 6:11 (NIV)

This chapter focuses on the application of existential therapy (ET) using the B-Well model. Key concepts of ET are presented to provide a basic understanding of ET's foundational principles. ET is not technique oriented but is philosophically driven based on human existence (Corey, 2016). After a brief ET review, a Christian integrative perspective and denominational lens relative to an existential approach to school counseling are shared. A case study of Faye, a high school junior, and her presenting concerns is provided. Cultural and ethical considerations pulled from the American School Counseling Association (ASCA) Ethical Standards are shared in support of a school counselor's work with Faye. An illustration of how ET and the B-Well model for a case conceptualization and a working action plan for Faye are provided. To conclude our work, an observational response to the implemented action plan is offered.

Background of Existential Therapy (ET)

Existential therapy evolved from the humanistic movement. The humanistic movement is classified as the third force in psychotherapy (Jones-Smith, 2021), where Carl Rogers is acknowledged as the developer of the humanistic theory through his person-centered approach. The person-centered approach was to be in direct rejection of the behaviorism movement, which "treated people like animals or machines to be manipulated by control and reinforcement strategies" (2021, p. 179). Throughout this book, many authors highlight Roger's emphasis on showing empathy toward people and maintaining unconditional positive regard for others, which we believe are the foundational principles of counseling (Corey, 2016; Jones-Smith, 2021; Scholl et al., 2014). Humanism and existentialism together acknowledge "human existence." Both concepts also embrace the worldview that people have personal responsibility, free will, and the ability to strive toward personal growth and fulfillment (Jones-Smith, 2021), which are highlighted as some of ET's key concepts. Scholl et al. (2014) identify that within the humanistic understanding, person-centered therapy, gestalt therapy, and the American and European existential perspectives are creative therapies connected through their respect for the whole person, which is another continuous theme found throughout the pages of this book. According to Scholl et al. (2012), modern humanism includes these diverse theories focusing on not reducing a person to their behavior or individual parts of themselves as this limits a wellness approach.

Origins

Søren Kierkegaard, a Danish philosopher and the man identified as the father of existential philosophy, presented the truth of Christianity and the object of Christian faith as "the existence of God" (Zurcher,

© Anna Yordanova/shutterstock.com

n.d., p. 14). Friedrich Nietzsche, a German philosopher who followed Kierkegaard, believed religion's effect on people no longer served as the major influence on moral value due to "natural causality lacking" and the mystery of natural sequence being a religious cult (Jones-Smith, 2021; Nietzsche, 1910, p. 117). Nietzsche further argued in his book *Human All-Too-Human* (1910) that nature should be accounted as God because nature is "uncomprehended" (p. 118), irregular, and voluntary. Rollo May, an American theologian known as the father of American existentialism, was influenced by Alfred Adler, who believed "humans lived in a realm of meanings" (Jones-Smith, 2021, p. 64), became a follower of Kierkegaard when he was diagnosed with tuberculosis in 1938. May connected with Kierkegaard's belief about anxiety being the result of one's life feeling threatened by sickness and forwarded the belief that anxiety is a normal and essential experience to the human condition that forces one toward self-realization (Jones-Smith, 2021). Kierkegaard believed people can carve out their own destiny and are solely responsible for giving their life meaning but should live with integrity despite experiencing despair, angst, alienation, and meaninglessness (Corey, 2017; Jones-Smith, 2021).

© Natata/shutterstock.com

These theorists are only three of many existentialists whose work has left an imprint on the circling understandings of human existence and the human experience. Together, along with other philosophers such as Viktor Frankl—who is noted for establishing the theory of logotherapy prefacing the ideology that there is meaning in human suffering with a will to want to discover meaning (Jones-Smith, 2021)—and others, the pursuit of meaning in relation to "being in the world" was encouraged and continually researched.

View of Human Nature

Existentialists view human nature through one's anxiety (Jones-Smith, 2021). "Why am I here, in this current time and space, within this body, surrounded by these people, under these circumstances?" This is a question existentialists seek to understand and work to assist others in understanding. The goal is to establish authentic relationships that embrace an elevated level of trust and intimacy to experience the wholeness of self even with the experience of anxiety. More specifically, existentialism can be conceptualized through the four concepts of death, freedom, isolation, and meaninglessness (Corey, 2016; Jones-Smith, 2021):

- People are **alone** in the world and will eventually face **death.**
- "People are **free** when they choose freely and **accept the consequences of their actions**" (Corey, 2016, p. 188).
- People desire a sense of **meaning** in life and long to be in **connection with others,** or they otherwise may experience hopelessness, discouragement, or emptiness.

View of Change

When addressing ineffective behaviors, existentialists believe a person's anxieties concerning death, freedom, isolation, and meaninglessness should be confronted with authenticity. It is important to examine one's anxiety, values, believed freedoms, and responsibility to find meaning (Corey, 2016; Scholl et al., 2014; Stone & Dahir, 2016). If not, psychological disturbances may develop by avoiding truth and behaving according to others' expectations and values for oneself versus behaving according to one's own values and beliefs (Jones-Smith, 2021).

When considering working with students, school counselors should help students view presenting issues as opportunities for the student to learn, accept the truth of their personal responsibility, and work through any confusion or conflict (Stone & Dahir, 2016). The process of applying ET for change is not initially about changing behaviors; it is about processing the way one thinks about their suffering (Scholl et al., 2014); the existentialist lives their life through their thoughts, which influence their behaviors (Zurcher, n.d.). Through self-awareness (thoughts) a student can recognize how their responsibility is connected

© Colored Lights/shutterstock.com

to their freedom in choosing how they act (Corey, 2016). Additionally, change, for the existentialist, is to seek balance between the limits of one's human existence and the opportunities provided through one's suffering to transcend limitations into purpose (Corey, 2016). According to Douglas (n.d.), the truth of one's existence is reflected through a person's actual experience as a hoping, fearing, living, willing, anxious person.

Christian Integration Perspective

We are in alliance with other book contributors in that our Christian integration is founded on these truths: The Bible is the infallible and inspired word of God. Jesus Christ was born of a virgin, lived a life without sin, gave His life as the largest rescue mission to atone for the collective sin of humankind, and rose three days after His crucifixion. As believers, by faith in Christ through grace, we can achieve a restored relationship with God.

Beyond the Christian truths above, in reflection of the founding ET theorists' beliefs about human existence and the world, we are mindful to consider the era of times in which these philosophers presented in this chapter sought meaning in their lives through their own suffering. For example, much of Kierkegaard's work evolved from his experiences with anxiety and fear of being alone. He quotes, "Deep within every human being there still lives the anxiety over the possibility of being alone in the world, forgotten by God, overlooked by the millions and millions in this enormous household" (Kierkegaard, 1980, p. xiii). Nietzsche wrote *Human All-Too-Human* (1910) after his service in the Franco-Prussian war and other books while suffering from various illnesses: dysentery, syphilis, progressive paralysis, short-sightedness, indigestion, and migraine headaches (Figueroa, 2020). During May's bout with tuberculosis, he identified that he was not ready to die and positioned his mindset to believe he was able to choose, at his *will*, to live, and therefore, lived until the year 1994.

Cast all your anxiety on him because he cares for you

1 PETER 5:7

© Borsuk Renat/shutterstock.com

The experiences of the existential theorists can be connected to scripture. For example,

Jesus, when on the cross, cried out in a loud voice, "My God, my God, why have you forsaken me?" (*New International Bible*, 1978/2011, Mark 15:34). Upon the cross, Jesus felt abandoned by God, the Father, leaving readers of the Bible to witness Christ's existential experience of aloneness, isolation, forsakenness, and anxiety. We agree with Kierkegaard's belief that every human experience has a level of anxiety at some point in life. Though we have had our own individual experiences living with anxiety, (e.g., surviving a pandemic), our Christian perspective rests on the grace, mercy, love, faithfulness, and justice given by God the Creator and His truths from scripture that allows us to experience the anxiety with courage and hope. We "humble [ourselves], therefore, under God's mighty hand, that He may lift [us] up in due time. [We] cast all [our] anxiety on Him because He cares for [us]" (1 Peter 5:6-7).

A Case Study: Faye

Demographics

Faye is an 18-year-old Black American female born and raised in a southern urban township. She currently lives with her father and stepmother as she prepares for life after high school. Faye lived with her mother for the first 16 years of her life. Faye is single and has no children. After high school, she plans to relocate to a southern city. There are no college graduates in her immediate family and Faye does not desire to attend college. Faye has no religious affiliation and does not consider herself to be a believer of any faith.

Developmental Experiences

Faye was born to a single mother with a lower income status and has one sister. Her older sister, by six years, is an active military service member and is a positive influence in her life. As a child, Faye maintained above-average grades and considered herself more mature than her peers. Faye felt supported and nurtured by her parents throughout her early childhood until the split between her mother and father took place when she was 12. They were never married.

As reported by Faye, the split between her parents was traumatic due to her father's alleged infidelity, which caused her mother

© pkchai/shutterstock.com

to leave in the middle of the night. She, her mother, and her sister moved around a lot due to her mother's struggle with substance abuse. Faye indicated she spent a good amount of time by herself and had to find creative activities on her own. At some point, Faye and her mother's relationship became tumultuous. She stated she could not live with her mother as a teenager because "We are just alike." After living with different family members, once leaving her mother's care, Faye moved in with her father at age 16.

When asked about the most memorable moments throughout her childhood, Faye recalled always having to take care of herself and feeling resentment as a result. When she mentioned her father, she described him as a nonchalant and indifferent man who is unbothered by her actions. Faye desires better communication from her parents and additional support to help her make life decisions for her future.

Cultural/Generational Traditions

Faye was not raised in any religious or spiritual belief system and describes her family as "non-religious." When she lived with other family members, the topics of faith were not discussed as essential tools for meaning, value, and purpose. Faye believes in having a good heart and "Treating people right is what life is all about." She indicated that her family has generational cycles that are continually perpetuated due to a lack of social-emotional health. She believes her experiences with dating multiple men are a direct correlation to the disconnections she experiences within her family and dating multiple men will equate to the perfect man. She shared how a familial norm is to remain connected but simultaneously distant from one another. Faye wants her family to have a better value system and believes this will help strengthen her family. Faye reported that she does not want to perpetuate the current familial cycle.

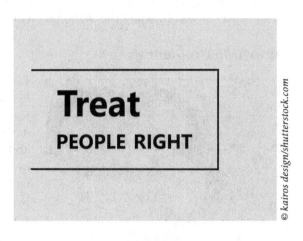

© kairos design/shutterstock.com

Social Relationships

Faye reported being with multiple men and believes that this is a means by which she can gain some of her emotional and material desires. She does not have a desire for monogamy and seeks independence but also connection.

She values her friendships but described herself as "always having to be the counselor or the strong one in the group." Faye wants to support her friends and assist with working out their issues but often feels unsupported when she is in need. At times she has stated, "I am my own person, so I have to learn to depend on myself."

Faye stated that anger has been a problem historically. She offered examples within her family and her peers at school, beginning in elementary school. She has been in verbal conflicts with her mother, father, sister, and classmates.

Psychological Abuse Historical Account

Faye reports no historical accounts of sexual abuse. She said she has experienced emotional and verbal abuse from her mother. Faye recollected experiencing these abuses when living with her mother. Often, her mother withdraws emotional support, calls her derogatory names, and exhibits aggressive/violent behaviors when she is engaging in substance abuse.

Substance Abuse Historical Account

Faye stated she began her risky behaviors and substance abuse during middle school. Faye reported that she has regularly used marijuana and experimented with alcohol. Although she engages in recreational drugs, she desires to "get clean" by the time she graduates high school due to her desire to become a real estate agent. She mostly indulges in substances when hanging out with her friends and family. There is no report of prescription drug use.

Mental Health Historical Account

There is no report of mental health diagnoses. She believes depression and bipolar could be evident within her family. She asserts that her family could benefit from seeking mental health support due to the strained relationships and the challenges with communication.

Presenting Problem(s)

Faye was referred to the school counselor by her father because of her continued anger outbursts toward her teachers and peers. She states she is committed to graduating high school on time but admits that her temper and anger continue to be an obstacle that she needs to overcome. Faye has tried belly breathing, walking, journaling, and separating herself from situations to manage her anger but cannot seem to find her best form of management. Faye wants to be a leader but fears that her lack of anger management will hinder her from achieving her goals. She struggles to set career goals for herself because of her desire to relocate. The concerns of the unknown future weigh heavily on her mind as she struggles to find the perfect time to discuss her plans for the future with her family. She believes she is at a disadvantage in making her own decisions to relocate because she believes her mother will be financially dependent upon her. Faye desires a closer relationship with her mother and father but not at the expense of her future. She perceives the demands placed on her required her to grow up faster than she wished.

Cultural and Ethical Considerations

Before addressing the application of existentialism and the B-Well model to Faye's case, a culturally competent, ethical, and intentional school counselor must first consider cultural and ethical expectations set forth by the American School Counselor Association (ASCA, 2022).

Cultural Considerations

When emotional and verbal abuse is experienced, one's perceived control is threatened as well as their predictability of life (Davis & McKearney, 2003). The perceived threat Faye experiences because of her mother's emotional and verbal abuse and her father's lack of engagement enacts specific behaviors that consist of, but are not limited to, anger, self-preservation, isolation, self-reliance, anxiety concerning the future, etc. These abuse experiences can result in a mental illness inclusive of post-traumatic stress disorder (PTSD), anxiety, depression, disassociation, etc. (Davis & McKearney, 2003; Fuller et al., 2018;

Nelson Goff & Smith, 2005; Sayed et al., 2015). Observably, there are clinical implications in Faye's case study that may appear out of a school counselor's scope of practice and may require a clinical referral.

Beyond abuse, a school counselor's awareness of how African Americans historically have been treated by the counseling profession is crucial as the school counselor considers one-on-one discussions and outside referrals. Research supports that work with African American females has typically been modeled as "1. Eurocentric masculine perspective of individualism, independence, and autonomy; 2. a marginalized multicultural perspective that compartmentalizes cultural variables from one another; and 3. a deficit perspective focused on economic despair, poverty, and violence" (Cholewa et al., 2015; Dye et al., 2017; Fuller et al., 2018, p. 40). Culturally sensitive school counseling should illustrate an affirmative approach that attends to normative developmental concerns, which includes identity development and relationship with parents. According to Fuller and colleagues (2018), when working with African American students who have experienced any form of abuse, topics such as racial socialization, resiliency, and self-efficacy should intentionally be incorporated into one-on-one counseling and group discussions for the benefit of increasing a positive self-image, awareness of internal strength, and instillation of hopefulness, all tenets of ET.

© Vitalii Vodolazskyi/shutterstock.com

Ethical Considerations

According to ASCA National Model (ASCA, 2019), school counseling programs should promote accountability, developmental mindsets, and behaviors expected of all students through the implementation of a school counseling program that is relevant, practical in activities, and thought-provoking when processing acquired knowledge in support of student's academic, career, and social/emotional development. In consideration of the presented case study, a culturally competent, ethical, intentional school counselor should be mindful of the following school counseling ethical standards (ASCA, 2022):

- In Responsibility to the Students (A.1 and A.6):
  - A.1.a. Have a primary obligation to the students, who are to be treated with dignity and respect as unique individuals.
  - A.1.c. Support all students and their development by actively working to eliminate systemic barriers or bias impeding student development.
  - A.1.e. Provide culturally responsive counseling to students in a brief context and support students and families/guardians in obtaining outside services if students need long-term clinical/mental health counseling.
  - A.1.f. Do not diagnose but recognize how a student's diagnosis and environment can potentially affect the student's access, participation and ability to achieve academic, postsecondary and social/emotional success.
  - A.1.h. Respect students' and families' values, beliefs and cultural background, as well as students' sexual orientation, gender identity and gender expression, and exercise great care to avoid imposing personal biases, beliefs or values rooted in one's religion, culture or ethnicity.
  - A.6.b. Provide a list of outside agencies and resources in their community, or the closest available, to students and parents/guardians when students need or request additional support. School counselors provide multiple referral options or the district-vetted list of referrals options and are careful not to indicate an endorsement or preference for one individual or

practice. School counselors encourage parents/guardians to research outside professionals' skills/experience to inform their personal decision regarding the best source of assistance for their student.

- A.6.e. Refrain from referring students based solely on the school counselor's personal beliefs or values rooted in one's religion, culture, ethnicity or personal worldview. School counselors maintain the highest respect for student cultural identities and worldviews. School counselors pursue additional training and supervision when their values are discriminatory in nature (e.g., sexual orientation, gender identity, gender expression, reproductive rights, race, religion, ability status). School counselors do not impose their values on students and/or families when making referrals to outside resources for student and/or family support.

- In Responsibility to Self (B.3):
  - B.3.i. Monitor personal behaviors and recognize the high standard of care a professional in this critical position of trust must maintain on and off the job. School counselors are cognizant of and refrain from activity that may diminish their effectiveness within the school community.
  - B.3.j. Apply an ethical decision-making model and seek consultation and supervision from colleagues and other professionals who are knowledgeable of the profession's practices when ethical questions arise.
  - B.3.k. Honor the diversity and identities of students and seek training/supervision when prejudice or biases interfere with providing comprehensive school counseling services to all pre-K–12 students. School counselors will not refuse services to students based solely on personally held beliefs/values rooted in one's religion, culture or ethnicity. School counselors work toward a school climate that embraces diverse identities and promotes equitable outcomes in academic, career and social/emotional development for all students.

Incorporating the practice of ET humanism into servicing students within schools should direct the attitudes of school counselors, educators, and interventionalists toward a "human potential movement" that believes each student can develop their greatest potential and views each student as a unique "creative" who is controlled by their values and choices (Jones-Smith, 2021) while maintaining respect for one's cultural beliefs and practices. This mindset begins with acknowledging that all students are first, creative. Secondly, school counselors should be clear about behaviors identified as misconduct. These behaviors can be learned behaviors stemming from an environment of low self-value where low self-valuing language is used, and therefore, the school counselor should not judge the student based on circumstances out of the student's control. In other words, avoid attributional bias.

Applying the B-Well Model Using Existential Therapy

As identified in Chapter 4, the tenets of the B-Well model—Heart, Mind, Strength, Soul, Neighbor, and Society—encompass the "whole person," aligning with existential therapy. Each facet engages the cognitive, emotional, physical, spiritual, and relational self. Below is a recommended description of how school counselors may apply an existential approach to the B-Well model in the case of Faye.

Heart

Faye is experiencing turmoil and isolation; this contributes to her emotional outbursts and disruptive accounts in the classroom. What is showing up in her disposition as insubordination in the classroom with her male teacher should be considered in context, given her desire to be loved by her father.

Her behavior is appearing as self-protection modeled through an ultimate desire for male protection, compassion, and connection. We also witness this emotional need reiterated in Faye's reporting about dating multiple men. Faye expresses her anger because she feels trapped (e.g., anger) by her mother's dependence upon her, which impacts her personal responsibility toward her goals and free will.

Mind

As we consider the Mind facet, it would be necessary to identify Faye's cognitive dissonance concerning her father and her future goals. She believes her father is not interested in what is going on with her; however, her father requested that she see the school counselor. Further examination with Faye to create meaning behind her father's request unlocks the aspects of her Mind that repeat untruths. Although these untruths influence her self-preservation, they also push her toward self-isolation, believing she has no support system. While processing Faye's Mind, highlighting how her mother's financial dependency upon her impacts her free will is notable.

Strength

Faye's Strength can be illustrated through no report of illnesses. However, her observable outbursts during class may be attributed to her behavior of avoidance or desire to seek attention. These outbursts of anger may be reflecting the perceived limitations of her free will and desire for meaning.

Soul

Though Faye does not have a religious/spiritual system, she is made in the image of God, which has certain attributes that can be evidenced across facets (e.g., problem solving, caring for others, etc.). Additionally, since Faye is unregenerated, she does not have the work of the Holy Spirit within her; therefore, she operates from the "flesh" and not the "spirit" (*New International Bible*, 1978/2011, 1 Corinthians 2:14), which could be influenced by her ideals of personal responsibility. Operating from the flesh may also be influencing her Heart, Mind, and Strength facets. She does have the work of the Holy Spirit upon her with God working via common grace.

Neighbor

The pattern of Faye's relationships displays incongruencies with her Neighbors. Though she reported being close to her sister when she was younger, her risky behaviors began in middle school, which appears to be when her sister departed the home and joined the military. This may be an influence of isolation and "death" with the removal of this important relationship that motivated her to act out. Additionally, Faye's Neighbor patterns illustrate a lack of reciprocity concerning offering support to friends and receiving support from friends. She believes she has no support from others and tells herself, "I have to learn to depend on myself." This belief maintains isolation in her life, apart from supportive Neighbors.

Society

An influential social construct that has an impact on Faye's free will includes her belief that dating multiple men is a strategy for gaining material items. Other societal influences may include Faye's historical living experiences with different family members and drug-accessible environments that support Faye's substance use. Both influences can have a dramatic impact on how Faye envisions her future after high school and influence the death of her dreams.

Recommended Goals and Interventions

Table 1 highlights three core problems we believe are the root causes of Faye's outbursts in class: anger, distressed relationships with parents, and self-preservation. Though ET therapists are not intervention specific, they do utilize interventions from other counseling theories (Murdock, 2017). Throughout the goals and interventions, we apply an assimilative integration of theory (Corey, 2017), borrowing interventions from other theories to assist with goal achievement by attending to each facet of the B-Well model and applying ET core concepts (Jones-Smith, 2021). For example, when highlighting Faye's anger as the presenting concern of her Heart, we suggest the goal targets Faye's existential observations by elevating her self-awareness concerning her behaviors and personal responsibility. This may be effective by applying the cognitive restructuring technique to provide Faye the space to process her Mind as her thoughts relate to the matters of her Heart. This will reveal Faye's experience with anxiety associated with her relationship with her parents, future, and lack of support system.

Faye's Case Revisited During Treatment Implementation

Faye and I met at the same time twice per week until we met for a total of 10 sessions. There were times she skipped our scheduled meetings. After I confronted her avoidance, she began looking forward to our weekly meetings. I kept our meeting times even while she was in In-School Suspension (ISS). Once, she shared that she was not in a talking mood. I respected her space and allowed her time to self-reflect and asked her to share her reflections at the end of our ISS meeting. Additionally, there was a time or two when we met, and she would not unpack anything. As I observed her resistance, I explained to her that I felt used and believed she only wanted to meet with me to avoid her fourth-period class, Career Management, where she experienced her greatest struggle and did not have a good rapport with her male teacher. She was informed that if she was not going to willingly work with me, I would need to terminate our sessions. She changed her attitude and became motivated with the process.

TABLE 1 Recommended Goals and Interventions Using Existential Therapy (ET)

Problem	Goal	Intervention
Anger	Assess Faye's matters of her heart to identify the source of her anger through *self-awareness.* [Heart, Neighbor]	• Cognitive restructuring • Top five social support • Journaling
Distressed relationship with parents	Improve Faye's *thought life* and communication skills to create *authentic* relationships through identifying *personal responsibility* and *meaningfulness.* [Heart, Mind, Soul, Neighbor]	• Role-playing • Empty chair technique • Reframing
Self-preservation	Identify strengths, purpose, and societal influences that hinder her freedom and will, creating isolation. [Mind, Neighbor, Society]	• Address cognitive dissonance between self-preservation and self-determined language. • Address abuse renarrative. • Connect with community resources such as career fair.

We began to meet weekly during fourth period (from 1:05-2:40 p.m.) upon completion of her class-work. Our time together became an incentive and a reward, in which she became motivated to complete her assignments quickly during that period, as opposed to later that day (as she had in the past). My goal was to check in with her by 2 p.m. when she was normally done with her work. As another incentive, I collaborated with her first-period teacher, a gracious female with whom Faye had a good relationship, and her fourth-period teacher. The collaboration was an agreement to allow Faye to be "bounced" to her first-period teacher as a safe space to decompress if Faye became too problematic to manage during fourth period. Faye was informed and encouraged to use this plan of action as her safe place to minimize problematic confrontations. She expressed relief toward this plan.

Through meeting with Faye for 10 sessions, the following occurred:

- We addressed the goal of minimizing outbursts and disruptive behaviors in class. As a substitute for disruptive behaviors, Faye uses email to communicate frustrations and questions to her teacher without disrupting the flow of the class. We also employed a thought log for cognitive restructuring.
- We implemented role play; however, she was humored by my impersonation of her teacher and asked to try another activity because she believed the portrayal was incorrect.
- We explored practicing positive phrases and "I statements" to reframe her communication tactics. She often feels disregarded when using an "I statement," so she chose to reframe her quotes and restate them by using positive phrases. For example, instead of saying to a teacher: "Why is this girl in my seat?" Faye restates: "I will find an empty workspace and send my teacher an email asking about changes in the seating arrangement." Another example would be that instead of saying, "WHY ARE WE DOING THIS ASSIGNMENT TODAY?" with attitude, Faye now sends her teacher an email inquiring about how the lesson relates to real-life situations.

Upon completion of our sessions, Faye explained that she only needed to be "bounced" once, and she took personal responsibility to maintain positive behavior. She has since developed a better rapport with her fourth-period teacher, and her grades have increased from a score of 76 to 84 in her fourth-period class. Both her fourth-period teacher and Faye have reported a better rapport and working relationship. Faye admits she needs to make changes, identifies that change has already occurred, and is focused on consistency. Additionally, Faye shared that she would accomplish her goal of minimizing outbursts in the classroom and will continue to send emails in times of frustration. This system seems to work for her. The fourth-period teacher reported Faye currently sends him emails and has not had any additional behavior referrals since the counseling intervention. He noticed the small changes and provided Faye with unsolicited feedback.

I noticed the change in Faye's attitude as well and have provided praise for the responsible, resilient, and mature behavior she displays. During one of my sit-ins within the classroom, I observed Faye asking to go to the bathroom instead of shouting out, "I'M GOING TO THE BATHROOM," as I had observed prior to our work. I have also observed Faye saying to her fourth-period teacher, "Have a good weekend," and using words and phrases such as "please" and "thank you." She now smiles when she talks about how she "used to" behave and looks forward to graduating high school.

Faye reported the relationship with her father as "better." However, she maintains that "He doesn't bother me much," and he remains indifferent about her actions. Faye described her relationship with her mother as strange and expressed that she needs a break from her mom.

Faye's change of behavior was noticeable after eight sessions. Two of her male teachers expressed reduced behavioral concerns. During her ninth session, Faye stated that she owned her change. She made the statement, "I'm getting better, aren't I?" To which I agreed and asked for her to share her observations. Before terminating, Faye was given a phone number to call for help with sobriety, which she said she would call after graduation. Faye believes her marijuana usage helps her to stay calm and sleep well. We discussed healthier coping skills at which she laughed.

As I think back to my work with Faye, I am reminded of Romans 12:2a, "And do not be conformed to this world, but be transformed by the renewing of your mind ..." (*New King James Bible,* 1982). Although Paul was talking about the lifestyle change that occurs spiritually, this idea can also be applied psychologically. Faye's behavior is being transformed as she renews her mind by addressing negative thoughts and reframing her thoughts in a more positive manner.

Summary

When mindfully examining the nature of existentialism, one will discover that the principles of ET are biblically supported and can be applied in schools. Through the lens of ET, we suggest working with students to assess and identify areas of personal responsibility and meaningfulness to therefore redirect the student's thoughts and behaviors toward a self-motivating, *willing* movement. While incorporating the B-Well model, school counselors can conceptualize students' needs holistically and choose necessary interventions that support the whole student. Being mindful of cultural and ethical considerations is necessary when working with students to ensure school counselors are modeling cultural sensitivity and ethical responsibility.

References

American School Counselor Association (ASCA). (2019). *ASCA national model: A framework for school counseling programs* (4th ed.). Author.

American School Counselor Association (ASCA). (2022). *Ethical standards for school counselors.* https://www.schoolcounselor.org/About-School-Counseling/Ethical-Legal-Responsibilities/ASCA-Ethical-Standards-for-School-Counselors-(1)

Cholewa, B., Burkhardt, C. K., & Hull, M. F. (2015). Are school counselors impacting underrepresented students' thinking about postsecondary education? *Professional School Counseling 19*(1), 144-154. https://doi.org/10.5330/1096-2409-19.1.144

Corey, G. (2016). *Theory and practice of group counseling* (9th ed.). Cengage Learning.

Corey, G. (2017). *Theory and practice of counseling and psychotherapy* (10th ed.). Cengage Learning.

Davis, C. G., & McKearney, J. M. (2003). How do people grow from their experience with trauma or loss? *Journal of Social and Clinical Psychology, 22*(5), 477-492. https://doi.org/10.1521/jscp.22.5.477.22928

Douglas, H. E. (n.d.). Faith as an existential experience. In *Existentialism: A survey and assessment* (pp. 15-23). The Biblical Research Institute. https://adventistbiblicalresearch.org

Dye, L., Fuller, L. B., Burke, M., & Hughey, A. (2017). Beyond social justice for the African American learner: A contextual humanistic perspective for school counselors. *African American Learners Journal of ISAAC, 6*(1), 1-15.

Figueroa, G. (2020). Nietzsche's mental disorders: Madness, being sick, how to become what you are. *Journal of Neuropsychiatry Chile, 58,* 4.

Fuller, L. B., Dye, L., Morris, J. R., Craig, S., & Dickson, J. (2018). Group counseling: African American adolescent females' resiliency, self-efficacy, and racial identity. *The Wisconsin Counseling Journal, 31,* 39-55.

Jones-Smith, E. (2021). *Theories of counseling and psychotherapy: An integrative approach* (3rd ed.). Sage Publications.

Kierkegaard, S. (1980). *The concept of anxiety: A simple psychologically orienting deliberation on the dogmatic issue of hereditary sin.* Princeton University Press.

Murdock, N. L. (2017). *Theories of counseling and psychotherapy: A case approach* (4th ed.). Pearson.

Nelson Goff, B. S., & Smith, D. B. (2005). Systemic traumatic stress: The couple adaptation to traumatic stress model. *Journal of Marital and Family Therapy, 31*(2), 145-157. https://doi.org/10.1111/j.1752-0606.2005.tb01552.x

New King James Bible. (1982). Thomas Nelson. https://www.thomasnelsonbibles.com/nkjv-bible/

New International Bible. (2011). The NIV Bible. https://www.thenivbible.com (Original work published 1978)

Nietzsche, F. (1910). *Human all—too—human: A book for the free spirits.* (Pt. I). Morrison & Gibb Limited.

Sayed, S., Lacoviello, B. M., & Charney, D. S. (2015). Risk factors for the development of psychopathology following trauma. *Current Psychiatry Reports, 17*(70), 69-75.

Scholl, M. B., McGowan, A. S., & Hansen, J. T. (2012). Introduction to humanistic perspectives on contemporary counseling issues. In M. B. Scholl, A. S. McGowan, & J. T. Hansen (Eds.), *Humanistic perspective on contemporary counseling issues* (pp. 3-14). Routledge.

Scholl, M. B., Ray, D. C., & Brady-Amoon, P. (2014). Humanistic counseling process, outcomes, and research. *Journal of Humanistic Counseling, 53*, 218-239. https://doi.org/10.1002/j.2161-1939.2014.00058.x

Stone, B. C., & Dahir, C. A. (2016). *The transformed school counselor* (3rd ed.). Cengage Learning.

Zurcher, J. R. (n.d.). Goals and spiritual values of existentialism. In *Existentialism: A Survey and Assessment.* (pp. 7-14). The Biblical Research Institute. https://adventistbiblicalresearch.org

B-Well Model in School Counseling Using Person-Centered Therapy

Angelica A. Greiner and Crystal Hatton

> "A new command I give you: Love one another. As I have loved you, so you must love one another. By this everyone will know that you are my disciples, if you love one another."
>
> — John 13:34-35 (NIV)

> "Love is patient, love is kind. It does not envy, it does not boast, it is not proud. It does not dishonor others, it is not self-seeking, it is not easily angered, it keeps no record of wrongs. Love does not delight in evil but rejoices with the truth. It always protects, always trusts, always hopes, always perseveres. Love never fails."
>
> — 1 Corinthians 13:4-8 (NIV)

This chapter will address how the B-Well model can be applied to person-centered school counseling. The authors will provide an overview of person-centered counseling, including special considerations for school counselors. The authors will utilize a case conceptualization to demonstrate the application of the B-Well model to person-centered school counseling. Lastly, the authors will conclude the chapter by highlighting recommended person-centered goals and interventions that align with the B-Well model.

Background of Person-Centered (PC) Therapy

Origins

Grounded within humanistic psychology, the person-centered approach was developed by Carl Rogers in the 1940s. This approach was revolutionary because it shifted away from the counselor being perceived as the expert in charge of the therapeutic process. Instead, the client directed the therapeutic process and was deemed capable of exercising autonomy, gaining insight into their problems, and making the necessary adjustments to improve their own situations. The person-centered counselor was nondirective and refrained from offering advice or suggestions to the client.

© Natata/shutterstock.com

View of Human Nature

Rogers (1951) believed that human beings are inherently good and have an innate ability to progress toward self-actualization and reach their highest potential. In addition, Rogers contended that people would develop in a positive manner if the therapeutic relationship created an atmosphere for growth to occur.

View of Change

Rogers (1957) emphasized that for positive change to occur for clients, counselors display an attitude that is characterized by three core conditions:

© arloo/shutterstock.com

- Unconditional positive regard—This is defined as the act of accepting clients as they are without rendering judgment. When counselors demonstrate unconditional positive regard, they demonstrate genuine care and concern for the client regardless of whether they agree with or approve of their opinions, life choices, or circumstances.
- Empathy—This is defined as the act of accurately understanding and identifying with the client's feelings and experiences through their worldview. Demonstrating empathy can yield growth for both the client and the counselor. More specifically, this empathic understanding enables the client to feel heard, understood, and valued within the therapeutic process.
- Congruence—This is defined as the counselor's ability to be authentic, real, and genuine within the therapeutic process. It is important to note that congruence is the most important core condition within the therapeutic relationship. When clients see counselors as authentic helpers, they are then able to build trusting relationships and fully engage in the therapeutic process.

Special Considerations for School Counseling

It is worth noting that counseling initially operated from a medical model approach, where the client was referred to as a "patient." However, as Roger's approach became widely accepted, there was a shift from using the term "patient" to "client." As school counselors, we provide counseling services to all students; however, we do not diagnose students. Accordingly, it is critical that we use the term "student" rather than "client," because the latter term has clinical implications.

Christian Integration Perspective

Both authors of this chapter are former school counselors and current school counselor educators who utilize Christian integration to inform their teaching and interactions with students. In addition to sharing similar professional paths, the authors also have parallel interpretations about Christian integration as it pertains to their biblical worldview and the role of the person-centered school counselor. The authors possess the core belief that God is the epitome of love. His love is steadfast, unconditional, and extends to all people. God's love was exemplified when his son, Jesus, gave his life to redeem humankind from sin. As person-centered school counselors who operate from a biblical worldview, the authors believe that it is their moral and ethical obligation to exercise inclusiveness by respecting all students' right to autonomy by exercising unconditional love and positive regard even when decisions, opinions, or beliefs may not align with a biblical worldview.

A Case Study: Marisol

Marisol is a 17-year-old Hispanic female. She is an only child and her parents immigrated to the United States from Mexico when she was five years old. Marisol's father is employed as a landscaper, and her mother is a homemaker. Although her parents did not graduate from high school, they always discuss the importance of education and encourage Marisol to do well in school. Marisol attends a local magnet school for science and technology and is in the ranking to become valedictorian. She plans to pursue higher education to become a pediatrician.

Marisol recently returned home from school to find her mother unconscious and lying on the kitchen floor. Marisol called 911, and this incident resulted in her mother being diagnosed with heart disease. Marisol's mother was placed on bed rest for two weeks, and Marisol was her primary caretaker.

Marisol visits the school counselor's office because she is concerned about her grade in calculus. She earned a low score on the midterm exam and is barely passing the course. Her recent trauma has caused her to have difficulty focusing, and her status as class valedictorian is in jeopardy. Marisol is accustomed to excelling in math and science, and her difficulty with calculus has caused her to question her college plans and future career choice. She fears that her parents will be disappointed in her because she has "let them down" and dishonored the sacrifices that they have made for her. In addition, she is worried about leaving her mom behind when she enrolls in college.

At the request of a family friend, Marisol continues to attend her church youth group and volunteer at the local food bank. Marisol also reads scripture and finds comfort through journaling. However, she no longer runs track after school, and this was a source of stress relief for her. Instead, she studies every night until she falls asleep and reports feeling very anxious. Marisol is normally considered "the strong one" in her family, and she has not shared her thoughts and feelings with anyone. However, Marisol has self-referred to the school counseling office because she feels that she is reaching a breaking point.

Applying the B-Well Model Using a Person-Centered Approach

When school counselors support their students with a person-centered approach, it is critical that they offer genuineness, unconditional positive regard, and empathy. By doing so, students feel safe to share their stories with the school counselor, including the six facets of the B-Well model (e.g., Heart, Mind, Strength, Soul, Neighbor, and Society).

Truax and Carkhuff (1967) suggest that there are five levels of empathic responses. A level one response is a very low-level empathic response. For example, the school counselor may give the student advice, change topics, judge the student, or not address the student's feelings. In contrast, a level five empathic response is a very high-level empathic response. Specifically, the school counselor will accurately paraphrase the student's story and feelings, explore possible issues and underlying feelings in a student's story, and offer an action step. By doing so, the school counselor and student can collaboratively set goals to address an issue. Striving to render empathic responses is an integral component of the person-centered school counseling approach. Thus, it is important for school counselors to craft their responses accordingly when counseling their students.

Let us take a closer look at how school counselors can apply a person-centered approach to the B-Well model in the case of Marisol. We will also showcase how school counselors can further advance the person-centered approach by offering level five empathic responses.

Heart

In order to view Marisol's situation through a person-centered lens, it would be important to further examine the aspects of her Heart that are pushing her toward self-actualization as well as the factors that are inhibiting this process. To address the Heart component of the B-Well model, it is important for the school counselor to explore Marisol's feelings about her current situation. Marisol is worried about her mother's medical condition and is fearful of leaving her alone at home while her father is away working. She also feels disappointed in herself and is ashamed of her academic progress. Marisol is typically driven and intrinsically motivated to succeed at home and in school; however, these feelings about her family and school are inhibiting her from reaching her full potential.

Mind

In order to view Marisol's situation through a person-centered lens, it would be important to further examine the aspects of her Mind that are pushing her toward self-actualization as well as the factors that are inhibiting this process. To address the Mind component of the B-Well model, it is necessary for the school counselor to assess how Marisol's thinking is impacting her outlook on her current situation. Marisol thinks that it is her responsibility to care for her mother, and this is causing her to reevaluate her plans to leave for college. In addition, Marisol also thinks that her family may be disappointed in her due to her current academic progress. Similarly, she thinks that she may not be equipped to attend college due to her current struggles with calculus. Marisol knows that her parents are supportive and want her to attend college and pursue a successful career. However, she is having a difficult time reconciling the negative thoughts she is having about leaving for college. Since thoughts can influence behaviors, it will be important for the school counselor to assist Marisol in reconciling the incongruencies in her thoughts and feelings.

Strength

In order to view Marisol's situation through a person-centered lens, it would be important to further examine the aspects of Strength that are pushing her toward self-actualization as well as the factors that are inhibiting this process. To address the Strength component of the B-Well model, it is necessary for the school counselor to explore the physical, physiological, and behavioral aspects of her life. Although Marisol was previously on the track team, she no longer runs. This was a self-care activity that helped Marisol manage her stress and anxiety. Additionally, she struggles to get adequate sleep each night. It will be important for the school counselor to help Marisol evaluate how a healthy sleep routine and exercise positively impacted her lifestyle. Furthermore, it will also be important for the school counselor to explore how poor sleep habits and a lack of self-care have negatively impacted her life. Ultimately, the school counselor's role would be to assist Marisol in reconciling the discrepancy between her current lifestyle and self-care activities needed for success.

Soul

In order to view Marisol's situation through a person-centered lens, it would be important to further examine the aspects of Soul that are pushing her toward self-actualization as well as the factors that are inhibiting this process. To address the Soul component of the B-Well model, it is necessary for the school counselor to explore religious and spiritual influences. Marisol has shared with the school counselor that she attends her church youth group every Sunday. Additionally, she has shared that her faith has helped her to navigate through challenging times. When the school counselor used open questions to explore religious and spiritual influences, Marisol shared that she often leans on Jeremiah 29:11 (*New International Bible*, 1978/2011) when she is going through difficult times. The school counselor's role would be to help Marisol see the aspects of her Soul that are strengths and how she can use them as she navigates through challenging times.

 ## Neighbor

In order to view Marisol's situation through a person-centered lens, it would be important to further examine the aspects of Neighbor that are pushing her toward self-actualization as well as the factors that are inhibiting this process. To address the Neighbor component of the B-Well model, it is essential for the school counselor to explore how Marisol engages, connects, and relates with others. Marisol's culture values family; this is evident as she has a healthy family system. Additionally, she has strong social connections with friends through her church youth group. Since Marisol's culture values family, she is struggling with the thought of leaving home. Marisol feels that it is her responsibility to stay and help her family. The school counselor's role would be to assist Marisol in balancing how she can remain connected with her family while also spreading her wings as she leaves home for the first time.

 ## Society

In order to view Marisol's situation through a person-centered lens, it would be important to further examine the aspects of Society that are pushing her toward self-actualization as well as the factors that are inhibiting this process. To address the Society component of the B-Well model, it is necessary for the school counselor to explore how societal influences may be preventing her from reaching her full potential. Marisol has shared with the school counselor that she will be a first-generation college student. Although Marisol is excited to be the first person in her family to go to college, she is experiencing barriers as she navigates finding the right school, completing the application process, and financing her education. The school counselor's role would be to help Marisol assess the societal barriers she is currently facing and connect her with resources to overcome them.

Recommended Goals and Interventions

Heart

Marisol is experiencing a myriad of feelings about her mother's illness, her current academic progress, and her future college plans. However, she has been holding her feelings inside because she does not want to cause additional stress to her family or appear to be vulnerable to them or her friends.

- **Empathic Response**: The school counselor validates Marisol's experiences and offers an open question to explore her feelings by saying,

"It sounds like you are feeling really stressed right now with your mother's health condition and your current academic progress. As you reflect on your mom and your future, can you tell me about some of the feelings that come to mind?"

Marisol says to the school counselor,

"I don't really know. I've always had to be the strong one in my family, so I've never really shared my thoughts and feelings with anyone. I just keep them bottled up inside of me. Usually, I'm OK, but these are big things that are happening in my life. My mom is sick, and I am nervous about leaving her alone. I am also feeling so disappointed in myself for bombing my calculus test. Now, I am fearful that I will not get into the college of my dreams. I don't tell anyone at home that these things bother me because I don't want them to worry about me. I feel so much better now just sharing these thoughts and feelings with you—thank you!"

The school counselor offers a level five empathic response by saying,

"It sounds like your mother's health condition and current academic progress are causing you to feel anxious about your future. I'm also hearing that you don't feel like you can share your thoughts and feelings with anyone but that it has been helpful for you to share them with me today. Would you like to come up with a plan to explore and manage your feelings?"

Marisol responds,

"Yes, I think that would be helpful. I don't think it's healthy for me to keep things bottled up inside anymore."

- **Goal:** Marisol will further explore her feelings to understand their origin, develop tools for managing them successfully, and achieve self-actualization.
- **Interventions:**
  ○ Marisol will "vent" about her feelings when meeting with the school counselor.
  ○ Marisol will write about her feelings in her journal.

Mind

Although Marisol's parents are very supportive, she worries that she will let them down. When she receives a poor grade, she immediately thinks that her parents will be disappointed and that she has dishonored them. In addition, she thinks that her mother's health will decline if she is not with her. Accordingly, it is critical that she work on reframing her negative thoughts.

- **Empathic Response**: After building rapport with Marisol, the school counselor says,

"I can see on your appointment slip that you wanted to talk about academics. Can you tell me a little about what's going on?"

Marisol responds,

"I completely bombed my calculus test. My parents worked so hard for me to get a great education. They are going to be so disappointed in me. I really let them down, and I completely dishonored the sacrifices that they made for me."

The school counselor offers a level five empathic response by saying,

"I can hear that you are disappointed in yourself for not getting a good grade on your calculus test. It also sounds like your parents are very supportive and want the best for you; however, you feel like you let them down with your calculus grade. Would it be helpful if we came up with a plan to address the thoughts and feelings you're having?"

The student responds,

"I don't always receive failing grades, but when I do, I always think I'll be a disappointment to my family. I think that's a good idea for us to come up with a plan."

- **Goal:** Marisol will replace negative thoughts with positive thoughts.
- **Interventions:**
  - The school counselor will teach Marisol how to reframe negative thoughts as positive thoughts.
  - Marisol will note in her journal each time she has a negative thought. When she has a negative thought, she will stop, reflect, and reframe it as a positive thought in her journal.

Strength

Since Marisol is struggling with self-care, her feelings of anxiousness have increased. Accordingly, it is important that Marisol integrate self-care into her daily routine. By doing so, she can use healthy coping skills to decrease her anxiety.

- **Empathic Response**: To explore Marisol's story and possible self-care activities, the school counselor says,

  "I know you excelled in track last year. How is it going this year?"

  Marisol tearfully responds,

  "Well, I sort of quit track. I loved running track, but there are just not enough hours in the day to keep up with practices and my schoolwork. I'm falling asleep with my head in my textbooks each night."

  The school counselor offers a level five empathic response by saying,

  "It sounds like you're sad that you're no longer running track. I'm also hearing that you're having some challenges putting yourself first. Would you like to come up with a plan that focuses on self-care strategies?"

  The student responds,

  "I miss track so much. It was always my outlet. I felt so good physically and mentally after my practices and meets. I think that it would be a good idea to come up with a plan to start taking care of me again. I think that might help with my anxiety, too!"
- **Goal:** Marisol will incorporate three self-care activities into her daily routine to decrease her anxiety.
- **Interventions:**
  - Since Marisol enjoys running, she will go for a 30-minute run at least four days each week.
  - Marisol will set a reminder alarm on her phone to go to bed at 10:00 p.m. during the school week. This will ensure that she gets at least eight hours of sleep each night.
  - Since Marisol leans on scriptures to navigate through challenging times, she will write down and reflect on one scripture in her journal each week.

Soul

The Soul is a strength for Marisol. Her healthy spiritual identity is an asset that will push her toward self-actualization. Marisol is engaged in self-care activities that fuel her sense of inner peace and wellness. Therefore, it is not necessary to set goals/interventions for her at this time. Instead, it would be beneficial for the school counselor to affirm her efforts and acknowledge that the Soul is a strength for her.

Neighbor

Marisol has a strong connection to her family and church. While they have instilled within her a zest to succeed, she worries about maintaining relationships with them while she is away.

- **Empathic Response**: Although the school counselor has worked with Marisol in the past, it is important that the school counselor initiates the session by building rapport, rather than jumping right into her issue or problem. Accordingly, the school counselor initiate the session with Marisol by asking her what she did over the weekend. Marisol responds by saying,

    "On Sunday, I went to church with my family. After church, my family and I got a quick lunch, and then I volunteered with my church youth group at the local food pantry. We volunteer once a month. I really enjoy spending time with my church family every Sunday and volunteering at the local food bank."

    The school counselor offers an empathic response by saying,

    "It sounds like it's important for you to spend quality time each weekend with your family and your church youth group. It also sounds like it's important for you to give back to the community by volunteering at the local food bank. Am I hearing you correctly?"

    The student responds,

    "When we came to the United States, I was just five years old—we had nothing. Although my parents work hard, we wouldn't be where we are today without the help of my church family and the local food bank. So, yes, you're right; it is important for me to give back to my community." The school counselor responds, "Since you have such a strong connection to your family and church, how are you feeling about leaving for college?"

    Marisol responds,

    "I've been struggling with this—I want to leave for college, but I'm worried about how I'll stay connected with them. My family and church mean everything to me, but I also know it's important for me to further my education by going to college."

    The school counselor offers a level five empathic response by saying,

    "It sounds like you're excited to go to college. However, I'm also hearing that you're worried about how you'll stay connected with your family and church. Would you like to come up with a plan for how to balance remaining connected with your family and church while you are away at college?"

    Marisol responds,

    "Yes, I would love to do that. I think that would help me feel less anxious about leaving for college next year, too!"

- **Goal**: The school counselor will help Marisol to envision how she will remain connected with family and her church youth group while she is away at college.
- **Interventions:**
    - The school counselor will help Marisol brainstorm ways that she can remain connected with her family and her church youth group. Marisol will select her top three choices and practice implementing them before leaving for college.

Society

Marisol will be a first-generation college student. It will be critical for the school counselor to ensure that Marisol has support to navigate the transition to college.

- **Empathic Response**: As the school counselor and Marisol discuss her calculus test, Marisol says,

  "I am so disappointed in myself for not doing well on my calculus test. Maybe I'm not meant to go to college; I don't even know where to start anyway."

  The school counselor offers a level five empathic response by saying,

  "I'm hearing that you are upset that you did not do well on your calculus test. I'm also hearing that you may have some apprehension about going to college because you are the first in your family to have this opportunity. Would it be helpful if we came up with a plan to help you navigate the college process?"

  Marisol responds,

  "Yes, I don't even know where to start. There are so many colleges out there—how do I know which one to pick, and how do I apply to them? Also, I know college is so expensive—there's no way that my family can pay for it."

- **Goal:** The school counselor will assist Marisol in navigating challenges and barriers that are connected to her identity as a first-generation college student.
- **Interventions:**
  - The school counselor will connect Marisol and her family with a Free Application for Federal Student Aid (FAFSA) liaison to help them complete the FAFSA application. Additionally, the school counselor will request that the FAFSA liaison discuss the FAFSA application process and the difference between loans, grants, and scholarships.
  - The school counselor will connect Marisol with the career development facilitator at school to help her explore colleges and fill out her college applications.
  - The school counselor will email Marisol the college tours that will be available this school year. Marisol will let the school counselor know which ones she would like to attend.
- **Goal**: The school counselor will assist Marisol in identifying how the intersectionality of various aspects of her cultural identity impacts her thoughts and feelings about her situation.
- **Interventions:**
  - The school counselor will assist Marisol in exploring if and how her thoughts and feelings are fueled by her life experiences and cultural beliefs.

TABLE 1 Recommended Goals and Interventions Using a Person-Centered Approach

Problem	Goals	Interventions
Marisol has been holding her feelings inside about her mother's health and her current academic progress. This has caused Marisol to feel anxious about her future.	Marisol will further explore her feelings to understand their origin, develop tools for managing them successfully, and achieve self-actualization. [Heart]	• Marisol will "vent" about her feelings when meeting with the school counselor. • Marisol will write about her feelings within her journal.

Problem	Goals	Interventions
Marisol's thoughts about her academic progress and her mother's health are always negative.	Marisol will replace negative thoughts with positive thoughts. [Mind]	• The school counselor will teach Marisol how to reframe negative thoughts as positive thoughts. • Marisol will note in her journal each time she has a negative thought. When she has a negative thought, she will stop, reflect, and reframe it as a positive thought in her journal.
Marisol no longer incorporates self-care activities into her daily routine, which has caused her to be very anxious.	Marisol will incorporate three self-care activities into her daily routine to decrease her anxiety. [Strength]	• Since Marisol enjoys running, she will go for a 30-minute run at least four days each week. • Marisol will set a reminder alarm on her phone to go to bed at 10:00 p.m. during the school week. This will ensure that she gets at least eight hours of sleep each night. • Since Marisol leans on scriptures to navigate through challenging times, she will write down and reflect on one scripture in her journal each week.
Marisol has a healthy spiritual identity.	This is a strength for Marisol; therefore, no goals are needed at this time. [Soul]	• This is a strength for Marisol; therefore, no interventions are needed at this time.
Marisol is worried about how she will remain connected with her family and her church youth group when she is away at college.	The school counselor will help Marisol to envision how she will remain connected with her family and her church youth group while she is away at college. [Neighbor]	• The school counselor will help Marisol brainstorm ways that she can remain connected with family and her church youth group. Marisol will select her top three choices and practice implementing them before leaving for college.
Since Marisol will be a first-generation college student, she is facing many obstacles as she prepares for college.	The school counselor will assist Marisol in navigating challenges and barriers that are connected to her identity as a first-generation college student. [Society]	• The school counselor will connect Marisol and her family with a FAFSA liaison to help them complete the FAFSA application. Additionally, the school counselor will request that the FAFSA liaison discuss the FAFSA application process and the difference between loans, grants, and scholarships.

Problem	Goals	Interventions
		• The school counselor will connect Marisol with the career development facilitator at school to help Marisol explore colleges and fill out her college applications. • The school counselor will email Marisol the college tours that will be available this school year. Marisol will let the school counselor know which ones she would like to attend.
	(2) The school counselor will assist Marisol in identifying how the intersectionality of various aspects of her cultural identity impacts her thoughts and feelings about her situation. [Society]	• The school counselor will assist Marisol in exploring if and how her thoughts and feelings are fueled by her life experiences and cultural beliefs.

Summary

School counselors have an ethical obligation to address the whole child. This means addressing their academic, social/emotional, career, and religious/spiritual development. A person-centered school counselor uses empathy, unconditional positive regard, and genuineness when working with students to draw out their stories and help them navigate issues or problems. The B-Well model is helpful because it provides the school counselor with a mental checklist of topics to explore in a student's story to determine whether they are protective or risk factors. In addition, it can also help to identify resources that may be available to support the student.

Once protective/risk factors are identified, the school counselor can use this knowledge to work collaboratively with students to navigate their issues or problems. When you combine the B-Well model with person-centered school counseling, it will benefit any student from any background. It allows the school counselor to better understand the student's worldview and life experiences, which ultimately helps the school counselor advocate for the student and navigate through their issues or problems.

References

New International Bible. (2011). The NIV Bible. https://www.thenivbible.com (Original work published 1978)

Rogers, C. R. (1951). *Client-centered therapy: Its current practice, implications, and theory.* Houghton Mifflin.

Rogers, C. R. (1957). The necessary and sufficient conditions of therapeutic personality change. *Journal of Consulting Psychology, 21*(2), 95-103. https://doi.org/10.1037/h0045357

Truax C. B., & Carkhuff, R. R. (1967). *Toward effective counseling and psychotherapy.* Aldine.

CHAPTER 9

B-Well Model in Clinical Mental Health Counseling Using Adlerian (Individual Psychology) Therapy

Courtney T. Evans

> "But by the grace of God I am what I am, and his grace to me was not without effect ..."
>
> — 1 Corinthians 15:10 (NIV)

Background of Adlerian Therapy (Individual Psychology)

Origins

Alfred Adler (1870-1937) was a medical doctor, psychotherapist, and founder of individual psychology. Adler grew up in a middle-class family in a poor Jewish section of Vienna, Austria, of whom he was the third child, and second son, in a family of seven children (Manaster, 1977). Adler was described as having a rivalry with his older brother, Sigmund, throughout his childhood. Adler experienced multiple life-impacting events at a young age, including suffering from rickets as a young child (which kept him from walking early on), witnessing the death of his brother in bed beside him, and battling a near-fatal case of pneumonia. Adler once overheard a doctor tell his father that Adler would be nothing more than a shoemaker. Adler attributed the influences of such experiences to his desire to become a physician (Ansbacher & Ansbacher, 1956). As will be seen later, his influences undoubtedly affected his theory of psychology.

Adler received his medical degree (MD) with a specialty in ophthalmology and began practicing as a physician at age 25 (Griffith & Powers, 2007). Two years later, at age 27, Adler married Raissa Timofejewna, a feminist and a political revolutionary (Bottome, 1939). Together, Adler and Raissa had four children, of whom two—Kurt and Alexandra—became psychiatrists and furthered Adler's work (Oberst & Stewart, 2012).

Adler was a pioneer and the first president of the Vienna Psychoanalytic Society alongside Sigmund Freud and Carl Jung (Cervone & Pervin, 2016). While Freud maintained that such depth psychology (i.e., taking the unconscious into account) was centered around seeking to understand deeply buried phenomena and psychic energy as driven by libido, Adler replaced the sex drive with the masculine protest (later named will-to-power, striving for superiority, striving for overcoming, or

perfection; Eife, 2019). Adlerian theory replaced preceding biological, external, and objective causal explanations with psychological, internal, and subjective causal explanations (Ansbacher & Ansbacher, 1956). In contrast to Freud and Jung, Adler was concerned about the social context, individual subjectivity, and expressions of discouragement. Adler stressed the conscious mind rather than the unconscious mind, social motives rather than sexual motives, and free will rather than determinism (Griffith & Powers, 2007). Due to such differing views, they parted after eight years of collaboration with Freud (Wedding & Corsini, 2014).

© Letter Logo/shutterstock.com

Individual Psychology. Individual psychology was introduced by Adler in 1912 (Wedding & Corsini, 2014). The Latin term "indivisible" was used by Adler to refer to the essential unity of a person (holism) (Sperry et al., 2015). According to Adler, there is one basic force behind all human movement—a striving from a perceived minus (inferiority) to a perceived plus (superiority) (Ansbacher & Ansbacher, 1956). The striving is directed by a largely unconscious goal of the individual, which is ideal and fiction.

Additionally, all humans have inferiority feelings and strive for superiority (i.e., feelings of adequacy and worth) (Adler, 1979). This goal-oriented striving offers a unifying direction to life movement. Adler describes the concept of personality from the perspective of the style of life or lifestyle. Lifestyle is the use of personality traits, temperaments, and psychological and biological processes to find a place in the social matrix of life (Griffith & Powers, 2007). Lifestyle is influenced by the degree of activity, organ inferiority, birth order and sibling relationships, family values, family atmosphere, and parenting style.

Progression of the Theory. In 1918, later in Adler's theory development, he introduced the term "community feeling" (Mosak & Maniacci, 1999). This introduction to community feeling shows how Adler's ideas progressed over time. As described by Adler, one's ability to cope with feelings of inferiority is largely dependent on community feeling (*Gemeinschaftsgefuhl* in German or social interest/community feeling in English) (Rasmussen, 2010).

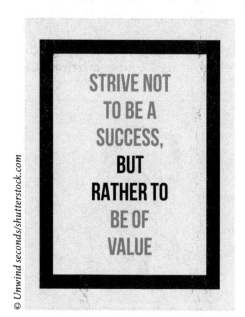

© Unwind seconds/shutterstock.com

The striving for superiority and the devotion to the community that relates the individual to others can be described as dual relatedness; in every psychological expression, we can find social interest and striving for superiority to be hand in hand (Miller & Taylor, 2016). Adler asserted that the criterion by which we measure individuals are determined by their value to humankind (Adler, 1927/2014; Ansbacher, 1992). Rudolph Dreikurs also expanded the concept of community feeling in individual psychology.

Rudolph Dreikurs was Adler's influential collaborator and the person who established Adlerian psychology in the United States. Dreikurs began his professional affiliation with Adler in 1927 while he and Adler both resided in Vienna. Rudolph Dreikurs systemized Adler's work by identifying four phases of psychotherapy: (1) building the relationship, (2) lifestyle assessment, (3) insight and development of client self-understanding, and (4) reorientation (Griffith & Powers, 2007). Additionally, to Dreikurs, superiority feelings were derived primarily through one's sense of belonging.

People feel capable and of worth (superior) when they feel a sense of belonging by those of whom they wish to be accepted.

A debate among Adlerians continues to surround whether belonging and superiority are different or the same or whether one is more important than the other (Ansbacher, 1992; Rasmussen, 2010). In fact, within Adlerian psychology, there is the *Dreikursian* theory camp and the *Classical Adlerian* theory camp. Overall, Adlerians agree that people strive to feel worthwhile, and these feelings are inseparable from relationships with others.

View of Human Nature

Adlerian theory takes an optimistic and phenomenological approach to human nature (Ansbacher & Ansbacher, 1956). Through a soft deterministic lens, Adler emphasized that humans are both creators and creations of their own lives. Adler opposed Freud's emphasis on biological and instinctual determination. Instead, he believed that individuals form an approach to life sometime during the first six years of living, and how individuals interpret early life events continues to influence present behavior. According to the theory, we do not just possess drives and instincts, but both the conscious and unconscious are influenced by subjective values and social orientation. This does not mean Adler did not look at objective factors such as physical attributes and inheritance of potential but instead thought of them as providing probabilities while the creative power of the self takes precedence.

Psychopathology. Adlerian therapists treat the person, not the symptoms. In every symptom, there is something to be found other than just what is observed externally, and no symptom means the same thing for two people. Unique to the individual is the lifestyle of which, upon examination, psychopathology can be understood. As defined by Griffith and Powers (2007), the lifestyle is the unique and self-consistent unity in the movement of an individual, which is created early in childhood in the context of genetic possibility and environmental opportunity (soft determinism) and is also organized and given direction by the subjective goal, based upon guiding fictions. In other words, the lifestyle is one's general orientation to life, a characteristic way of operating in a social field, and behavior based on those convictions. It is comprised of a person's belief about self, others, and the world and the behaviors based on those convictions (Kottman & Meany-Walen, 2016).

An Adlerian therapist spends time completing a lifestyle assessment in the beginning phases of counseling. Understanding the lifestyle is not only important for the clinician, but client insight is also pivotal to change. Therapists must have the complete picture in view before drawing any conclusions about its parts (Adler, 1927/2014). Humans cannot be understood apart from their social context and relationships (Watts, 2003).

A lifestyle assessment can help therapists—and clients during the insight phase—understand maladjustment, which is understood in terms of discouragement. Psychopathology exists on a continuum, with healthy on one end and severe on the other. Discouragement may be a result of the inability to find a useful way of belonging, a lack of social interest, overwhelming feelings of inferiority, and mistaken beliefs about self, others, and the world accompanied by abnormal behavior to protect feelings about the self (i.e., safeguarding) (Carlson et al., 2006; Kottman & Meany-Walen, 2016; Wedding & Corsini,

2014). A maladaptive or dysfunctional lifestyle is an inflexible lifestyle in which a person bases problem solving on self-protective private senses. Self-protective coping patterns may become entrenched (Sperry et al., 2015). The individual is unconscious of all these events.

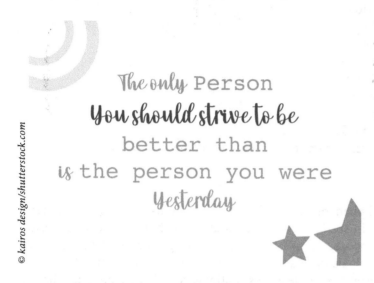

The only Person You should strive to be better than is the person you were Yesterday

© kairos design/shutterstock.com

Adler believed that the hallmark of the healthy, nonpathological person is the capacity to move through life, meeting the various life tasks with courage and common sense, which Adler called "social interest" (Sperry et al., 2015). While, according to Adler, there is not such a thing as a perfect or self-actualized person (as imperfections and failures are part of being human), healthy persons can use their private logic, experience some discouragement and a sense of inferiority, and compensate in a socially useful way. The theory is optimistic in terms of inferiority feelings; rather than being seen as a sign of weakness, they can be the wellspring of creativity and motivate us to strive for success (Kopp & Kivel, 1990). Adler optimistically asserted that any person can be better than they are at any given point, no matter how discouraged or dysfunctional they appear to be (Nystul, 1994). Education, encouragement, teaching new choices, empathy, understanding, helping to compensate for organic inferiorities, and acquisition of new skills can all help people become better (Adler, 1958). Increasing social interest provides a sense of connectedness to other people and humankind (Kottman & Meany-Walen, 2016).

Role of the Counselor. In Adlerian therapy, the client-counselor relationship is egalitarian, collaborative, optimistic, and respectful (Watts, 2003). The therapeutic relationship is a joint journey between the client and counselor. In fact, the beginning phase of Adlerian counseling is dedicated to building the relationship.

Throughout counseling, the relationship is vital for client insight and reorientation.

According to Adler, nothing is more likely to arouse resentment—and nothing will attract greater criticism—than brusquely presenting individuals with the stark facts we have discovered in the exploration of their psyche (Adler, 1927/2014). Adlerians honor that the client is always the expert in their own life; an excellent way to acquire a bad representation is to carelessly misuse one's knowledge. As clients slowly begin to understand their lifestyle and take small steps toward new thoughts and behaviors, the counselor is supportive and encouraging (Belangee, 2012).

Christian Integration Perspective

Entwistle's (2010) Allies model of Christian integration is used to guide this author's work with clients, and in particular, this conceptualization and treatment plan. This model poses that the Truth is inherit in God's Word and God's Work, therefore, valuing theology and counseling as a foundation for understanding human behavior. Such a model lays a foundation for a more comprehensive understanding.

Adler explained that the fundamental motivation of all human beings is to belong, have a place, and contribute to the welfare of society (Ferguson, 1984). The Bible highlights the importance of community feeling through the biblical principle of being kind and good to others (*New International Bible*, 1978/2011, James 1:27). Being good to someone else helps us overcome the pain, loss, or disappointments we may experience; it also releases joy in our lives. God has called us to "outreach." When we reach out to others, God reaches into our souls and heals us.

The Bible emphasizes the importance of sewing His seeds everywhere. In Acts 20:35, the Bible says,

> In all things I have shown you that by working hard in this way we must help the weak and remember the words of the Lord Jesus, how he himself said, 'It is more blessed to give than to receive.' (*English Standard Bible,* 2001)

Philippians 2:2-8 is another example of the importance of social interest in the Bible as it reads:

> Complete my joy by being of the same mind, having the same love, being in full accord and of one mind. Do nothing from rivalry or conceit, but in humility count others more significant than yourselves. Let each of you look not only to his own interests, but also to the interests of others.

The Bible indicates that people have a responsibility to God, others, and themselves (Watts, 2000). According to the Bible, the very nature of humankind is to live in harmony with others (Grenz, 1994). In the teachings of Jesus, it can also be understood that humans are responsible for one another.

Additionally, just as Adlerian theory helps clients to identify growth-inhibiting life themes and replace them with more life-enhancing ones, the Bible teaches that healthy behaviors and emotions result from healthy thoughts (Watts, 2000). Both the Bible and Adlerian theory value encouragement and stress its influence on human growth and development.

Both Christianity and Individual Psychology look at cognitive, psychodynamic, and systemic perspectives of human functioning; both conceptualize humans as creative, holistic, socially oriented, and teleologically motivated; and both perspectives emphasize the value of equality, value, and dignity of all human beings. (Watts, 2000, p. 319). Therapists who integrate Christianity into counseling should use a psychotherapy theory most compatible with Christianity. Individual psychology is one of the most adaptable systems for working within a religious or spiritual framework (Watts, 2000).

A Case Study: Alani

Alani is an eight-year-old girl in second grade in a small rural town. Her parents are separated, and she lives in the home with her mother, two sisters, a baby brother, and maternal grandparents. Her father struggles with drug use and has been in and out of her life since she was born. There are no custody arrangements, but the client lives with her mother and only sees her father occasionally (mainly on holidays)—and only with the mother present. Her father does not work, is homeless, and pays no child support. The family receives child welfare and has low income. Alani's mother works part-time at a preschool and is in college full-time,

© Dubova/shutterstock.com

studying to become an elementary school teacher. Alani typically attends a Title I school but, at the time of counseling, was schooling from home due to the COVID-19 pandemic. Alani performs well in school, and her mother reports that it is "really important" to Alani that she makes good grades and has good behavior. Alani is the middle child.

Alani's mother reports that Alani is a "perfectionist," which sometimes causes conflict in the family when "She has to have things an exact way or she has a meltdown." Alani's mother reports that Alani acts like she is left out and sometimes withdraws or "back talks." Alani's mother describes that when Alani feels left out, "I try to hug her, but sometimes she just gets stiff and won't let anyone touch her. Then I get frustrated and tell her to get up and that it is enough." Alani's mother reported that Alani is extremely "picky" over her clothes and what she wears, always wanting to "dress up in her own style." Her mother also reports that Alani is a picky eater and "even has to have her food heated an exact way or she refuses to eat it. Sometimes she microwaves it while it is still hot; it makes no sense." As reported by her mother, Alani has lost significant weight in the previous month.

Her mother describes that Alani gets along okay with her older sister, who is one year older than her, but even the two of them argue at times. Her mother reports that the arguments between Alani and her older sister are usually concerning Alani's perception of things being unfair. Her mother reports that

Alani frequently argues with her younger siblings and "always tells me that I am unfair." As described by Alani's mother, when Alani feels left out or perceives things as unfair, she often finds comfort in "snuggling" with her maternal grandma. However, Alani's mother said, "Sometimes I feel like she makes things worse with Alani and makes me look like the bad guy." Overall, Alani's mother reports that she wants to find ways to help Alani "not want everything to be a certain way all the time and to start feeling more like she belongs instead of feeling left out among her siblings."

Applying the B-Well Model Using Adlerian (Individual Psychology) Therapy

As a part of a B-Well case conceptualization, Alani was assessed as a whole in terms of the Mind, Heart, Strength, Soul, Neighbor, and Society facets. These facets will be discussed in detail below. As a part of the therapy provided for Alani, a *DSM-5* diagnosis was not required. This is in accordance with Adlerian theory, in which the therapist treats the person holistically, not the symptoms. If a diagnosis or categorization were required for reimbursement or other reasons, Alani would have most closely met the diagnostic criteria for F43.25 adjustment disorder with mixed disturbances of emotion and conduct, Z62.820 parent-child relational problem, Z62.891 sibling relational problem, Z63.5 disruption of family by separation or divorce, and Z59.6 low income.

Regarding differential diagnosis, although Alani has many symptoms of obsessive-compulsive personality disorder (e.g., preoccupation with details, maladaptive perfectionism, rigidity, etc.), it should be recognized that most personality disorders are not diagnosable in individuals younger than 18, as features of personality usually become recognizable and more persistent during adolescence or early adult life (American Psychiatric Association, 2013). In addition, the onset of Alani's symptoms was in response to identifiable stressors, which included her and her family leaving their home to move in with her maternal grandparents.

Utilizing the decision tree offered as a part of the B-Well model and following data collection and assessment, themes were organized according to B-Well model facets. These include Heart, Mind, Strength, Soul, Neighbor, and Society. Any applicable assets in each facet are also noted as important to client wellbeing and healing.

Heart

From Adlerian theory, Alani's elevated sadness, frequent anger, and feelings of isolation would be looked at in terms of movement in the lifestyle. For example, when Alani is sad, angry, or isolates herself, what might be happening in terms of safeguarding? If Alani's mistaken beliefs in this area are, "I am not my mother's favorite; I am left out; I am not wanted," then her private logic might be, "I must act out or withdraw to get attention; I must earn my mother's love by being perfect; I must keep myself safe by withdrawing." In the Bible, Proverbs 100:3 (*New International Bible*, 1978/2011) says, "Know the Lord is God. It is he who made us, and we are His; we are His people, the sheep of his pasture." This Bible verse can also be used to help encourage Alani that she always has a place and belongs.

 ## Mind

As reported by her mother, Alani was preoccupied with details and expressed perfectionism in maladaptive ways. When working from an Adlerian lens, Alani's preoccupation with details and maladaptive perfectionism would also be viewed in terms of the client's lifestyle convictions, mistaken beliefs, and private logic. According to the Adlerian theory, imperfections are a part of being human. In Alani's case, she is meeting a life task with "self-focus" rather than "other focus," known as social interest. As Alani displays maladaptive perfectionism, it is important to help her begin to define herself by God's standards. In God, we can identify as His beloved child (*English Standard Bible*, 2001, Ephesians 1:3-6; Romans 8:14-17; 1 John 3:1-3). Children have a special place in God's heart. When Jesus' disciples tried to keep children from coming to Jesus, He rebuked them and welcomed the children to His side, saying, "Let the little children come to me, and do not hinder them, for the kingdom of God belongs to such as these" (*New International Bible*, 1978/2011, Mark 10:14).

 ## Strength

Alani demonstrates rigid eating patterns and weight loss. Alani's rigidity about her eating patterns can be targeted from an Adlerian lens in terms of private logic. Alani is currently feeling discouraged about inferiority feelings; however, in Adlerian theory, it is clear that inferiority feelings can be used as motivation for success. Biblically, the client can be pointed to scripture that will help her believe that she is remarkably and wonderfully made (*New International Bible*, 1978/2011, Psalm 139:14; Song of Solomon 4:7) and mediate on God's Word regarding the fleeting nature of beauty and the everlasting love of God (Proverbs 31:30).

Soul

Alani endured the lasting impact of her father's drug abuse (Soul). According to Adlerian theory, the lifestyle is formed during the early years and is highly influenced by the family constellation. Alani's father abuses drugs, provides no support, and is absent in her life. This results in a lack of attachment as well as a lack of support. As Alani's spirituality (i.e., an Adlerian life task) was a strength in her life, this could be interwoven into the treatment plan to help with healing. With spiritual integration, a Christian therapist is reminded that God is the only one who can heal the brokenhearted and make the wounded better than new. The most important support is God, our ultimate healer and counselor. David wrote, "From the ends of the earth I call to you, I call as my heart grows faint; lead me to the rock that is higher than I. For you have been my refuge, a strong tower against the foe" (*New International Bible*, 1978/2011, Psalm 61:2-3). It is our responsibility to exercise faith in God, stay in the Word, cry out to God in prayer, and maintain fellowship with other believers. In this sense, Alani's spiritual practices such as attending church and using prayer are pivotal in her healing. We go to God in our distress and make use of the resources He provides.

Neighbor

Alani's estranged relationship with her father and withdrawal from her mother and siblings (Neighbor) would be viewed in terms of her lifestyle and private logic. Alani's experiences during young childhood motivated her movement in life. As family is a life task, according to Adlerian theory, the resolution is social interest.

As social interest is a key concept in Adlerian theory, a goal might include encouraging belonging. Increasing social interest provides a sense of connectedness to other people. It is important for her to remember the truth of God's sovereignty and that He has a purpose for everyone's life. It is important to replace the lie that we are unworthy with the truth that God has a plan for each of us (*English Standard Bible*, 2001, Ephesians 2:10; 5:15-16). Through parent consultation, it will be important to discuss this loss too. Loss does not mean everything in life is over, just that one part of it has ended. In Ruth 3:1-5, Ruth stepped into God's plan of restoration for her life. The Bible teaches that faith moves us to take God-inspired action (James 2:17-18). One season has passed, and another will begin if you are willing to believe you can go forward.

Society

Alani and her family have low income. She lives in a food desert and attends an impoverished school system. From an Adlerian perspective, although each person does possess the creative power of the self, physical factors can have an impact. In this case, safety and food needs are vital to the client's well-being.

Client Assets

As far as assets in each facet of the B-Well model, Alani is curious, caring, and trusting (Heart). She is persistent, thoughtful, intelligent, responsible, and creative (Mind). Alani is, overall, physically healthy with no chronic ailments (Strength). She is friendly and has many friends at school and church; her mother describes that she even keeps in touch with them through the closings occurring alongside the COVID-19 pandemic (Neighbor). Alani loves attending church and regularly uses prayer (Soul). Alani is also Caucasian, a race most often benefitting from societal advantages in the United States due to racism and social inequality (Society).

B-Well Treatment Plan

Because of the Lord's great love we are not consumed, for his compassions never fail. They are new every morning; great is your faithfulness.

Lamentations 3:22-23

© SoulPhotos/shutterstock.com

Following the case conceptualization using the B-Well model, a treatment plan was made (see Table 1). The goals, objectives, and interventions are directly related to the B-Well conceptualization. While this section is not a comprehensive treatment plan, it will show some examples of how individual psychology can be integrated with the B-Well model. Through an Adlerian lens, important components of therapy, in addition to assessment, are building a relationship, lifestyle assessment, client insight, and client reorientation. These are integrated into each part of the treatment plan below.

In terms of life stress, Adler wondered less about the serious event itself; instead, he wondered more about why some individuals become fixated on the event while others do not, indicating a failing in the lifestyle (Hjertaas,

2013). As such, unhealthy or mistaken self and world views may predispose an individual to undesirable responses. Alani has experienced many stressful life events, including witnessing drug abuse by her father, experiencing an estranged relationship with her father, leaving her home to move in with her maternal grandparents, and sensing tension in the relationships between her mother and grandparents as far as parenting values. From an Adlerian lens, Alani's symptoms manifest in terms of movement in her lifestyle based on lifestyle convictions, mistaken beliefs, and private logic. The Bible aligns with Adlerian theory in this reference as compared to Paul's "thorn in the flesh" (*New International Bible*, 1978/2011, 2 Corinthians 12:7-10). Thorns are painful, but we can continue to go to God and remind ourselves of His faithfulness (Lamentations 3; 1 Corinthians 1:4-9).

TABLE 1 Recommended Goals, Objectives, and Interventions

Problem	Goal	Objective	Intervention
Elevated sadness, frequent anger, and feelings of isolation [Heart]	Increased belonging	Objective 1 – The client will gain insight into private logic. [Mind] Objective 2 – The client will replace mistaken belief/s with common sense. [Mind] Objective 3 – The client will have increased social interest. [Heart, Mind, Neighbor]	• The therapist will use encouragement to convey acceptance and belief in Alani regarding her assets. • The therapist will use meta-communication about the goals of behavior. • The therapist will use shared storytelling to help the client gain insight into how demanding attention sometimes backfires. • The therapist will use sand trays to help the client describe ways she gets attention and how negative and positive attention feels. • The therapist will use "spitting in the [client's] soup" (i.e., she really does not get the attention she wants when acting out or withdrawing).
Maladaptive perfectionism [Mind]	Healthy view of the self	Objective 4 – The client will move toward healthy expression of personality priority (control). [Heart, Mind, Strength] Objective 5 – The client will exhibit the courage to be imperfect. [Heart]	• The therapist will use meta-communication to help the client see her need for control in situations and any undesirable effects. • The therapist will direct the client to complete a sand tray on assets (to be used to foster healthy expression of behavioral patterns). • The therapist will use bibliotherapy to help the client see that a person can be out of control and still be safe.

Rigid eating patterns [Strength]	Healthy eating patterns and body weight	Objective 6 – The client will gain insight into private logic. [Mind] Objective 7 – The client will replace mistaken belief/s with common sense. [Mind]	• The therapist will use "spitting in the soup" to point out when behavior patterns are unhelpful. • The therapist will model the courage to be imperfect.
Impact of lack of/ estranged relationship with father on life tasks [Soul]	Use of spiritual strengths as a source of resilience and coping	Objective 8 – The client will increase prayer when experiencing overwhelming emotions. [Soul]	• The therapist will explore the client's spirituality (including what helps her feel calm). • The therapist will use encouragement to increase use of strengths for coping.
Estranged relationship with father and withdrawal from mother	Gain a sense of belonging Increased social interest	Objective 9 – The client will name her assets. [Mind] Objective 10 – The client will list her contributions in the family. [Heart, Mind] Objective 11 – The client will brainstorm ways to enhance communication with mother. [Mind]	• The therapist will play games with the client. • The therapist will have the client create a sand tray of ways to communicate with the family. • The therapist will use co-storytelling or mutual storytelling to encourage connection. • The therapist will use creative characters in stories as storytelling devices. • The therapist will use the relationship as a tool for connection and show excitement to see the client. • The therapist will do a sand tray for the client on what they believe is the client's impact on the world. • The therapist will ask the client to teach them about things that are important to and contributions to the family. • The therapist will consult with the parent (mother), asking her to give the client responsibilities and acknowledge contributions.

Lack of resources for healthy living [Society]	Optimal physical health and safety	Objective 12 – The client will identify things that are important to her health. [Mind, Strength] Objective 13 – The client will create a safety plan. [Mind] Objective 14 – The client will collaborate with mother in healthy meal planning. [Mind, Neighbor]	• The therapist will provide a list of resources to assist the client in times of need. • The therapist will provide psycho-education on the psychological impact of physiological health. • The therapist will encourage healthy meal planning as a shared activity between the client and mother.

Summary

Core components of individual psychology, or Adlerian theory, include that people are socially embedded and have a need to belong; people are self-determining and creative; all behavior is goal-directed; reality is perceived subjectively; and people are unique and integrated parts that cannot be separated into distinct parts (Kottman & Meany-Walen, 2016). In another way, the theory of individual psychology can be described using the acronym SUPER: Social interest, Unity, Private logic, Equality, and Reason or purpose (Eckstein & Kern, 2009). Although considered to be one of the three depth therapies (i.e., those that take the unconscious into account), Adlerian theory shares many similarities with other psychological theories, including humanistic, cognitive, and constructivist approaches (Obserst & Stewart, 2012). Adlerian theory, a part of the psychodynamic force of counseling, has been followed by many other theories; however, it is still widely used today. Upon close examination, it seems that many ideas in other theories are found in individual psychology, perhaps packaged in a different way (Carlson, 2000). Individual psychology encompasses the therapeutic strengths of many schools of psychotherapy while avoiding many of their limitations (Mansager, 2014). In this case study, individual psychology was used as a part of the B-Well model case conceptualization rather seamlessly, as the theory already takes into consideration so many factors as a part of the lifestyle assessment. The B-Well model provided a framework to understand the Adlerian theory concept of lifestyle while also providing a seamless way to use Christian integration.

References

Adler, A. (1958). *What life should mean to you.* Capricorn.

Adler, A. (1979). *Superiority and social interest: A collection of later writings* (3rd ed.). W. W. Norton.

Adler, A. (2014). *Understanding human nature.* Oneworld publications. (Original work published 1927).

American Psychiatric Association. (2013). *Diagnostic and statistical manual of mental disorders* (5th ed).

Ansbacher, H. L. (1992). Alfred Adler's concepts of community feeling and social interest and the relevance of community feeling for old age. *The Journal of Individual Psychology, 48*(4), 402-412.

Ansbacher, H. L., & Ansbacher, R. R. (1956). *The individual psychology of Alfred Adler: A systematic presentation in selections from his writings.* Harper Perennial.

Belangee, S. (2012, July 1). Individual psychology: Relevant techniques for today's counselor. *Counseling Today: A Publication of the American Counseling Association.* https://ct.counseling.org/2012/07/individual-psychology-relevant-techniques-for-todays-counselor/

Bottome, P. (1939). *Alfred Adler, a biography.* Putnam.

Carlson, J. (2000). Individual psychology in the year 2000 and beyond: Astronaut or dinosaur? Headline or footnote? *Journal of Individual Psychology, 56*(1), 3-13.

Carlson, J., Watts, R. E., & Maniacci, M. (2006). *Adlerian therapy: Theory and practice.* American Psychological Association. https://doi.org/10.1037/11363-000

Cervone, D., & Pervin, L. A. (2016). *Personality: Theory and research.* John Wiley and Sons.

Eckstein, D., & Kern, R. (2009). *Psychological footprints.* (6th ed.). Kendall Hunt Publishing Company.

Eife, G. (2019). *The development of Alfred Adler's individual psychology: Theory of personality, psychopathology, psychotherapy (1912-1937).* Vandenhoeck & Ruprecht.

English Standard Bible. (2001). ESV Online. https://esv.literalword.com/

Entwistle, D. N. (2010). *Integrative approaches to psychology and Christianity: An introduction to worldview issues, philosophical foundations, and models of integration* (2nd ed.). Cascade.

Ferguson, E. D. (1984). *Adlerian theory: An introduction.* Adler Professional School of Psychology.

Grenz, S. J. (1994). *Theology for the community of God.* Broadman & Holman Publishers.

Griffith, J., & Powers, R. L. (2007). *The lexicon of Adlerian psychology: 106 terms associated with the individual psychology of Alfred Adler.* Adlerian Psychology Associates, Ltd., Publishers.

Hjertaas, T. (2013). Toward an Adlerian perspective on trauma. *The Journal of Individual Psychology, 69*(3), 186-201.

Kopp, R. R., & Kivel, C. (1990). Traps and escapes: An Adlerian approach to understanding resistance and resolving impasses in psychotherapy. *Individual Psychology, 46*(2), 139-147.

Kottman, T., & Meany-Walen, K. (2016). *Partners in play: An Adlerian approach to play therapy* (3rd ed). American Counseling Association.

Manaster, G. J. (1977). *Adolescent development and the life tasks.* Allyn & Bacon.

Mansager, E. (2014). A narrative survey of classical Adlerian depth psychotherapists. *Journal of Individual Psychology, 70*(4), 323-331. 10.1353/jip.2014.0028

Miller, R., & Taylor, D. D. (2016). Does Adlerian theory stand the test of time?: Examining individual psychology from a neuroscience perspective. *The Journal of Humanistic Counseling, 55*(2), 111-128. https://doi.org/10.1002/johc.12028

Mosak, H. H., & Maniacci, M. P. (1999). *A primer of Adlerian psychology: The analytic-behavioral-cognitive psychology of Alfred Adler.* Brunner-Routledge.

New International Bible. (2011). The NIV Bible. https://www.thenivbible.com (Original work published 1978)

Nystul, M. S. (1994). Increasing the positive orientation to Adlerian psychotherapy: Redefining the concept of "basic mistakes.". *Individual Psychology: Journal of Adlerian Theory, Research & Practice, 50*(3), 272-278.

Oberst, U. E., & Stewart, A. E. (2012). *Adlerian psychotherapy: An advanced approach to individual psychology.* Routledge.

Rasmussen, P. (2010). *The quest to feel good.* Routledge.

Sperry, L., Carlson, J., Sauerheber, J. D., & Sperry, J. (2015). *Psychopathology and psychotherapy: DSM-5 diagnosis, case conceptualization, and treatment.* (3rd ed). Routledge.

Watts, R. (2000). Biblically based Christian spirituality and Adlerian psychotherapy. *The Journal of Individual Psychology, 56*(3), 316-328.

Watts, R. (2003). Adlerian therapy as a relational constructivist approach. *The Family Journal, 11*(2), 139-147. https://doi.org/10.1177/1066480702250169

Wedding, D., & Corsini, R. (2014). *Current psychotherapies* (10th ed.). Cengage.

CHAPTER 10

B-Well Model in Clinical Mental Health Counseling Using Cognitive Behavioral Therapy

David E. Jones

> "Therefore, I urge you, brothers and sisters, in view of God's mercy, to offer your bodies as a living sacrifice, holy and pleasing to God— this is your true and proper worship. Do not conform to the pattern of this world but be transformed by the renewing of your mind. Then you will be able to test and approve what God's will is—his good, pleasing and perfect will."
>
> — Romans 12:1-3 (NIV)

This chapter will focus on the application of cognitive behavioral therapy (CBT) using the B-Well model. In this chapter, you will find a brief overview of CBT, a refresher. I will then offer my Christian integration approach and my denominational lens. Then I will provide a case study on Sam. After the case study, I will apply CBT within the B-Well model to conceptualize Sam's presenting problem and other clinically relevant factors. Finally, I will offer a B-Well/CBT treatment plan example for you.

Background of Cognitive Behavioral Therapy (CBT)

Origins

As a practicing clinical mental health professional counselor, my primary theoretical approach is Beck's cognitive theory (created in the 1960s and 1970s), one of CBT's primary theories (Beck, 2020). Initially, when Aaron Beck developed cognitive theory, his focus was on cognitions. Currently, cognitive therapy is identified as cognitive behavioral therapy with the merging of both cognitive therapy and behavioral therapy. CBT is a present-based, short-term form of counseling.

View of Human Nature

When applying Beck's CBT approach, the view of human nature—specifically pathology—is based on the cognitive model (Beck, 2020). The cognitive model suggests that the root of emotional, behavioral, and physiological dysfunction is influenced by the client's thoughts.

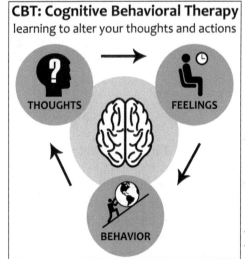

CBT: Cognitive Behavioral Therapy
learning to alter your thoughts and actions

THOUGHTS — FEELINGS — BEHAVIOR

© desdemona72/shutterstock.com

View of Change

If a client's presenting problem is viewed through the cognitive model, then the root is maladaptive thoughts or perceptions that are eliciting the problems. A CBT clinician aims to assist the client in their appraisals (Beck, 2020). Adjusting their thinking process will bring about healthy changes in mood, behaviors, and physiology. CBT focuses on cognitions to understand the client's problems (case conceptualization) that have at least three levels of understanding—automatic thoughts (words or images), intermediate beliefs (conditions, assumptions, rules, attitudes), and core beliefs. When a specific event or situation triggers the client, an appraisal of the event happens. This event appraisal can elicit a shift in

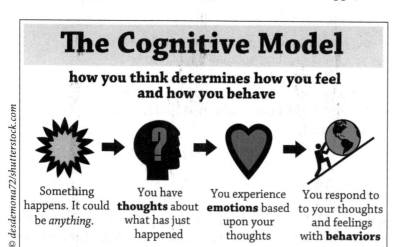

mood, behavior, and/or physiology that can be maladaptive. For example, a client may have asked a person on a date. The client was rejected. This event then elicits a negative appraisal of self, which moved the client to a depressive state (emotion), seeking isolation (behavior), and change in sleep patterns (physiological). Beck recognizes the focus on cognitions as a therapeutic "heuristic," and there is an interaction of mood, physiology, behavior, and thinking that affects our clients.

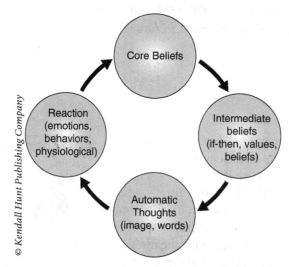

From a CBT lens, the client had an automatic thought of "Nobody will date me," which connected to a conditional assumption (if-then orientation to reality). The conditional assumption could be, "When I am rejected, then I avoid others." The conditional assumption can be driven by a maladaptive core belief of being unlovable, worthless, or helpless. For example, let's assume the client identifies the core belief of "unlovable." The client was rejected, which led to a maladaptive appraisal of self, which then triggered an if-then condition of avoidance driven by the maladaptive core belief of being perceived as unlovable.

The process of change through CBT is to move from the core maladaptive beliefs of self, others, and the world to more adaptive, accurate core beliefs of self. As Beck (2020) states, clients develop "flexible, helpful, reality-based beliefs about themselves, their worlds, other people, and the future" (p. 31). Working with the client to adjust their maladaptive automatic thoughts, such as "Nobody will date me," to more flexible, adaptive automatic thoughts, such as "I am good enough, and there are other fish in the sea," will change the if-then condition from isolation to a continued engagement in a prosocial manner. This can then bring about, over time, a change in the unlovable maladaptive core belief to one where the client perceives self as "lovable" by others by testing their thoughts, replacing maladaptive thoughts, and engaging in helpful behaviors.

The example above is a single event. Generally, our clients have had repeated events throughout their lifespans that reinforce the maladaptive core beliefs of unlovable, worthless, or helpless. The client above may have been previously rejected by his mother, father, peers, and/or coworkers, which helped establish the client's negative view of self, others, and the world that became persistent and unmalleable. The client then engaged in repeated maladaptive thinking, inculcating problems with mood, behaviors, and physiology.

Cognitive Behavorial Therapy is focused on learning to alter your thoughts (cognitions) and actions (behavior)

without CBT: negative thinking

NEGATIVE OUTCOMES

with CBT: reframed thinking

POSITIVE OUTCOMES

© desdemona72/shutterstock.com

Christian Integration Perspective

Christian Integration

As a practicing Christian counselor, one of the first steps I took was establishing my Christian counseling approach. There are a number of Christian counseling approaches (e.g., Entwistle, 2015; Hawkins & Clinton, 2015). Yet, I have operated from an integration view (Jones, 2010). In essence, this view advocates for Christianity and science. I see the biblical worldview as the foundation, but I can also find "truths" in science when working with my clients. Jones refers to Collins (1977), which captures my integration approach. Collins called for,

> Christians to draw on all the riches of scripture to develop, in as much depth as possible, a fundamentally Christian understanding of the human condition, and then seek to engage and rebuild [counseling] in a way that honors God and functionally places Jesus as Lord over our work as [counselors]. (p. 104)

From an integration view, the Bible is a starting place. Through God's special revelation (e.g., scripture), we are to be obedient to Christ's lordship (*New International Bible*, 1978/2011, Ephesians 1:20-23; Matthew 28:18; 2 Timothy 3:16). This includes obedience, out of love, of our mind, body, and soul and the creative works we discover and do (e.g., science). We are to make our work as counselors and the associated science obedient to God, who shapes reality and our understanding of being human.

We can see this when we counter the secular understanding of humankind—our clients. For example, a Rogerian practitioner would focus on self-actualization and hold a metaphysical belief that our clients are "... basically good, that dysfunction is the result of the socialized environment and not of the person, and that the core human motivation is that of seeking self-actualization" (Jones, 2010, p. 103). Many of these presuppositions are contrary to a Christian worldview of a fallen world and sin. There are a number of other "correctives" the Bible offers to the counseling field. This includes that humans are not only matter but also body and soul (*New International Bible*, 1978/2011, Ecclesiastes 12:7; Matthew 10:28, Romans 8:10); humans are made in the image of God (Genesis 2:7); and humans have free will and are inclined to do evil (Leviticus 19:4; James 1:14-15; 1 Corinthians 6:9).

Yet, the Bible does not have all the answers when we conceptualize and treat our clients. McMinn (2012) offers a clear picture to discriminate by offering the following: when a client is in deep suffering, he can view the person from a biblical lens with the impact of the fall, sin, and our deepest desire for redemption (*New International Bible*, 1978/2011, Romans 8:22-34); but when working with PTSD, for example, the cognitive and behavioral therapies equip the counselor to assist in healing the client by offering evidence-based treatments that are found efficacious (e.g., prolonged exposure therapy, cognitive processing therapy, CBT, and EMDR therapy). The Bible does point to the importance of relationships (Genesis 2:18; Psalm 23; 1 John 4:16), but through the science of counseling, we have discovered the essential counseling skills, ingredients (e.g., alliance, collaborative goals, empathy, positive regard, congruence) to bring about healing (Wampold, 2015).

As a Christian integrationist, I seek to conceptualize the client through a biblical lens. This includes inherent value (*imago Dei; New International Bible*, 1978/2011, Genesis 2:7) as well as using scripture to have a true understanding of what being human means, body and soul. This foundation, then, informs my work with a client. With the client's being both body and soul, and if the client is a Christian, then, with consent, spiritual disciplines can be employed in sessions that engage the mind, body, and soul. Yet, I would also integrate a cognitive behavioral lens and appropriate clinical interventions as needed based on the disorder. There is a dance between a biblical worldview, the truths of scripture, and evidence-based counseling treatment. Moreover, as a Christian counselor, my own walk with Jesus, the process of sanctification or holiness, is imperative. As I grow in Christ (Ephesians 4:13-15; 2 Peter 1:5-8), I will bear more of the fruit of the Spirit (Galatians 5:22-23). As the Holy Spirit works in my life, I am able to offer peace, joy, love, patience, kindness, goodness, gentleness, faithfulness, and self-control to my client. This engenders rapport and a safe haven where the client can grow, heal, and if a Christian client, will have the potential to become more like Christ, further sanctified through treatment. Even if the client does not profess to follow Christ or is indecisive about their faith, I am still demonstrating God's love through acceptance and safety.

Denominational Influence

An implicit backdrop to my Christian integration approach is my denominational lens. As an evangelical restoration movement protestant, certain biblical tenants influence my Christian worldview. Some of these align with evangelical Protestantism at large, but others may be unique to the conservative restoration movement. As a conservative evangelical, I hold to the following Christian beliefs—the Bible is the inspired word of God; the Bible is infallible; and Jesus Christ was born of a virgin, lived a sinless life, died on the cross, and was resurrected in three days. I also hold that faith in Christ through grace is the path for salvation. I believe in the historical Adam and Eve who disobeyed God, bringing about sin into the world. I also hold that sin permeated all creation, particularly humans.

Beyond the essentials above, the American Restoration movement had a central aim of returning back to the New Testament church (*New International Bible*, 1978/2011, Acts 2:1-14) and a focus on scripture as the foundation of faith versus church history, denominational creeds, etc. We, generally, hold to the cessations of the gifts (e.g., speaking in

tongues, etc.) at the end of the apostolic period. The restoration movement also affirms full emersion for baptism, the sacrament of communion, and God's written Word ending with the New Testament.

A Case Study: Sam

Sam is a Black female, age 56. She lives in an urban, inner-city environment. Sam is on Medicaid-based disability (e.g., a chronic back condition) and receives monthly social security checks for her income, which places her below the federal poverty line. Sam has a history of counseling and has been diagnosed with bipolar I disorder and a history of sexual abuse by her uncle. The client self-referred because of increased depressive symptoms triggered by the loss of her mother about four weeks ago. The client recalled that she has been sleeping much of the day, has experienced an increase in crying episodes, and has had an increase in irritability that occurs nearly every other day.

During the assessment interview, the client appeared unkempt with poor grooming, unclean clothing, and disheveled. The client was alert and oriented times four (i.e., person, place, time, event). The client reported feeling sad daily for the past three weeks. I observed that the client's affect was depressed with slower speech than would be expected and several occurrences of crying during the assessment session. The client stated she feels lethargic most days and sleeps about 10 to 12 hours daily. Prior to the initial session, the client completed a semi-structured adult assessment form and a battery of assessments: the Beck's Depression Inventory-II (score = 22), PCL-5 (score = 27), and the Altman Self-Rating Mania Scale (score = 2), in addition to a problems checklist noting concerns with anxiety, generally unhappy, grief, sleeping problems, and irritability. Sam also completed the Discover the Lies worksheet (Campbell, 1993). There were a number of negative views of self, others, and the world. She marked "Almost All the Time" in the following areas: "I'm totally helpless;" "I'm no good. I never have been;" and "I'm a bad person."

Sam is currently single. She has two children (son, 22, and daughter, 24). She offered that she has a healthy and supportive relationship with her children. She lives by herself in a subsidized apartment. Her mother, father, and stepfather have passed away. She did disclose that she was abused by an uncle from the ages of eight to 11. She reported a few friends and some connections at her local church. Yet, she noted that she finds it difficult to connect with her friends or church consistently because of her fear of

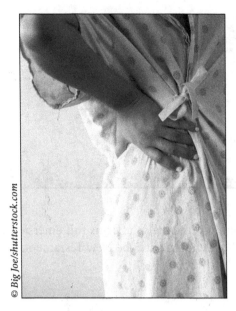

© Big Joe/shutterstock.com

© Leka Sergeeva/shutterstock.com

being judged. She attends church sporadically because of her fear of stigma for bipolar disorder and dysgraphia. The client stated, "If people really knew me, they would not like me," yet, the client claims to have a strong Christian faith. She reported listening to her Bible daily and praying.

She is unemployed and has been for the past 15 years due to her chronic back condition. She has had several back surgeries with some relief but continues to have daily back pain that affects her functioning and quality of life. The client stated that her chronic back pain contributes to her depressive states and irritation.

Sam was diagnosed with bipolar I disorder when she was 21. Over time, she has experienced several manic and depressive episodes. Her last manic episode was seven years ago. Currently, she is able to manage her manic episodes with her prescribed medication. Her psychiatrist has prescribed her Trazadone (300mg per day) and Abilify (10mg per day). Sam is compliant with taking the medications and does not report any side effects. Sam did report shopping sprees during her past manic phases. She stated that in the past, she used credit cards during those times. Purses are her particular focus when shopping during a manic phase. The client reported continued credit card debt as a stressor.

Sam has completed her high school GED but struggled throughout school. She was diagnosed with a learning disorder, dysgraphia, when she was eight years old. The client has difficulty with written assignments and when reading assignment instructions. The client stated she does not generally read and limits her writing. The client prefers oral exchanges.

When asked about her assets, using the lens of the six facets of the B-Well model, the client hesitated to suggest any. After some reflection and assistance, the client stated she has "grit." She is able to attend to most of her daily duties throughout her life, even with her continued struggles with bipolar disorder, dysgraphia, chronic back pain, and perceived stigma. She offered her "spirituality" as a source of empowerment. Through her relationship with God, she finds comfort, peace, and some social resources at her church. She stated that she is able to gain food, clothing, and other necessities from her church pantry. She recalled that the church has assisted in paying bills through their benevolence fund in the past.

Applying the B-Well Model Using CBT

The aim of case conceptualization, or case formulation, is to "explain" what drives and maintains the clinical problems. To do this, a CBT counselor, operating from a Beck CBT focus, uses a cognitive case diagram (CCD) in the conceptualization process. During assessment and beyond, the therapist uses the CCD for situations where problematic emotional, behavioral, and physiological reactions occur. Additionally, the therapist is looking for associated maladaptive automatic thoughts (ATs) and the meaning of those ATs associated with the problems and linked signs and symptoms. The therapist identifies the client's maladaptive core beliefs, conditional assumptions/rules, and associated maladaptive coping strategies along with clinically relevant client historical factors. Using CBT within B-Well, the counselor evaluates situations for maladaptive responses of the Heart, Mind, Strength, Soul, Neighbor, and

Society. This approach expands beyond thoughts, emotions, behaviors, and physiology to a more robust, holistic understanding of the client's problems, assets, and associated context.

Sam's Problem Areas

Heart

Starting with the Heart, Sam's antecedent event, the presenting problem, was the loss of her mother. Sam has a history of depressive episodes, with the most recent associated with grief. She is currently in a depressed state, which was supported via a semi-structured interview and a battery of assessments. She had an elevated Beck Depression Inventory-II score of 22, which indicates moderate depression, and her problems checklist identified concerns with generally unhappy and grief. Biblically, Sam is experiencing the consequences of the fall and how we all experience death and the associated grief. We see this evidenced in John 11 (*New International Bible*, 1978/2011) and the death of Lazarus. When Mary came to Jesus, and he saw her weeping, grieving over her brother's death, "Jesus wept" (v. 35).

Mind

From a CBT lens, we see the "Mind" driving these changes in Heart and Strength. During the semi-structured interview, the client offered automatic thoughts of "If people really knew me, they would not like me." From the battery of assessments, other automatic thoughts were offered: "I'm totally helpless;" "I'm no good. I never have been;" and "I'm a bad person." These automatic thoughts and maladaptive behaviors point to conditional assumptions, "When I (Sam) feel sad, it is best if I avoid others." "If I avoid others socially, then I will not be judged negatively because I am an unlikeable person." This then points to a couple of maladaptive core beliefs that are driving her conditional assumptions, behaviors, and automatic thoughts. Beck (2020) suggests there are three primary maladaptive core beliefs (helpless, worthless, and unlovable). For Sam, there is evidence of unlovable and helpless.

From a biblical lens, the mind is in a fallen state (*New International Bible*, 1978/2011, Genesis 3:6-7). The mind can be controlled by the flesh or the Spirit (Ephesians 4:17-19; Romans 8:6-7), and the mind has the capacity to be renewed (Romans 12:2). However, the renewing Paul refers to is, in part, limited to Christians. For our client, she evidences a number of false beliefs of self: "I'm no good. I never have been;" "I'm a bad person;" and "If people really knew me, they would not like me." We can interpret these beliefs as the work of the flesh in the client's life, which is increasing the likelihood of a depressed state.

Strength

We can see evidence of maladaptation through the lens of Strength. The client has increased her daily sleep intake to about 10 to 12 hours per day. Alongside this avoidant behavior, the client has reduced her attendance at church and frequency of connecting with her social connections. She is also crying, irritable, lethargic, disheveled, and has slowed speech.

She has also experienced trauma—sexual abuse by her uncle. Traumatic experiences have biological plausibility for increasing the likelihood of bipolar disorder as well as other concerns (Aas et al., 2016). Trauma may influence a number of biological pathways such as the "Hypothalamic–pituitary–adrenal (HPA) axis, serotonergic transmission, neuroplasticity, immunity, calcium signaling, and circadian rhythms ..." (p. 1) that contribute to the likelihood of bipolar I, as well as impacting the production of dopamine, which is essential in motivation and goal-directed behavior.

The intersection of science and a biblical worldview has a potential connection with bipolar disorders. Preston et al. (2017) state that bipolar disorders are biologically based, which is why pharmacological interventions are primary indicators for treatment. We can potentially connect this biblically; the fall had consequences and may be discoverable at the biological and physiological levels. Rae (2006), a chaplain, offers this perspective effectively:

> The Bible affirms a general connection between sickness and sin—that death, disease, and decay were not part of God's original design for human beings. Beyond that, it is hard to generalize, since some illness does result from sin, some from being sinned against, and most through no fault of the patient. (p. 156)

Soul

There were no direct religious or spiritual concerns offered by the client. What is found in the case study is more assets, or resources, in this facet. These will be offered below in "Assets."

Neighbor

The Neighbor facet informs the relevant life history of the CCD. The client's history of being judged by others for her learning disorder, dysgraphia, and her diagnosis of bipolar I have elicited a stigma that engages her compensatory behavior of avoidance and reinforces her maladaptive belief of unlovable and helplessness. Her history of sexual abuse and potential trauma also maintains her current approach to others through her perception of others. This is evidenced in her ATs of "I'm no good. I never have been;" "I'm a bad person;" and "If people really knew me, they would not like me," which would generate avoidant behaviors. This decreases her social connections and increases the likelihood of isolation and depressive symptoms.

A key biblical point here is the sin of the neighbor against Sam. Grudem (1994) states that "Scripture is primarily a history of [humans] in a state of sin and rebellion against God [and one another]" (p. 490). We see this in how others treat Sam because of her fallen state experiences of bipolar I, trauma, and difficulties in writing. From her interactions with others who are operating in the flesh, it informs us of how her beliefs of self and others have, in part, developed her core maladaptive belief of helplessness and unlovable that then engenders a lack of interactions with others as well as how others may be avoiding her.

Society

Finally, there are a number of potential Society influences. Sam is a single, Black woman. The intersectionality of being a Black woman may have consequences such as gendered racism and society norms that bring about microaggression and the expected roles offered by Dr. Ford in Chapter 20—"Mammie, Jezebel, Safire, and Strong Black Woman"—that interact with the Mind, Heart, and Neighbor facets (Lewis et al., 2017). These two factors may contribute to her view of self and others. Sam did not explicitly report these experiences, but there could be implicit biases toward her and discrimination that have helped solidify her low view of self: "If people really knew me, they would not like me," and "I am a bad person." Her experience of poverty may also contribute to her low view of self. Each of these potential contributing factors would need further investigation to verify their influence and how it would contribute to the treatment plan.

Sam's Assets

CBT is primarily a problem-based theory when it comes to case conceptualization, but with CBT embedded within the B-Well model, we account for client assets through the six facets. This allows a counselor to identify client resources when conceptualizing and use the identified client's resources for treatment planning. Below I will offer both explicit and implicit resources by facet.

Mind

The client is able to recognize her emotional disturbances, depressed mood, and manic state; she evidences insight. Through this awareness, she has humility by seeking help; we see her taking action. This may indicate motivation to change. Sam noted she has "grit" or determination to get better and comply by taking her psychotropics as required to manage her manic episodes. She is also alert and oriented times four (i.e., person, place, time, event) and a reliable historian. We also know from Romans 12:2 (*New International Bible*, 1978/2011) that a Christian has the capacity for "renewing of [the] mind" and that non-Christians have the ability to change their thoughts based on *imago Dei*.

Soul

Her Soul facet points to her strong faith in Christ, her engagement in the Bible, and prayer. There is also the working of the Holy Spirit within her as a believer (*New International Bible*, 1978/2011, Acts 2:38; Galatians 5:22-23; John 14:15-17) and the loving relationship she has with God the Father.

Neighbor

Viewing the client from the Neighbor facet, she has effective connections with her two children, who provide her with social, emotional, cognitive, and physical support. She has connections at her church; those may not be as strong.

Society

Finally, Sam noted Society factors that are a boon—church food pantry, church assistance with paying bills, access to medical care, Medicaid, housing assistance, and SSI income.

B-Well Treatment Plan

Developing the treatment plan for Sam using the B-Well model and CBT offers a unique and more robust approach to treatment than CBT alone. The B-Well model calls for the therapist to attend to both the client's assets and the problems, allowing for a focus on the most pressing concerns. Sam has a number of assets to apply during the treatment. She has "grit" during the trials of life to be a survivor of sexual abuse, discrimination, and chronic health conditions. Through her faith, Sam can find succor, hope, empowerment, and growth. Finally, she has resources such as her children, church, and community (e.g., Medicaid). As a B-Well CBT counselor, I will use these assets implicitly and explicitly in the treatment based on the client's consent. For this case study, we will take the stance that Sam wants to integrate her Christian faith into treatment.

When examining the client's presenting problem, treatment focuses on the depressive symptoms. The treatment plan will address this main concern using CBT interventions and the client's assets to reduce and overcome her current depressive state. When creating interventions and objectives, I aim to apply, when possible, each facet of the B-Well model (Heart, Mind, Strength, Soul, Neighbor, and Society). I document in the treatment plan where each facet is applied for clarity to the reader. Yet, there will be a focus on "Mind" in that CBT perceives changes in the mind will elicit changes in Heart and Strength facets. Table 1 is a treatment plan for Sam.

TABLE 1 Recommended Goals, Objectives, and Interventions

Problem	Goal	Objective	Intervention
Major depressive disorder	Reduce depressive symptoms to baseline.	Objective 1 – The client will have a clear understanding of depression associated with bipolar disorder as well as the effectiveness of CBT for treatment. [Mind]	• Psychoeducation
		Objective 2 – The client, in session, will examine her current daily schedule for the week to determine potential behavioral changes. [Mind, Strength]	• Behavior modification
		Objective 3 – The client will identify maladaptive strategies, rules, assumptions, and core beliefs that may be increasing depressive and anxiety symptoms and reframe. [Mind]	• Socratic questioning • Values assessment • Testing Your Thoughts worksheet
		Objective 4 – The client will complete a mastery and pleasure survey to identify and apply the top three from each area across treatment to reduce depressive symptoms. [Mind, Heart]	• Mastery and Pleasure survey
		Objective 5 – The client will reframe maladaptive automatic thoughts, assumptions, and core beliefs of self, others, and the world. [Mind]	• Socratic questioning • Reframing • Test Your Thoughts worksheet • Cost-benefit analysis
		Objective 6 – The client will attend her quarterly medication evaluation with her psychiatrist to determine if changes are needed for current medication for bipolar I disorder management. [Mind, Strength]	• Release of Information • Monitor existing and new medication for side effects, efficacy, and compliance.

Problem	Goal	Objective	Intervention
		Objective 7 – The client will identify emotional states associated with key areas of dysfunction and learn to accurately label past and present experiences. [Heart]	• Emotion chart • Emotional granulation
		Objective 8 – The client will identify, expand, and engage with key individuals for social support aiding in the reduction of depressive symptoms and improvement of self-esteem. [Mind, Strength, Neighbor]	• Circle of Social Connections worksheet • Brainstorming • Rank order opportunities • Small group
		Objective 9 – The client will identify and utilize key spiritual disciplines based on her understanding of her Christian beliefs as an aid to overcoming depressive symptoms. [Mind, Heart, Soul]	• Bible • Pastoral Care • Bibliotherapy using *Celebration of Discipline* by R. Foster (2008)
		Objective 10 – The client will continue to utilize existing community resources (e.g., Medicaid, church) and engage in other community resources identified as beneficial. [Neighbor, Society]	• Psychoeducation • Medicaid • Church beneficence • Sexual abuse help groups • Black women support groups • Bipolar support groups

Summary

In the practice of counseling, it is essential to have competency in at least one theoretical approach, such as CBT. Understanding the theory's essential ingredients (e.g., view of human nature, theory of change, and interventions) and having a foundational understanding of a biblical worldview equips you to operate from a Christian counseling integrated lens. This naturally lends itself to working within the B-Well model and its six facets. The facets offer a heuristic to assess, conceptualize, and treat a client in a holistic approach. We can understand Sam's problems and her assets during the intake phase, then evaluate those facets using CBT embedded within the B-Well model. The result is an encompassing treatment plan that will assist in bringing about better outcomes for Sam through an expanded treatment plan created by examining the six facets. Clear assessment and targeted conceptualization provide CBT interventions, plus other interventions, to attend to each client facet—her Heart, Mind, Strength, Soul, Neighbor, and Society.

References

Aas, M., Chantal, H., Andreassen, O. A., Bellivier, F., Melle, I., & Etain, B. (2016). The role of childhood trauma in bipolar disorders. *International Journal of Bipolar Disorders, 4*(2), 1-10. https://doi.org/10.1186/s40345-015-0042-0

Beck, J. (2020). *Cognitive behavior therapy: Basics and beyond* (3rd ed.). Guilford.

Campbell, B. (1993). *Discover the lies.* https://counseling4christians.com/Videos/IntegrationDiscovertheLies.html.

Collins, G. R. (1977). *The rebuilding of psychology.* Tyndale House.

Entwistle, D. N. (2015). *Integrative approaches to psychology and Christianity: An introduction to worldview issues, philosophical foundations, and models of integration* (3rd ed.). Cascade Books.

Foster, R. J. (2008). *Celebration of discipline: The path to spiritual growth.* Hodder & Stoughton.

Grudem, W. (1994). *Systematic theology: An introduction to biblical doctrine.* Zondervan.

Hawkins, R., & Clinton, T. (2015). *The Christian counselor: A fresh biblical & transformational approach.* Harvest House.

Jones, S. (2010). An integration view. In E. L. Johnson (Ed.), *Psychology and Christianity: Five views* (2nd ed., pp. 101-128). IVP.

Lewis, J. A., Williams, M. G., Peppers, E. J., & Gadson, C. A. (2017). Applying intersectionality to explore the relations between gendered racism and health among Black women. *Journal of Counseling Psychology, 64*(5), 475–486. https://doi.org/10.1037/cou0000231

McMinn, M. R. (2012). *Psychology, theology, and spirituality in Christian counseling.* Tyndale House Publishers, Inc.

New International Bible. (2011). The NIV Bible. https://www.thenivbible.com (Original work published 1978)

Preston, J. D., O'Neal, J. H., & Talaga, M. C. (2017). *Handbook of clinical psychopharmacology for therapists* (8th ed.). New Harbinger Publications.

Rae, S. B. (2006). On the connection between sickness and sin: A commentary. *Christian Bioethics, 12*(2), 151-156. https://doi.org/10.1080/13803600600805310

Wampold, B. E. (2015). How important are the common factors in psychotherapy? An update. *World Psychiatry, 14,* 270-277. https://doi.org/10.1002/wps.20238

B-Well Model in Clinical Mental Health Counseling Using Acceptance and Commitment Therapy

Ken D. Miller

> "Now may the God of peace himself sanctify you completely, and may your whole spirit and soul and body be kept blameless at the coming of our Lord Jesus Christ."
>
> — 1 Thessalonians 5:23 (ESV)

Background of Acceptance and Commitment Therapy (ACT)

Origins

People have avoided uncomfortable emotions since the Fall. Adam's attempt to avoid the pain of his unpleasant emotions became a common pattern of response for most throughout human history. People avoid painful thoughts, feelings, and emotions in many ways: worrying, abusing substances, overeating, binging and purging, engaging in obsessive and compulsive behaviors, and creating alternate realities. In response to the inescapable suffering of being a human, Hayes and colleagues (Hayes & Wilson, 1994; Hayes et al., 2013) developed acceptance and commitment therapy (ACT) to help clients to accept the inevitable pain and suffering of being human. ACT leads clients through six processes (self-as-context, the present moment, defusion, acceptance, values, and committed action) with the hope of leading the client toward psychological flexibility (Hayes et al., 2011). The scope of ACT interventions includes couples therapy, anxiety, panic disorder, depression, obsessive-compulsive disorder (OCD), chronic pain, posttraumatic stress disorder (PTSD), and borderline personality disorder (BPD) (Gordon & Borushok, 2017; Hayes et al., 2011).

View of Human Nature

ACT was created to help people effectively deal with the effects of human misery and reframe their view of suffering. The creators of ACT recognize that the Judeo-Christian tradition view of human suffering as ubiquitous and inherent in the human condition precipitated because of the Fall (*English Standard Bible*, 2001, Genesis 3; Hayes et al., 2011). One of the foundational premises is that human beings engage in pain and suffering by pursuing their values or escaping their pain through maladaptive avoidance behaviors (Hayes & Wilson, 1994; Hayes et al., 2011, 2014; Tan, 2016). ACT theory holds the medical model of psychiatric disease at arm's length and suggests that "Human suffering predominantly emerges from normal psychological processes, particularly those involving human language" (Hayes et al., 2011, p. 11). While the creators agree that organic (brain injury, etc.)

Although the world is full of suffering, it is full also of the overcoming of it

© Naaz001/shutterstock.com

and abnormal psychological conditions and processes exist, how a person responds to their experiences and thoughts directly impacts emotional and psychological well-being. This is best described by the ACT idea of the assumption of destructive normality (Hayes et al., 2011). Normal thoughts and experiences and their associated language are interpreted as positive or negative, with the latter progressing into maladaptive beliefs and actions that compound human suffering.

View of Change

© Billion Photos/shutterstock.com

The client deciding to engage their psychological distress through ACT is recognized by the ACT therapist as the first committed action to change (Hayes & Wilson, 1994; Hayes et al., 2011, 2014). Change can take place in each of the six processes of ACT. By investigating and analyzing the language of their fused thoughts and feelings, the client can defuse and change their literal interpretation/ thought-identity belief and inspect thoughts as they occur. Learning to be present involves the client changing their thinking from predominantly about the past or future to the present moment. In ACT theory, primal change for the client results in a view of self-as-context that comes from changing their maladaptive views of thought/identity fusions and experiential avoidance. The client can change their valued direction by choosing to accept their unpleasant thoughts and circumstances and pursue who and what they value the most. Accepting thoughts, feelings, sensations, and experiences takes a willingness to change.

While not one of the six ACT processes, willingness plays a significant role in the change process. One type of willingness to change is the willingness with your feet, which means engaging in an activity even though it is psychologically and/or physically distressing (Tan, 2016). Willingness with your heart, although metaphorical and known only to the client, defines the inner motivation for change (Tan, 2016). The change process of ACT then is compatible and congruent with the Soul facet of the B-Well model. Change in the Soul (Heart, Mind, Strength) takes place as the client learns to actively pursue the fruit of the Spirit (*English Standard Bible*, 2001, Galatians 5:22-23).

Christian Integration Perspective

My pursuit of integrating psychology and Christianity began as a third-generation pastor's son growing up in a small Pentecostal denomination based in the southwest. The denomination was heavily influenced by the Azusa Revival, with an emphasis on the outworking gifts of the Spirit. One of the influential leaders of the denomination was my father, who also served as my primary spiritual influence in my early years. While he only had an eleventh-grade education, he was a voracious reader of theological classics and prominent theologians. Since there were few prominent Pentecostal theologians in the 1950s and 1960s, he turned to other evangelicals for theological inquiry and training. His example of being intellectually curious and theologically competent influenced me to challenge the prevailing anti-psychology mindset of evangelical Christianity during college and serve local churches as a volunteer and pastor.

The example of my father provided the motivation to question and look beyond my spiritual roots. That search resulted in adopting a Baptist-oriented core theology and synthesizing it with some of my Spirit-informed upbringing. Both the Pentecostal and Baptist denominations provided me with a wonderful foundation for faith and life. That foundation included the view that everything I needed for any aspect of life could be found in scripture. However, a personal existential crisis and emotional health struggles sent me on a quest for something that seemed to exist beyond memorizing scripture to mitigate anxiety and depression. There were truths I was discovering in the counseling sessions I was attending that led me to believe that there were truths about the human condition that existed outside of scripture, *and* they were congruent with scripture.

As I moved from being a client toward becoming a clinical mental health counselor, it became evident that I was adopting the view that science and, particularly counseling, was an ally of and could partner with, in many cases, sound doctrine (Entwistle, 2021; Johnson, 2007). The special revelation of scripture provided me with an ability to speak to the deepest of soul needs and questions that counseling does not address (Collins, 1993; Grenz, 1994; Grudem, 2000; Guthrie, Jr., 1968). General revelation, which is insight and knowledge that God provides to us about human nature outside of special revelation, helps clinicians address the human problems not addressed in scripture. It seems reasonable, and even necessary, to integrate faith and counseling so that holistic therapy can be provided to everyone through an interdisciplinary, reciprocal interaction (Carter & Narramore, 1979; Johnson, 2007; McMinn & Campbell, 2007; Miller, 2016).

In my personal quest to find a core psychotherapy that would allow me to conceptualize client cases and seamlessly integrate my belief in faith and science, I came across ACT. As I began to study ACT, I soon learned that it was an evidence-based treatment modality grounded in Judeo-Christian philosophy. ACT philosophically is grounded in the Biblical story of the fall of humanity, specifically, how the human desire to know as much as God resulted in human suffering (Hayes et al., 2014). Hayes and colleagues posit that suffering is painful, and that is why humans prefer avoiding pain rather than accepting and growing from their pain. As I studied ACT, I saw that it not only aligns philosophically with my own view of psychological pain but also provides me with a flexible case conceptualization template that allows me to integrate other treatment modalities and concepts based on a client's specific need. In the case of Christopher, his deep Christian faith was the reason I chose to help us conceptualize his psychological pain by synthesizing ACT and the B-Well model.

A Case Study: Christopher

Intake

Christopher is a 39-year-old Caucasian male who called to inquire about counseling upon a referral from one of the pastors at his church. In our initial intake session, he stated he had reservations about talking to a clinical mental health counselor, but he was told I was a "counselor that was Christian." He recently visited his physician for a checkup and an anxiety/depression medication refill assessment. During his exam, Christopher told his physician that he had experienced what he described as a "nervous

© Krakenimages.com/shutterstock.com

breakdown." His doctor gave him a clean bill of health otherwise but thought Christopher's additional complaints of restlessness, frequent headaches, irritable bowel, and numbness and tingling in his extremities may be related to job stress and the result of untreated anxiety. Christopher's physician suggested that he consider seeing a counselor for anxiety and job stress. Christopher told his doctor he was hesitant to see a clinical counselor. His doctor said he should at least seek the counsel of a pastor at his church. After a few sessions of pastoral counseling, the pastor told Christopher that a clinical mental health counselor would be able to help him best and that he knew of a counselor in the area that was a Christian.

After hearing his reason for calling, I asked Christopher to tell me what he thought was the cause of his anxiety and stress. Christopher says, "My anxiety is killing me right now." He explains that he is overwhelmed with his job and wants to quit. He constantly worries about work and his family. Christopher worries that his lack of energy and irritability are negatively affecting his wife and children. He is deeply spiritual but states he has questioned his belief in God for years despite being an avid student of the Bible. He is disturbed by his inability to end his prayers, whether they be simple food blessings, prayers of confession, or attempts to simply communicate with God. Life seems hopeless for Christopher at times. His sense of helplessness and hopelessness lead him to think, "What if I wasn't around anymore?" He was also concerned about physical symptoms that he did not discuss at his recent physical. In the last few months, Christopher began experiencing twitching and embarrassing vocalizations. He is concerned that these symptoms and other physical symptoms may be related to his anxiety and job stress, so he believes counseling might bring relief and help him see things more clearly. A thorough bio-psycho-social-spiritual assessment was conducted to aid in conceptualizing the primary diagnosis and subsequent treatment plan.

© Colored Lights/shutterstock.com

Assessment

The assessment process began with an online battery of anxiety, depression, and worry questionnaires. The *DSM-5* Level 1 Cross-Cutting Symptom Measure was administered as a funnel assessment to give context and to compare the results of the Penn State Worry Questionnaire (PSWQ), Generalized Anxiety Disorder-7 (GAD-7), Depression Anxiety Stress Scale (DASS-21), and Beck Anxiety Inventory (BAI) for clinical direction. The Acceptance and Action Questionnaire-II (AAQ-II) was administered to determine the client's level of thought fusion. I conducted a Mental Status Exam that resulted in the client being within normal limits.

The assessment battery revealed that Christopher was struggling with moderate to high anxiety, excessive worry, a high level of thought fusion, and mild to moderate depression that had been lingering for almost two years. Christopher and I reviewed the results together. During our conversation, he revisited his physical symptoms and reiterated his concerns about the other physical manifestations of ticks and vocalizations, which he had mentioned during his initial conversation with me. When asked about anything else that might inform the treatment process, Christopher offered that he has some obsessive tendencies: checking to see if the family van is locked three times before walking away and checking the outside doors of his home three times before going to bed. He did not report any other obsessive-type behaviors, so we collaboratively agreed that we would not assess for obsessive-compulsive disorder (OCD) unless it was warranted with further discovery during treatment. We discussed ancillary information that Christopher provided and investigated the proximal and distal factors that are contributing to his psychological distress.

Factors Leading to Counseling

Stress at Work

Christopher has taught middle school math for thirteen years. His perfectionist tendencies serve him well at his school, where he attained teacher of the year for the largest school system in his state. The population of the school where he teaches is from fractured families with predominately low incomes. In Christopher's words, "We're understaffed, and we've had three principals in the last five years." The instability of leadership, lack of administrative support, and nominal parental involvement have taken a toll on Christopher. Worrying about his job has become invasive. He finds himself losing his train of thought in lectures and has difficulty concentrating in lectures and personal conversations, which he finds embarrassing.

© Arsenii Palivoda/shutterstock.com

To compound the stress, virtual learning instituted by his school district due to the COVID-19 pandemic dramatically increased his stress level and workload. He is working more hours configuring curriculum and lecture delivery to an online platform. Communication with parents is tenser due to their increased uncertainty and the stress of adding the role of tutor to their home duties. This causes unique stressors for Christopher at home.

Stress at Home

Being a teacher and now a parent/tutor of two boys, ages 10 and six, in an at-home learning environment adds to Christopher's stress. Compounding the new stress at home, Christopher's wife, Frances, is a vice president of operations of a large corporation. Her long commutes and increased demands of her job contribute to the overall level of stress in their family. She is less involved with the children due to her extended work hours and the commute to her office. Christopher and Frances' stress levels are making them irritable and degrading their communication and family decision-making. They have decided as a couple to put up with the extra stress because of his wife's large salary. To relieve these combined life stressors, they are planning to move closer to Frances' work. However, the current housing shortage has put their plan on pause. Throughout the family stress, Christopher is committed to being present with his children since he did not experience that in his family.

Family History

Christopher grew up in a traditional family with a father, a mother, and a sister. His father was a high school coach who was distant from Christopher through middle school. Once he reached high school, the relationship began to be much stronger, but he often had anxious thoughts regarding his relationship with his father. His mother stayed at home to raise the children. While not officially diagnosed, Christopher presented his mother as emotionally turbulent, fraught with anger, depression, and elevated levels of anxiety. He reports that he and his sister were unable to be sure "which Mom we were going to get." Christopher did not report any abuse and that, other than a distant father and emotionally unstable mother, things were normal.

Spiritual/Religious Factors

Christopher's family of origin attended church regularly at what he described as a traditional Southern Baptist church that leaned heavily toward legalism. Grace did not abound except for salvation. The pastor preached fiery "turn or burn" sermons that scared Christopher as a child. He remembers the pastor preaching against tangential social issues as sin, "lumping them in with other sins in the Bible." Christopher said, "I began to ask Jesus into my heart daily." That practice diminished as the family began to attend church less but resurfaced after he got married and increased church attendance with his wife. He theologically understood that salvation occurred once, but thoughts of his childhood drove his theological anxiety. This led to an inability to finish prayers both in solitude and in groups, which resulted in significant shame and anxiety.

Client Concerns and Problem Areas

Christopher feels overwhelmed and stressed, constantly worries about his work, and thinks of quitting his job often. He worries about his family and the future of his children. Christopher struggles to end his prayers and has questioned his belief in God for years. He finds himself irritable, tired, and restless and reports some suicidal ideation. Christopher presents with physical diagnostic features that include headaches, irritable bowel, and twitching, along with numbness and tingling in his extremities. He has developed a pattern of constant worry for his children, employment trajectory, and spiritual faithfulness.

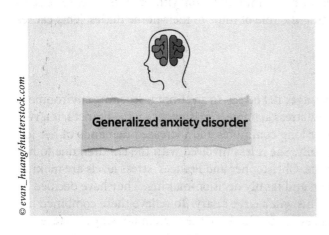

Generalized anxiety disorder

© evan_huang/shutterstock.com

Descriptive Diagnosis

Christopher's assessment battery results reveal a high level of anxiety, thought fusion, and a mild to moderate level of depression. Distal environmental factors of anxious attachment to both parents and religious struggles rooted in his childhood continue to influence proximal environmental factors of job and family stress and current religious struggles. He has developed excessive worry in most life domains and has been depressed for the last two years. Christopher's assessment results, life narrative, and associated physical features are indicative of generalized anxiety disorder (GAD) with comorbid moderate major depressive disorder (MDD) (American Psychiatric Association, 2013; Patriquin & Mathew, 2017).

Applying the B-Well Model Using ACT

Christopher's presenting issues include a high level of anxiety and worry in his relationships at home and work. As a devout Christian, he insisted on seeing a clinical mental health counselor that was a Christian. ACT is an effective treatment modality for conceptualizing and treating generalized anxiety disorder, but my clinical opinion was that the client would be more likely to adhere to a treatment plan interpreted through biblical constructs. I chose to synthesize ACT and the B-Well model since there is a strong congruence in how they approach case conceptualization.

For instance, Christopher has fused maladaptive cognitions (ACT—fusion/defusion; B-Well—Mind/Heart) with his identity (ACT—self-as-context; B-Well—Mind/Heart/Soul) while attempting to avoid his high anxiety and depression (ACT—acceptance; B-Well—Heart/Mind) with worry (ACT—being present; B-Well—Mind). His excessive worry adversely affects his spouse, children, and coworkers (ACT—values; B-Well—Neighbor), and he reports frequent headaches, irritable bowel, numbness and tingling in his extremities, vocalizations, and twitching (B-Well—Strength). Christopher exercises and runs to reduce his anxiety (ACT—committed action; B-Well—Strength) but senses that he needs to implement other means to manage his anxiety (ACT—committed action; B-Well—the fruit of the Spirit). The congruencies provide him with a familiar biblical heuristic to explain and implement the necessary evidence-based ACT interventions.

Christopher in Context: ACT/B-Well Therapeutic Lens

Heart

Christopher came to counseling for self-reported anxiety and depression. A diagnostic interview and empirical assessments for anxiety and depression (*DSM-5* Level 1 Cross-Cutting Symptom Measure PSWQ, GAD-7, DASS-21, BAI, AAQ-II) supported comorbid diagnoses of generalized anxiety disorder and moderate major depressive disorder. Christopher has been unable to accept and regulate anxious and depressed thoughts and has developed a pattern of excessive worry that perpetuates emotion dysregulation (Lissek et al., 2014).

Mind

Christopher responds to his suffering, or present context, with cognitive rigidity (Hayes et al., 2013). His cognitive rigidity has caused him to create an external locus of perspective, which fundamentally affects his ability to regulate his anxiety (Hovenkamp-Hermelink et al., 2019). Christopher's excessive worry is promoting experiential avoidance (Borkovec & Inz, 1990; Hayes & Wilson, 1994). Christopher's neuroticism and constant "what if" thinking (Newman et al., 2013) overlap with painful thoughts of "I'm not good enough" and "If I don't do this perfectly, I won't be accepted." These thoughts merge into Christopher's overarching thought fusion of "My anxiety is driving me crazy" (Newman et al., 2013). Christopher has fused his experiences of anxiety with his identity (Hayes et al., 2013). He frequently uses fused phrases like "my anxiety" that reflect an inability to differentiate his emotions from his identity. Christopher is unable to observe and tell the difference between experiences and emotions, and this is causing a sense of isolation in the major life domains of work, family, and spirituality.

Strength

Case conceptualization in ACT requires that the clinician explore what actions the client is willing to commit to or is already doing. In Christopher's case, he is committed to counseling and is willing to commit to pursuing a combined ACT and B-Well treatment plan. Christopher has realized that physical activity is important in managing anxiety and depression. An avid runner (fifteen miles per week), Christopher takes his sons, ages 10 and six, to hike in nearby parks and occasionally visits state parks for day hikes. Christopher's high level of physical activity, combined with a healthy diet, has resulted in long-term overall physical fitness.

Soul

Christopher's religious struggles may emanate from his fused self, perceiving God through his self-perceived identity rather than from the loving, transcendent, and limitless God who has gifted humans with the *imago Dei* (Hayes et al., 2013). Additionally, Christopher states he has a strong relationship with God despite worrying about his worthiness in approaching God in prayer.

Neighbor

Christopher's wife, children, extended family, and coworkers have endured Christopher's increasing irritability. Strained relationships at home and work were a primary motivation for Christopher to seek counseling. Christopher values his relationship with his wife, children, and coworkers, but his constant irritability and growing isolation are problematic for those he values the most. His constant worry about his employment trajectory has also caused a strained relationship with his school's administration.

Society

The onset of the COVID-19 pandemic contributed to Christopher's excessive worry about his family's physical health and how he should best respond as a father and husband. The changes caused by the pandemic to how school was conducted dramatically affected Christopher as a teacher. The stressors of delivering middle school math through underdeveloped online classroom delivery systems while teaching his own children during the lockdown were significant.

B-Well Treatment Plan

The treatment plan designed for Christopher is a synthesis of treatment plans that incorporate a standard ACT twelve-session plan (Meyer et al., 2018; Twohig & Crosby, 2010; Wetherell et al., 2011) and the B-Well model. The treatment plan is implemented after the initial intake session and an integrated psycho/spiritual education of the six components of ACT and the B-Well constructs and how they work together. The goal of the psychoeducation session is to provide hope for change through engaging and transforming the brain toward psychological flexibility through ACT/B-Well therapy.

Treatment Goals

Christopher wants to decrease the intense distress of his anxiety. He wants to "be there" for his students and especially his family. Christopher wants to be able to finish his prayers and move from an intellectual relationship with God to a true soul connection with Him. Table 1 provides an ACT/B-Well treatment plan for Christopher.

Treatment goals that focus on change for Christopher are:

1. Defuse thoughts from identity.
2. Decrease and hopefully eliminate "what if" thinking.
3. Incorporate mindfulness and biblical peace activities into his health routine.
4. Take responsibility for committed actions (Hayes et al., 2014).
5. Develop healthy spirituality.
6. Pursue the fruit of the Spirit instead of perfection (B-Well).

Working with Christopher

The journey toward soul change for Christopher was, at best, difficult. His thought/identity fusion was deeply entrenched in his soul. Although there was willingness to change, his presenting issues were multi-faceted. His intelligence, coupled with an analytical personality, allowed him to interpret the ACT/B-Well treatment plan easily, but they also inhibited change because of endless paralysis by analysis.

TABLE 1 Recommended Goals, Objectives, and Interventions

Problem	Goal	Objective	Intervention
Generalized anxiety disorder	Reduce worry and anxiety symptoms to baseline.	Objective 1 – The client will have a clear understanding of ACT rationale and how it integrates with B-Well. [Mind]	• Psychoeducation
		Objective 2 – The client, in session, will engage in values clarification and B-Well/fruit of the Spirit integration. [Mind]	• Cognitive reframing and restructuring using the whiteboard technique
		Objective 3 – The client will identify persistent sin patterns and maladaptive worry strategies, behaviors, and emotion-dysregulation that have inhibited the pursuit of well-being. [Mind]	• Cognitive reframing and restructuring using the whiteboard technique
		Objective 4 – The client will defuse maladaptive automatic thoughts, assumptions, and core beliefs of self and others, to increase internal locus of control and self-as-context. [Mind, Heart]	• Cognitive defusion using whiteboard externalization of thoughts, thought inspection, thought challenging, and thought restructuring • Leaves on a stream
		Objective 5 – The client will accept and reduce feelings of anxiety and practice self-regulation through Christian meditation [Heart, Mind, Strength, Soul]	• Self-regulation and meditation through body scan and the Jesus-in-the-room meditation technique
		Objective 6 – The client will, in session, expand thought defusion skills [Heart, Mind]	• Defusion practice using the "take your mind for a walk" exercise
		Objective 7 – The client will construct and apply a plan to pursue values and biblical wellness (fruit of the Spirit). [Mind, Soul]	• Whiteboard responsibility for sin and emotion regulation • Complete self-forgiveness (Enright) and others forgiveness (Worthington) worksheets
		Objective 8 – The client will identify and implement a Committed Action plan to integrate and apply ACT processes and B-Well facets to overcome barriers and expand commitment to wellness. [Heart, Mind, Soul]	• Small group • Use the Living Room analogy/exercise to address both sin and psychological impairments and barrier

Objective eight included the Living Room metaphor intervention that was important to Christopher's progress, as the metaphor guided him to ~~view his soul as both spiritual and emotional~~. As he considered decluttering his soul by processing his sin in the context of grace and forgiveness and cleaning up his emotional baggage using the ACT processes, Christopher began a movement toward self-as-context as the result of a healthy soul.

Since Christopher's intelligence and analytical personality were always waiting to hijack progress, the mindfulness and defusion techniques used in sessions five through eight were pivotal to Christopher's change. A defining moment that began the move toward psychological flexibility and spiritual health was his willing participation in the body scan and Jesus-in-the-room interventions. Being mindfully aware of his body position and sensations allowed him to be present in a way he had never experienced before. During his calm and present state, the Jesus-in-the-room intervention was introduced. Christopher was encouraged to envision that Jesus was in the room, as he was when he appeared to the disciples after his resurrection. Christopher was reminded that the first words spoken to the disciples after his resurrection were, "Peace be with you" (*New International Bible*, 1978/2011, John 20:21). This exercise impacted Christopher significantly and was the beginning of change in his anxious relationship with God.

The valued direction of living out the fruit of the Spirit in the pursuit of emotional health in the B-Well model was integral to Christopher's growth toward emotional health. He began to pursue the fruit of the Spirit by taking responsibility for his emotions and engaging in mindful inspection of his thoughts and experiences.

Summary

Acceptance and commitment therapy (ACT) is an evidence-based therapy and a case conceptualization process that uses six constructs—acceptance, cognitive fusion/defusion, values, self-as-context, being present, and committed action—to assist counselors in interpreting and treating client suffering. ACT's interpretation of the origin of human nature, human suffering, and the human change process aligns with a biblical worldview. The six facets of the biblically based B-Well model seamlessly integrate with ACT offering the clinical mental health counselor a contextualized case conceptualization and treatment planning aid for Christian clients.

We evaluated Christopher's case study by integrating ACT and the B-Well model. Incorporating the six facets of the B-Well model (Heart, Mind, Strength, Soul, Neighbor, Society) taken from the Great Commandment as a primary case conceptualization tool gave the highly religious client familiar themes to interpret the evidence-based diagnostics and interventions of ACT. Using the B-Well model with this client provided a contextualized and comprehensive treatment plan that met his spiritual, emotional, and physical treatment goals. Christopher eagerly engaged with the treatment plan, made significant progress, and incorporated both spiritual and psychological interventions to obtain his goal of biblical wellness.

References

American Psychiatric Association (APA). (2013). *Diagnostic and statistical manual of mental disorders* (5th ed.). https://doi.org/10.1176/appi.books.9780890425596

Borkovec, T. D., & Inz, J. (1990). The nature of worry in generalized anxiety disorder: A predominance of thought activity. Retrieved from https://ac-els-cdn-com.ezproxy.liberty.edu/000579679090027G/1-s2.0-000579679090027G-main.pdf?_tid=db693e54-d0e3-4abe-8555-a7ef8785d84a&acdnat=1541 257433_91711e 771bc503b6cb268fedd00ebf66

Carter, J. D., & Narramore, B. (1979). *The integration of psychology and theology: An introduction.* Zondervan.

Collins, G. R. (1993). *The biblical basis of Christian counseling for people helpers.* Navpress.

English Standard Bible. (2001). ESV Online. https://esv.literalword.com/

Entwistle, D. N. (2021). *Integrative approaches to psychology and Christianity: An introduction to worldview issues, philosophical foundations, and models of integration.* Wipf and Stock Publishers.

Gordon, T., & Borushok, J. (2017). *The ACT approach: A comprehensive guide for acceptance and commitment therapy.* PESI Publishing & Media.

Grenz, S. J. (1994). *Theology for the community of God.* Broadman & Holman Publishers.

Grudem, W. (2000). *Systematic theology: An introduction to biblical doctrine.* Zondervan.

Guthrie, Jr., S. C. (1968). *Christian doctrine.* John Knox Press.

Hayes, S. C., & Wilson, K. G. (1994). Acceptance and commitment therapy: Altering the verbal support for experiential avoidance. *The Behavior Analyst, 17*(2), 289–303. https://doi.org/10.1007/bf03392677

Hayes, S. C., Levin, M. E., Plumb-Vilardaga, J., Villatte, J. L., & Pistorello, J. (2013). Acceptance and commitment therapy and contextual behavioral science: Examining the progress of a distinctive model of behavioral and cognitive therapy. *Behavior Therapy, 44*(2), 180-198. https://doi.org/10.1016/j.beth.2009.08.002

Hayes, S. C., Strosahl, K. D., & Wilson, K. G. (2011). *Acceptance and commitment therapy* (2nd ed.). Guilford Publications.

Hayes, S. C., Strosahl, K. D., & Wilson, K. G. (2014). *Acceptance and commitment therapy: The process and practice of mindful change (mindfulness).* Desclée de Brouwer.

Hovenkamp-Hermelink, J. H., Jeronimus, B. F., Spinhoven, P., Penninx, B. W., Schoevers, R. A., & Riese, H. (2019). Differential associations of locus of control with anxiety, depression and life-events: A five-wave, nine-year study to test stability and change. *Journal of Affective Disorders, 253*, 26-34. https://doi.org/10.1016/j.jad.2019.04.005

Johnson, E. L. (2007). *Foundations for soul care: A Christian psychology proposal.* InterVarsity Press.

Lissek, S., Kaczkurkin, A. N., Rabin, S., Geraci, M., Pine, D. S., & Grillon, C. (2014). Generalized anxiety disorder is associated with overgeneralization of classically conditioned fear. *Biological Psychiatry, 75*(11), 909-915.

McMinn, M. R., & Campbell, C. D. (2007). *Integrative psychotherapy: Toward a comprehensive Christian approach.* InterVarsity Press.

Meyer, E. C., Walser, R., Hermann, B., La Bash, H., DeBeer, B. B., Morissette, S. B., Kimbrel, N. A., Kwok, O., Batten, S. V., & Schnurr, P. P. (2018). Acceptance and commitment therapy for co-occurring posttraumatic stress disorder and alcohol use disorders in veterans: Pilot treatment outcomes. *Journal of Traumatic Stress, 31*(5), 781-789. https://doi.org/10.1002/jts.22322

Miller, K. D. (2016). *Biblical foundation for Christian integration: A theology of Christian counseling* [Unpublished manuscript]. Liberty University.

New International Bible. (2011). The NIV Bible. https://www.thenivbible.com (Original work published 1978)

Newman, M. G., Llera, S. J., Erickson, T. M., Przeworski, A., & Castonguay, L. G. (2013). Worry and generalized anxiety disorder: A review and theoretical synthesis of evidence on nature, etiology, mechanisms, and treatment. *Annual Review of Clinical Psychology, 9*, 275. https://doi.org/10.1146/annurev-clinpsy-050212-185544

Patriquin, M. A., & Mathew, S. J. (2017). The neurobiological mechanisms of generalized anxiety disorder and chronic stress. *Chronic Stress, 1*, 2470547017703993. https://doi.org/10.1177/2470547017703

Tan, S.-Y. (2016). *ACT for clergy and pastoral counselors: Using acceptance and commitment therapy to bridge psychological and spiritual care.* New Harbinger Publications.

Twohig, M. P., & Crosby, J. M. (2010). Acceptance and commitment therapy as a treatment for problematic internet pornography viewing. *Behavior Therapy, 41*(3), 285-295. https://doi.org/10.1016/j.beth.2009.06.002

Wetherell, J. L., Liu, L., Patterson, T. L., Afari, N., Ayers, C. R., Thorp, S. R., Stoddard, J. A., Ruberg, J., Kraft, A., Sorrell, J. T., & Petkus, A. J. (2011). Acceptance and commitment therapy for generalized anxiety disorder in older adults: A preliminary report. *Behavior Therapy, 42*(1), 127-134. https://doi.org/10.1016/j.beth.2010.07.002

CHAPTER 12

B-Well Model in Clinical Mental Health Counseling Using Psychodynamic (Jung) Therapy

Robin Switzer

> "But the fruit of the Spirit is love, joy, peace, forbearance, kindness, goodness, faithfulness, gentleness, and self-control. Against such things there is no law."
>
> — Galatians 5:22-23 (NIV)

Background of Psychodynamic Theory

The psychodynamic theory focuses on unconscious thoughts, emotions, motivations, and patterns in events and relationships. Unconscious drives are dynamics that affect present behaviors and relationships. Past relationships affect current relationships and include universal considerations of the human experience. Within the profession, psychodynamic theory can be referred to as the works of Carl Jung or can be grouped with contemporaries of the period: Freudian (psychoanalysis) and Adlerian. This clinician's work is from the Jungian psychodynamic viewpoint; throughout this case analysis, references to psychodynamic will refer to the works of Carl Jung, but other psychodynamic therapy constructs will be offered as well.

Origins

Jung was a mentee and colleague of Sigmund Freud. Jung struggled with what he considered the restrictions of sexual only motivations in psychoanalytical theory and the dynamics of a personal friendship with Freud (Stevens, 2001). Although there was personal conflict within the relationship between Freud and Jung, there were also differences in theory. Jung branched off personally and professionally with psychodynamic theory. A notable difference is that the underlying unconscious forces are considered creative vs. sexual and include a place for spirituality (Clinton & Hawkins, 2011).

Carl Jung was born in 1875 in the small town of Kesswil, Switzerland (Stevens, 2001). While his father was a pastor, his paternal grandfather was a physician, and his mother's side of the family worked as theologians or clergymen. His parents'

marriage was tumultuous, and his mother suffered from a breakdown when he was three. Jung noted having a difficult relationship with his father, a pastor; however, there is scholarly debate as to the influence of this relationship and the perspectives on religion included within the theory. Regardless of the details of each dynamic within his family, his upbringing exposed him to medicine, religion, and relationship dynamics, which influenced his work.

© Svjatoslav Andreichyn/shutterstock.com

View of Human Nature

The view of human nature within the psychodynamic theory is an internal one of many parts, blending conscious and unconscious drives and experiences called the Psyche (Stevens, 2001). One way to understand it is to envision it as a house. The Self is both the physical house and the architect of the mind working to develop the mind, heart, and soul. The Self is responsible for integrating experiences and personality into a healthy whole. The Ego is the caretaker, making conscious decisions to fix and plan tasks. The Persona is the home's exterior, how one expresses themselves and acts in the world. The Shadow is the unseen electricity and water pipes, so common that it is often unnoticed; however, when it requires our attention, it can be complicated to understand and takes a great deal of effort to address. All of these parts of the Psyche, the whole house, are integral in understanding a person and are considered in case conceptualization from a psychodynamic perspective.

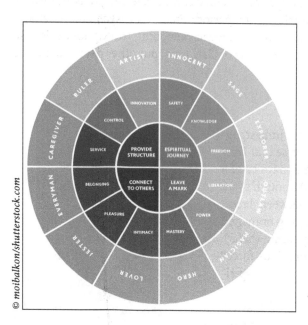

© moibalkon/shutterstock.com

Personality is formed by conscious and unconscious forces. Within the unconscious, Jung proposed multiple components of expression through roles, including the expression of masculine and feminine components known as anima/animus and archetypes that express the experience of human beings throughout existence, such as the Hero or the Maiden. The unconscious often communicates in a representation or characteristics. The Myers-Briggs Inventory is a demonstration of the identification of psychological types of personality described by Carl Jung (Stevens, 2001).

View of Change

In psychodynamic theory, the focus is for the unconscious to become conscious, the unrealized to be known, and insight to be gained as to who the client is and what they desire to be. The use of the relationship between the therapist and client is paramount as corrective relational experiences assist in healing. It is a developmental theory that begins with childhood but recognizes growth and development in all stages of life. Jung engaged in a lifetime of self-exploration, and to be a psychodynamic clinician is to do the same—lifelong development as a clinician and a person. The therapist supportively accompanies the client on their journey and utilizes knowledge from their own life to assist the client in this journey.

Christian Integration Perspective

This clinician's guiding principle for Christian integration is the Allies model (Entwistle, 2015)—All truth is God's truth; therefore, truth found in counseling is God's truth, and there is no conflict. Within the Allies model, counseling can focus on the acts or works of God, allowing clinical work to walk alongside the client and utilize the counseling process to support the client's journey. In this clinician's practice with trauma survivors of various ages, the privilege is to collaborate with the clients, not to be a spiritual leader. In application, balancing a calling to the profession and the legal limitations of the profession means following the client's lead. With children, parental teachings on faith may offer a direction during treatment. With adults, a starting place is assessment and consent to see if faith is to be used and, if so, how.

For example, trauma survivors often have complicated relationships with faith or God. This can be from the pain they suffered and when others have used God as a weapon of abuse. To force discussions regarding faith, religion, or spirituality could reinforce violating dynamics that could harm the client and derail the therapeutic relationship. The therapist can provide a passive, integrative approach by reflecting the joy, love, and respect God has for all His people. Additionally, focusing on recognizing and reflecting the client's worth is utilized as a corrective relationship experience and to build trust. In this clinician's experience, many clients who are survivors of trauma initially state that they do not wish to discuss their relationship with God, yet many return to this topic as part of the healing process. By following a supporting and trusting process, the client can arrive at meaning and connection that would far outweigh the clinician's opinion. It is not my job to direct this path; it is my job to show the client they are loved and worthy of this journey.

Psychodynamic Principles and the B-Well Model

When considering the use of the B-Well model within a psychodynamic lens, one must remember that interventions themselves rarely line up perfectly with each theory but can be utilized to connect to the main components embraced by that theory. Since the psychodynamic approach is based on the works and explorations of Jung, speculation on his viewpoint toward the model would be an inappropriate application and consideration of his work. However, there are main components of the theory that we can utilize and integrate with the B-Well model.

Individuation

The psychodynamic theory recognizes and aspires to a lifelong personal journey of growth and development entitled individuation. Development is not viewed as achieving certain goals but as unlocking inherent potential (Stevens, 2001). As one reflects, explores, and learns, an understanding of personal and collective experiences can be found, and how one interacts within that context can be developed. The B-Well model focuses on a continued journey of growth and wellness with a focus on internal and external development that effectively integrates the concept of individuation.

The B-Well model includes biblical wellness and a focus on the soul and spiritual matters. Many works have included

> Spiritual growth requires the development of inner knowing and inner authority. It requires the heart, not the intellect.

© Aysezgicmeli/shutterstock.com

Jung's lifelong exploration of Christianity and spirituality, from his relationship with his father, his faith, and his questions. While many return to his works with varied lenses and interpretations of conclusions on Jung's beliefs, to create a conclusion would be an overstep and incorrect application of the work. The point and the clear component are the importance of such focus (e.g., spirituality) in development. To ignore the relationship with faith is to ignore a pivotal component of a person, and spiritual growth and development were a priority in both theory and practice (Jung, 1963; Jung & Stein, 2012).

Integration

Throughout the development of psychodynamic theory, the Psyche was established as a self-regulating process that attempted to achieve balance. As components in life become off-balance, the Psyche will compensate emotionally and mentally. This process, called integration, is not always on a conscious level, but one can be aware of it by reflecting on known laws of nature: Where there is a vacuum, it will be filled by projected meaning (Green, 2014; Stevens, 2001). Like how a body will compensate for an injury, the mind will adjust to emotional and mental struggles. However, in the Psyche's attempt to gain balance, compensation is not always healthy in the long term, and adjustments can become injurious. A review of wellness that includes a focus on multiple areas—Heart, Mind, Strength, Soul, Neighbor, and Society—can offer an assessment of integration, including what areas have become off-balance for the client and the compensations that have occurred. This allows the client to gain insight—engaging the unconscious in the conscious process.

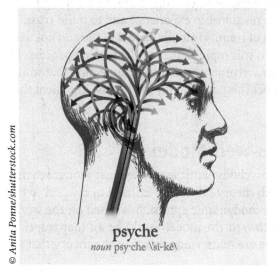

psyche
noun psy·che \sī-kē\

Integration also explores how each part of us can be unified into one whole psychic person. Traumas, stressors, and struggles can fracture or wound sections of a person's Psyche as development occurs throughout life. Exploration of the Self, insight into the experience, and the work of lifelong growth help unlock who a person is. It is not about becoming; it is about understanding and developing what is already present (Jung, 1963; Stevens, 2001). The B-Well model focuses on various roles and areas but brings together one picture of wellness—all parts feed into a whole person embedded within their context seeking integration vs. disintegration.

Relationship

The third main component of the psychodynamic theory that can be assisted by the B-Well model is the focus on relationship patterns (Jung, 1915/2016). The relationships explored in psychodynamic theory are internal, social, and anthropological. The relationship between the conscious or unconscious, the parts, the components, the experiences, and the insight into personality can be assisted by the focus on mood (Heart), thoughts (Mind), health (Strength), and spirit (Soul). The Mind and Heart connections are present and dynamic (Green, 2014). The relationships—successes, failings, and struggles—can be explored through the connections with others, as well as the corrective relational experience with the clinician (Neighbor).

All humans experience a connection to the inherent experiences of being human, continued development from past human victories, and repetition of destructive patterns throughout history (Jung, 1933). While a personal exploration of the collective unconscious is required, it needs to be contextualized in the client's waking life with relationships with others and within society. Although the work is internal, it must connect to external relationships. How one fits in or is viewed by society, and in turn, how one views society, can be a continued pattern of relationship that requires examination (Jung, 1970). The B-Well model allows exploration of internal processes, relationship patterns with others, and external influences (Society) on the client.

A Case Study: Beth

Beth is a 35-year-old Caucasian woman, married with two children. Beth entered therapy due to intense reactions and fears that have isolated her to the extent of hiding in her home and rarely venturing out or socializing. She does not have friends, has a strained relationship with her family, and is afraid to drive, walk, or be alone. She fears for her safety and the safety of her children due to her history of trauma. She is not living the life she wants and wishes to provide for her family.

© Anna Nahabed/shutterstock.com

Beth suffers from the effects of complex trauma. She was sexually assaulted at a college holiday party as a young adult. She received little to no support or services at the time. After the sexual assault, Beth returned home from college because she struggled to heal and cope, and her mother berated her, accusing her of causing the assault.

Beth was raised in a neglectful home that included psychological and emotional abuse. Beth's parents were divorced when she was four, and her parents provided separate homes. Life consisted of a father who was an alcoholic and a mother who blamed the client for many issues. Her mother used God as a weapon to condemn. From this environment, Beth internalized the belief that she caused many negative aspects of their home life and that she was a burden upon her parents and older siblings.

Since the sexual assault in college, Beth reported intense, consistent fear and regular dreams reliving the attack. However, Beth was able to cope due to her love of outdoor running. She felt strong, able to outrun potential future attacks, and emotionally stable. Within the last three years, Beth has been diagnosed with medical conditions that affect the inner ear, resulting in a loss of balance and hearing. Beth is afraid to run due to feeling physically unstable and is afraid to be alone because she cannot hear a potential attacker. Over the last three years, Beth has increased her isolation by retreating into her home and avoiding social events. Beth reported that when she does have to attend a school event, she sweats excessively and feels panicky. She is afraid to be alone inside her home and afraid to be outside of her home. She continues to have regular dreams reliving the sexual assault and associates the event with weather patterns occurring that evening. When the weather turns, her memories intensify, and her fear increases. Beth states that she fears her children will be harmed like she was (i.e., the assault) and by her current state. She worries that she cannot be the mother they deserve, and that is why she decided to try counseling.

Applying the B-Well Model Using Psychodynamic Theory

To begin, it is important to understand the depth and impact the experiences of life have on the client's current conditions. The primary aim is to conceptualize (e.g., to explain, to understand) Beth's problems and identify her resources using the six facets of the B-Well model and psychodynamic theory. We will do this by attending to each facet below.

Heart

The client freely shares the fear associated with daily life, the fear of being harmed, the fear of those she loves being harmed, and the disconnect from what others tell her and how she feels. This disconnect is patterned throughout her life as, during childhood, the client shared emotions and was informed that she was wrong. Even with the assault, a pattern of what the client felt was disregarded as unimportant. Through the psychodynamic theory lens, trauma can cause fractures within the Psyche, as the emotions are intense and overwhelming; the compensation can be to avoid these emotional states. Additionally, attempts to contain emotional arousal can cause numbness or emotional overreactions.

 ## Mind

Exploration of what the client thinks highlights an understanding that, rationally, many situations are non-threatening, but the concept of safety is inconceivable. The client reported that, based on her experiences, she does not think of herself as allowed to have her boundaries; others can take as they please regardless of what she thinks or wants. She is concerned that her current state of survival is unrealistic (isolation) and inappropriate for her children. The client may lack insight into the many drives that are influencing her interior across her lifespan. Her Ego may incorrectly attempt to be a "caretaker" by increasing the cognitive limitations that lead to increased isolation. Through these experiences, she would have limited individuation and integration because her "Self" development was limited by her historical family dynamics and the experience of sexual trauma.

 ## Strength

Through the Strength lens, a number of factors are at play that are problems and assets. Based on Beth's presenting problem, she has regularly re-experienced items from her traumatic history and describes a continued autonomic physiological reaction, or fight-or-flight responses. From a psychodynamic lens, Beth's response to trauma can be understood as a reaction of her unconscious to seek control and reduce or eliminate threats (Spermon et al., 2010). The trauma has further limited her integration. The impact of the trauma remains in the unconscious, which is then expressed physiologically.

The client identified that, in the past, running made her feel strong and helped her process her emotions. Her current medical conditions interfere with balance, which has made running almost impossible for the client. However, the client takes the initiative concerning health and continues with medical appointments, medications, and follow-ups. As exercise is a way that she had felt strong and coped in the past, the psychodynamic approach would recognize a healthy relational pattern between the client's ability to cope, her perception of strength, and physical exercise.

Soul

Beth stated that she is unsure of an individual relationship with God and shared the many ways she has fallen short of God's love, per her parents. Beth avoids this relationship or connection as it is a reminder of what she cannot do right and what a disappointment she is. The church has been used as a weapon against the client and a way to keep her expression limited. Beth does not feel worthy of love. Through the dysfunctional exchanges with her mother, the client's personality formation may have been impacted. In particular, her anima (feminine) and animus (masculine) archetypes may not be equally developed. This may fracture her view of self in relation to God as well as support an unhealthy view of God's character (e.g., blaming, critical, judgmental, hurtful).

Neighbor

Beth struggles to connect across systems outside her nuclear family of husband and children. Anyone outside this system is assessed as a potential threat, and fear occurs. There are no friends, no neighborhood relationships, and no connections with children's friend's parents; social situations induce fight-or-flight responses. There is a relationship with her mother that makes the client feel inadequate and judged. The client is isolated. She loves and adores her children and is driven to change to make a better life for them. Psychodynamic theory views concerns, struggles, and solutions as relational. Exploring this area highlights patterns of isolation and restriction in connection with others. Because interpersonal relationships are so important for the development of the Psyche, the client's unhealthy interactions within her family system—and then the trauma event—may have limited her insight, disrupting her integration. Yet, the client does have a strong, healthy relationship with her husband.

Society

According to the client's self-assessment, she is struggling to function as a mother, as expressed by fears that she will harm her children by never being the mother they deserve. She is faulting herself as inadequate despite her dedication and attention to their needs. Although she did not experience a healthy relationship with her mother as a child, she perceives motherhood as something that ought to occur automatically. It is possible that the client is experiencing a heightened awareness of the societal idea that since motherhood is natural, all women are born with the innate knowledge to parent successfully, which could negatively impact her Psyche's attempt at integration.

B-Well Treatment Plan

The B-Well model can be used to assist the client in individuation, integration, and improvement of relationships. The client may lack insight but is aware that the current state of life is neither realistic nor desired. Within the client complex, opposite forces arise:

- The client is unable to conceptualize safety but wishes to provide that for her children.
- The client perceives herself as unworthy of love and yet loves her husband and children bravely and in a healthy manner.
- The client notes the flaws of her parents, but the parental information is infallible.
- The client's strength has been impaired by medical conditions that she confronts and manages directly.
- The client cannot conceptualize how to connect to others, yet she reached out to therapy.

The client's role as a mother provides a large amount of strength and motivation to make changes in her various roles—wife, mother, daughter, friend, neighbor, and member of society. Jung and Hoffman (2003) suggest that "the greater the tension, the greater is the potential. Great energy springs from correspondingly great tension between opposites" (p. 104). This tension has the potential to bring about change in the client's life.

The B-Well model integrated with psychodynamic therapy provides focus areas to develop and grow to assist the client in confronting her wounds and integrating the past into the whole. The dynamics of past relationships continue to leave a mark, and current relationship dynamics are frayed. Beth struggles to have a relationship with herself and with others. The past trauma is overshadowing her current reality. Confronting and challenging the patterns and pain will be needed to integrate the pain into the person and move forward.

Heart and Mind

Treatment Goal #1: The client will process thoughts and feelings associated with trauma, abuse, and neglect within individual weekly sessions utilizing creative and/or verbal expression.

The emotions and cognitive effects of trauma, abuse, and neglect require processing. In sessions, trust can be developed within the therapeutic relationship and begin to simulate and demonstrate safety to the client. The therapist-client relationship will be nurtured and utilized to combat fear and mistrust with developed trust and safety within the protected relationship of therapy. Techniques will include verbal and non-verbal, focusing on both conscious and unconscious processes. The non-verbal techniques will draw upon her reported interest in drawing and crafts, utilizing creative endeavors. The need to have the client explore and understand her experience as legitimate is required for her to trust her own experiences and her journey of development. This goal will work to assist the client in experiencing a beneficial relationship and integrating her wounds as a victim and strengths as a survivor. This goal encompasses both Heart and Mind because the conscious and unconscious processes of emotions and cognitions will be intertwined. While they may volley between emotional and cognitive, the process is fluid and responsive to the client; thereby, the treatment goal can reflect the process in its entirety to ensure appropriate assessment of progress.

Strength

Treatment Goal #2: The client will regain confidence and develop an exercise regimen to return to pre-medical condition levels of activity.

Each facet of the B-Well model can be utilized to structure treatment goals and interventions. Within the Strength facet, it will be important to focus on the client finding what will work within the limitations of her situation. Currently, Beth does not have confidence in herself or her abilities. However, although situations cannot necessarily be altered, such as her medical conditions, the client's ability to try and adapt is within her power. Focusing on physical exercise will help build confidence and provide a coping skill as the client can adjust to her limitations and engage in activities that previously made her feel empowered. If the client struggles to do this, an adaptive idea is to find a physical activity to complete with the children, as teaching them physical health is potential motivation.

Although internal work could be initially construed as mental or emotional only, the connection to the body in trauma work is significant. This is an initial step in differentiating between control and power; the client cannot control the external world but has the power to adapt, adjust, and innovate to meet her own needs. Finding an exercise routine allows her to take charge and return to a coping skill previously utilized. Understanding and recognizing her power can assist in her journey of individuation and integration.

Soul, Neighbor, and Society

Treatment Goal #3: The client will work to identify and engage in healthy relationship patterns and parameters in individual weekly sessions.

Beth has past and current relationships that are unhealthy and need to be managed in a manner to avoid damage. She also has healthy relationships that serve as motivation but are limited in size. To understand healthy relationships, the client must begin by identifying the differences between the relationships that serve her and the relationships that harm her. Focus on healthy dynamics, appropriate boundaries, and connection will assist the client in navigating vulnerability when it is appropriate or needed for relationships. This evaluation and realignment of the intrapersonal will further her integration process.

This goal can grow and adapt to "Apply healthy boundaries" and "Communicate with a new person" as growth and healing occur. If the client struggles with the adaptation of learning, being able to instruct her children can be utilized to assist the client and stay connected with her strongest motivating factor. Connections will also be necessary to increase the children's social circles and can be used as motivation or possible new connections (parents of friends).

This goal encompasses the Neighbor and Society facets as forming and determining healthy boundaries in relationships will allow a support system to continue navigating the relationships of a larger society and her place in it. If the client can place healthy boundaries, the client can gain confidence to form friendships and a support system (Neighbor). The support system and ability to identify unrealistic expectations can lead to confronting false norms and allow Beth to feel more connected and a part of Society.

This goal can also move into the Soul facet and pose considerations of relationship with God. The relationship with God will need to be determined by the client (Jung, 1963). A direct approach to the current relationship may be harmful if the client is not ready; therefore, this area is listed as a provisional objective in the treatment plan to ensure client readiness and approval. However, exposure to toxic faith is an unhealthy relationship dynamic that can be addressed in review and work on identifying healthy relationships. Through corrective relational experiences, Beth can heal her view of God in relationship to self, even if it is not directly discussed. This will enhance her relationships with others, herself, and potentially her view of God, advancing her individuation and integration.

TABLE 1 Recommended Goals, Objectives, and Interventions

Problem	Goal	Objective	Intervention
History of trauma, neglect, and emotional and psychological abuse	The client will process thoughts and feelings associated with trauma, abuse, and neglect within individual weekly sessions, utilizing creative and/or verbal expressions.	Objective 1 – In individual therapy, the client will explore and identify the impact and effect of trauma, neglect, and abuse on identity and relationships. [Heart, Mind] Objective 2 – In individual therapy, the client will process emotions and events associated with trauma, abuse, and neglect. [Heart, Mind]	• Talk therapy • Free association • Art • Sand tray • Music • Sculpture • Relational pattern identification
Loss of confidence combined with medical conditions that interfere with the self-care strategy of exercise	The client will regain confidence and develop an exercise regimen to return to pre-medical condition levels of activity.	Objective 3 – The client will explore and attempt one form of exercise per week that fits within medical parameters. [Strength] Objective 4 – The client will utilize motivating relationships to identify and engage in one group physical activity per week. [Strength]	• Talk therapy focused on identifying feasible, realistic strategies • Identification of strengths and interests • Clarification of limitations

Problem	Goal	Objective	Intervention
Exposure to unhealthy relationship dynamics, false norms, and toxic faith	The client will work to identify and engage in healthy relationship patterns and parameters in individual weekly sessions.	Objective 5 – In individual therapy, the client will work to identify unhealthy and healthy relationship patterns in past and current relationships. [Neighbor, Society] Objective 6 – In individual therapy, the client will work to identify health needs and boundaries. [Neighbor, Society] Objective 7 – The client will work to communicate and implement one boundary or request one need per week. [Neighbor] Objective 8 – (Provisional) The client may explore unhealthy relationship dynamics with raised faith and review relationship with God. [Soul]	• Talk therapy • Role play • Free association • Corrective relational experiences

Summary

The focus on wellness may seem trivial when considering the immensity of traumatic history. However, as a mother, Beth can do for others what she cannot provide for herself. The relationship with her children is a large motivating factor. Utilizing the strengths provided by the role of mother, Beth can confront and nurture her personal growth and development. The need to be a good mother to her children provides the motivation that can assist with healing, gain insight into her potential, empower her to integrate, and improve dynamics with others. The strength she finds for her children can also be used for herself.

The B-Well model utilized with psychodynamic theory can be used as an assessment tool and a conceptualization tool for treatment goals. The model's focus on wellness in different facets aligns with the psychodynamic tenet of integration: multiple elements of a person working to be whole. The B-Well model connects users to an understanding of themselves and their needs, fostering a continued internal expedition of knowledge experience known as individuation. The relational aspect of wellness aligns with psychodynamic therapy's use of corrective relational experiences and healthy connection to loved ones, neighbors, and society. Therefore, psychodynamic theory can utilize the B-Well model's focus on internal wellness and connection to others.

References

Clinton, T., & Hawkins, R. (2011) *The popular encyclopedia of Christian counseling*. Harvest House.

Entwistle, D. N. (2015). *Integrative approaches to psychology and Christianity* (3rd ed.). Cascade Books.

Green, E. (2014). *The handbook of Jungian play therapy with children and adolescents*. Johns Hopkins University Press.

Jung, C. (1933). *Modern man in search of a soul*. Harcourt, Inc.

Jung, C. (1963). *Memories, dreams, and reflections*. Random House.

Jung, C. (1970). *Analytical psychology: Its theory and practice* (the Tavistock Lectures). Vintage.

Jung, C. (2016). *The theory of psychoanalysis* (Classic Reprint). Forgotten Books. (Original work published 1915)

Jung, C., & Hoffman, E. (2003). *The wisdom of Carl Jung*. Kensington Publishing.

Jung, C., & Stein, M. (2012). *Jung on Christianity*. Princeton University Press.

New International Bible. (2011). The NIV Bible. https://www.thenivbible.com (Original work published 1978)

Spermon, D., Darlington, Y., & Gibney, P. (2010). Psychodynamic psychotherapy for complex trauma: Targets, focus, applications, and outcomes. *Psychology research and behavior management, 3*, 119–127. https://doi.org/10.2147/PRBM.S10215

Stevens, A. (2001). *Jung: A very short introduction*. Oxford University Press.

CHAPTER 13

B-Well Model in Clinical Mental Health Counseling Using Solution-Focused Brief Therapy

Yulanda Tyre, Deborah A. Braboy, & Krista E. Kirk

> "Let the words of my mouth and the meditation of my heart be acceptable in your sight, O Lord, my rock and my redeemer."
>
> — Psalm 19:14 (ESV)

This chapter will provide an overview of solution-focused brief therapy (SFBT) using the B-Well model. Consistent with many other theory-based chapters in this text, a Christian integration approach, and denominational lens will be provided. This is followed by a case study that provides an example of the use of SFBT with the B-Well model that conceptualizes the client's presenting problem and relevant clinical factors, followed by an SFBT/B-Well example treatment plan.

Background of Solution-Focused Brief Therapy (SFBT)

Origins

Solution-focused brief therapy (SFBT) is also called solution-focused therapy (SFT) and was developed in the late 1970s by Steve de Shazer (1940-2005) and Insoo Kim Berg (1934-2007). They founded the Milwaukee Brief Family Therapy Center to collaborate and train others in future-focused, goal-directed therapy that focuses on solutions rather than on the problems that bring clients in for therapy.

SFBT is a short-term, goal-focused, evidence-based therapy that incorporates principles from positive psychology. It helps clients change by focusing on solutions (rather than problems) and exceptions, and it is present and future-oriented. Essentially, SFBT is a hope-friendly, positive emotion eliciting, and future-oriented treatment used for framing, motivating, exploring, accomplishing, and maintaining desired behavioral change. SFBT uses a language of *change*. This approach focuses on *how* clients change instead of concentrating on a diagnosis and treating the client's problems (de Shazer, 1986).

FOCUS ON THE SOLUTION NOT THE PROBLEM

© Yusnizam Yusof/shutterstock.com

A solution-focused (SF) counselor recognizes that the client is the expert in their life. Unlike earlier therapeutic models, the SF counselor takes the position of collaborator and consultant with the client. The counselor takes a stance of "not knowing" and uses solution-focused questions and responses to guide the client toward solutions to achieving their goals. The emphasis is not problem-oriented but rather on the new, desired client experiences. These emerging narratives will be in a language that allows for personal capability and responsibility (Walter & Peller, 2000).

View of Human Nature

SFBT counselors believe that people construct reality with language, and many of their clients' problems are maintained as the result of their reality construction that discounts the competence and resources they already possess. SFBT counselors also believe that clients are competent and able to form solutions.

> There are exceptions to every problem, or times when the problem was absent. By talking about these expectations, clients can get clues to effective solutions and can gain control over what seemed to be an insurmountable personal difficulty. Rapid changes are possible when clients identify expectations instead of around the problem. (Corey, 2021, p. 373)

View of Change

SFBT posits that all people come to therapy wanting to change their situation, but their attempts at change have failed to bring desired results. Since the client comes to counseling in hopes of finding a resolution to their problems, the counselor helps the client construct solutions to alleviate complaints, building hope and inner strength for future endeavors (de Shazer, 1978, 1986; Franklin et al., 2017; Joubert & Guse, 2021). Change occurs when the client alters the way they interact or behave, so a solution can be achieved, resulting in overall well-being. It is only when the behavior can be viewed from multiple perspectives that the client and the counselor can interpret the meaning behind the behavior, opening the door for a reconstruction of the belief that large change is required into an understanding that only a small change is necessary. Counselors using the SFBT approach believe that one small change will lead to a larger change in the person's overall well-being, and effective therapy begins with asking the question: "How will we know when the problem is solved?" (de Shazer, 1986, p. 3).

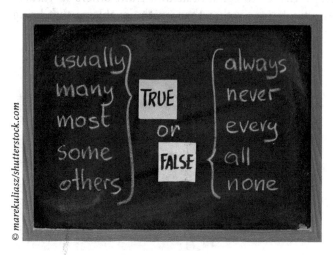

A general assumption in SFBT is that the client's complaint has exceptions—exceptions that they struggle to notice (i.e., "I am always depressed" versus "I know I'm feeling depressed because I used to enjoy ... "), and the counselor helps co-construct solutions based upon the details of these exceptions. The counselor helps start the solution process, collaborating with the client on developing a more "workable view" (p. 4) of their situation, leading to a solution to their complaints. Similar to a cognitive approach, SFBT counselors work to help clients gain insight to solutions by exploring "talk difficulties" using strengths and resources to identify alternatives to reality by identifying exceptions that engender change talk and behavioral changes.

Christian Integration Perspective

When considering integration, I, the first author, am reminded of a core belief regarding my purpose. I view my skills as a talent bestowed upon me by God. My work, and the use of that talent, is an extension of my beliefs and values, used to honor Him. In other words, God provided the talent, and I choose to use it to serve others as a representative of Him. James 1:17a tells us, "Every good and every perfect gift is from above [God]" (*New International Bible*, 1978/2011). We each have different talents and God-given gifts, which can be used for the kingdom. Ephesians 2:10 states, "For we are God's handiwork, created in Christ Jesus to do good works, which God prepared in advance for us to do."

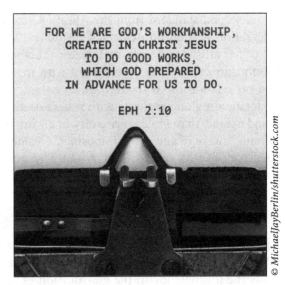

Professionally, I am a licensed professional counselor operating from a Christian worldview. This definition can be used by someone who obtains professional licensure as a counselor and is submitted to the requirements and ethics codes of credentialing bodies and professional organizations yet operates from a Christian worldview (Simmons et al., 2019). As several previous chapters have noted, Entwistle's (2015) Model of the Disciplinary Relationship speaks to this in the Allies Model, noting that Christian theology and counseling can coexist and inform one another. Similarly, Jones and Butman's (2011) ideal scenario for Christian integration is that both faith and scholarship should "naturally mix" (p. 19). The Association for Spiritual, Ethical, and Religious Values in Counseling (ASERVIC), a division of ACA, also supports this and provides standards of practice in its competencies (ASERVIC, 2009). The competencies

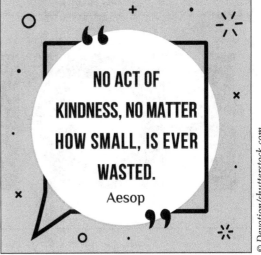

entitled "Addressing Spiritual and Religious Issues in Counseling" state that its standards are designed to complement ACA standards and are established to "recognize diversity and embrace a cross-cultural approach in support of the worth, dignity, potential and uniqueness of people within their social and cultural contexts" (p. 3). This statement aligns with my desire to serve the "kingdom" in a manner that represents the character of Christ—with humility, kindness, and understanding (Jones & Butman, 2011). Taking on this approach allows me the opportunity to see each client as a child of God from the onset of the therapeutic relationship. This approach prompts me to formally and/or informally assess spiritual/religious values and beliefs and use them during therapy, starting in the intake process and continuing through the implementation of interventions as directed by the client. For clients that do not desire spiritual or religious integration, I allow myself to be led by the Holy Spirit as noted in John 16:13 (*New International Bible*, 1978/2011): "But when he, the Spirit of truth, comes, he will guide you into all the truth. He will not speak on his own; he will speak only what he hears, and he will tell you what is yet to come."

A second standard from the ASERVIC competencies that resonates with me and my approach to integration is the Counselor Self-Awareness standard: "The professional counselor actively explores his or her attitudes, beliefs, and values about spirituality and/or religion." (ASERVIC, 2009, p. 1). This prompt for exploration is consistent with my ongoing journey to expand both my understanding of and my relationship with God, which enhances my overall wellness. In doing so, I have increased my understanding and patience with others on the same journey, allowing me to view them holistically. I understand that while spirituality is an important part of their overall wellness, I must be sure to remain "aware of and avoid imposing … values, attitudes, beliefs, and behaviors" as supported by the ACA code of ethics (ACA, 2014, A.4.b). These combined steps provide me with a foundation for competent and ethical practice.

The Intersection of SFBT, B-Well, and a Biblical Worldview

The B-Well model describes humans being created in the image of God (*New International Bible*, 1978/2011, Genesis 1:26-27) as a person's physical and spiritual nature fully culminates when the soul finds the ultimate joy in the glorification of God. The biblical narrative asserts that the fall of man severed our ability to find ultimate joy as sin separated humanity from its Creator (Genesis 3). Then,

in Matthew 27, Jesus restores our connection to God the Creator, redeeming a person's ability to reflect the image they bear more fully. According to the B-Well model, wellness emerges through sanctifying the soul, including the heart, mind, and body (1 Thessalonians 5:23), and hoping for future glory (Romans 8:19-25). The ongoing sanctification and hopeful knowledge (2 Peter 1:3) mimic the hope of counseling in solution-focused language. Specifically, SFBT operates on the construct of hope, categorized as *future-thinking*, allowing the person to see beyond their present world and focus on what could be.

In this hope-focused approach, SFBT parallels the connection between Galatians 5:21 (works of the flesh) and Galatians 5:22-23 (fruit of the Spirit), where Paul describes redemption leading to sanctification (*New International Bible*, 1978/2011). SFBT recognizes that the redemption experienced in brief counseling will continue to be "sanctified" even after counseling ends, just as the soul is redeemed through Christ and sanctified to develop the healthy characteristics of a redeemed person (i.e., love, joy, peace, etc.). Furthermore, Paul acknowledges the fruit of the Spirit will take time to grow, but the real change will occur, nonetheless. Similarly, SFBT therapists believe that real, lasting change will inevitably grow, no matter how small the initial change is. The parallel is undeniable: from planting the fruit seed (redemption) to harvesting the healthy fruit (wellness), a person who actively engages in personal growth will eventually bear healthy fruit. Likewise, just as a fruit tree grows deeper roots when exposed to harsh weather conditions, an SFBT therapist will not focus on stopping rain or strong winds but will help clients develop a desired vision of the future, strengthening their inner resources in the storm.

It is important to note that Galatians 5:22 (*New International Bible*, 1978/2011) describes this growth as a singular "fruit," not the plural "fruits," despite listing nine different qualities. Paul, the writer of the letter to the Galatians, emphasized that a person cannot have just one fruit of the Spirit, but all will grow together. Similarly, SFBT asserts that one small change, no matter how slowly the change is made, will affect other areas of life; the tree that withstands a hurricane deepens its roots and will result in a more fruitful harvest.

Conceptually, the integration of SFBT and the B-Well model can be outlined simply:

1. The planter (therapist) **trusts** that a seed (client's wellness), by nature, was created to grow into fruit if cared for well. (*SFBT: If it isn't broken, don't fix it.*)
2. The planter actively plants the seed and waters it to help it grow. (*SFBT: Building the therapeutic relationship*)
3. The planter must **empower** the seed to open and make its way to the surface without interfering. (*SFBT: Encourage the client to make reasonable changes; the client is the expert.*)
4. The planter helps remove barriers that might **impede** the seed's ability to get enough sunlight. (*SFBT: If it's not working, do something different; look for exceptions.*)
5. The planter then trusts that the fully grown **fruit tree** (client's overall wellness) will strengthen and deepen its roots when needed. (*SFBT: Resiliency and strength already exist; small steps can lead to big changes*).

A Case Study: Karly

Karly presented to the university counseling center with complaints of apprehensions about going to class and work. Karly revealed that she was encouraged to attend the counseling center by a roommate, her mother, and her faculty advisor after a private conversation—all on separate occasions. Karly admitted that she did not initially see herself as having an issue that warranted counseling; however, after noting the same concern from each of them, she thought that she should take their advice, supporting a high motivation for change.

© Dikushin Dmitry/shutterstock.com

Karly revealed that she is struggling with anger outbursts. She notes that she finds herself struggling with her emotions the most when in class and at work. In both places, she has found herself shouting at classmates and co-workers. On several occasions, she has kicked things when angry (e.g., desk, doors, walls, etc.) and stormed out of the room to "cool down."

Karly noted that she believes her classmates and co-workers "hate her" and "have no confidence in her." She has shared, "They think that I am dumb. I don't care about what they think. I just hate making mistakes in class and at work, and it seems to keep happening. I really get frustrated with myself when I get things wrong." She states that while she has

© Dikushin Dmitry/shutterstock.com

been pressing herself to go to both places, she feels that the symptoms are getting worse. She wants to get some help so she can continue to carry on with her life in a way that does not become volatile. Instead of being asked, "What is bothering you?" Karly was asked, "What do you hope to see happen?" In response, Karly stated that she is living like a crockpot at a high temperature, currently set at a 10, and would like to slow down to a warming temperature of three and enjoy life more. When asked how she would know if she was moving down on the scale, she noted enhanced laughter in her day-to-day life.

During the intake, Karly shared that she is a 21-year-old, White, heterosexual female. She is the oldest of five children and notes being very close to her siblings and parents. She is from a small town in Kansas and is now attending a college of over 25,000 students, working to gain a veterinary science degree. She is attending college on an academic scholarship and works part-time in the university cafeteria to supplement what the scholarship does not cover. She notes that her desire to maintain the scholarship gives her the courage to face her issues. Although she is experiencing issues at the cafeteria, she also finds pride in having this job as many other students also vied for the opportunity to work there.

When asked, when is "the problem" not so much of a problem, (incorporating the six facets of the B-Well model), she noted that she enjoys outdoor activities such as running, biking, fishing, caring for the animals on her farm, and spending time with family and friends, when possible. She also offered that the problem is not as much of an issue when she attends church or spends time in a devotional or Bible study. Karly recognized that focusing on her values has helped her manage "the problem," at least for a bit, so far, when she can remain calm. When asked what the most important people in her life would say about her, she stated they would confirm that she is a hard worker and perfectionist and that she loves animals, family, and friends. She also noted that she likes to have fun and sees laughter and her ability to make others laugh as a superpower.

Applying the B-Well Model Using SFBT

In this section, we will explore Karly's scenario through the six facets of the B-Well model, which provides a biblical worldview lens and is grounded in wellness, and an SFBT perspective in a clinical, college counseling setting. In conceptualizing any case, it is important to consider how the counselor's values and beliefs intertwine or integrate into their clinical framework. Doing so aligns with and promotes competent, ethical practice as outlined in the ACA (2014) and ASERVIC (2009) ethical codes. Similarly, the combined use of B-Well and SFBT provides the therapist with a congruent avenue to holistically serve the client in the therapeutic process by exploring the client's problems with a specific focus on solutions and strengths.

Heart

From the B-Well lens, Heart speaks to the emotional state of the client concerning the problem. Karly presented to the counseling center with troubles related to anger and angry outbursts. She noted that her anger originated from "mistakes" and beliefs that classmates and co-workers "hate her," "have no confidence in her," and view her as "dumb." Karly's emotional state is compounded with feelings of hopelessness about how to achieve her goal of engaging with others positively after mistakes are made. She does find "pride" in her part-time job, which is a strength, her love of others (e.g., animals, family, and friends), and her superpower of engaging in humor may assist Karly in overcoming her problems.

Mind

In consideration of Mind, Karly has some maladaptive beliefs about how she sees herself and incongruent language regarding how she feels about her interactions with others. These stated beliefs are supporting distress: "I don't care about what they think;" "I hate to make mistakes in class and at work, and it seems to keep happening;" and "I really get frustrated with myself when I get things wrong;" and "I feel like a crockpot on high temperature." Though Karly struggles in her view of self and others, she does have some positives. She can focus on her "values," which can be a strength in addressing the problem.

Strength

Conceptualizing Karly through the lens of Strength will provide an anchor to identify and address effective and ineffective physical and behavioral choices. Karly's anger outbursts displayed through shouting, storming out of the room, and kicking desks, doors, and walls are current maladaptive coping choices that perpetuate challenges in developing and maintaining positive peer relationships. A positive aspect of Strength is that Karly is young and healthy. She does not report any disability or health conditions. She is physically able across domains—school, work, and social.

Soul

Although Karly noted a strong relationship with God and spiritual values, there is an incongruence and delay in displaying these factors when angered. Karly seems to lean on her "works" and "efforts" to maintain calmness yet becomes "a crockpot" when mistakes occur. Yet, when asking Karly about exceptions to the problem, it is limited when at church, during devotions, and Bible study.

Neighbor

From the B-Well perspective, Karly is experiencing issues in the area of Neighbor. She reports issues of anger and aggressive behavior toward those at work and home. Yet, during the intake, Karly shared that she has strong relationships with her family, friends from home, and her Sunday school group. While she is struggling to connect with current classmates and co-workers, she does express a desire to do so and a motivation for a solution, which is consistent with an SFBT approach.

Society

From the B-Well facet of Society, the university's contextual factors can indirectly influence her wellness. Her scholarship and standing prompt an incongruence with family and self-expectations. Karly is from a rural town in Kansas and has moved to a large university with 25,000 students. This may have negative and positive indirect influences on Karly. Though not reported by Karly, a part of her anger and acting out could be associated with this transition. Guiffrida (2008) stated that students who move from a rural small town to a large university may "[feel] lost and out of place ..." (p. 3). Guifridda noted that many rural students may drop out at a large university. Yet, the large university setting is also a resource for Karly. She has the opportunity for part-time employment and on-campus counseling.

B-Well Treatment Plan

Solution-focused therapy combined with the B-Well model provides a unique way of working with Karly's presenting issues. B-Well articulates several defining principles that support a collaborative approach to holistically assess and conceptualize the client, thereby enhancing the observation and use of her assets through various parts of the treatment process. The following sections outline those points.

Heart

Just as the B-Well model describes a person's emotional state as a continuum of wellness, the SFBT therapist trusts that the client is the expert on their own life. Wellness arises when there is the freedom to reconstruct solutions to feel contentment. From an SFBT approach, the client only can define the feelings of progress and contentment. Scaling is one technique that can be used with Karly in the SFBT process, allowing her to evaluate her progress and subjectively measure how solutions are working. Although the SFBT therapist would not explore the underlying components of what contributed to the number scaled, the SFBT therapist recognizes that the client, Karly, is the expert on how they feel about whether or not a solution is working.

Mind

SFBT thrives on the premise that future-oriented thinking drives the ongoing attainment of a client's goals. The fundamental belief that problems are best solved by identifying what is already working is the hallmark of SFBT, and the Mind is a crucial component of developing solution-focused change. In working with Karly, the SFBT therapist can help her build hope for what *could be*, reorienting past thinking into an active reconstruction of solutions for lasting change.

Strength

In the B-Well model, Strength is defined as the physical and behavioral component of the client, a highly valued component of SFBT. The maintenance of positive and long-term change can only be sustained when the client continues their useful behavior habits. In SFBT, therapists believe that the solution already exists for clients. In this case, the therapist and Karly can work together to find alternatives to the undesired pattern of behavior, and her desired future becomes a reality through ongoing behavioral changes. The SFBT therapists can encourage Karly to find exceptions to her problems and to develop small changes that eventually lead to long-term changes and the utilization of resources (e.g., ableness).

Soul

The Soul, which according to the B-Well model, includes the heart, mind, and body, is an imperative part of wellness. As aforementioned, addressing incongruencies in thinking and behaviors will help produce sanctification and hope within the Soul. The hopeful nature of this approach resonates with the SFBT therapist. Developing and maintaining a positive, strengths-focused therapeutic alliance with Karly will enable her to focus on current positive thinking, behaviors, and resources that can be used in the future (to plant and maintain the seed). Spending time in nature and with God in prayer and devotion are current behaviors that support calm and peace for her. These encouraging actions can be combined with skills to enhance positive thinking that helps to mitigate explosive emotions, maladaptive beliefs, and behaviors.

Neighbor

SFBT therapists see clients in an egalitarian way, collaborating with them to achieve their goals and acting as a consultant, regardless of the nature of the complaint. The B-Well model describes this part of the person as the "how" of engagement with others. A distinct difference with SFBT, as compared to other models, is what others might consider the "resistance" of a client. SFBT therapists consider these natural protective mechanisms, and it is the therapist's responsibility to be cooperative and maintain a collegial stance. Working with Karly in this manner will support the therapeutic alliance, helping her to identify the inner strengths that she may already have.

Society

SFBT centers on the premise that modifications of the cognitive and behavioral aspects of an individual will bring about positive outcomes and long-term change. A weakness in this model is that the primary focus does not incorporate the whole of the person (Heart, Neighbor, and Society). The indirect effects of this model on Society may not be clearly outlined in SFBT literature; however, we believe that the use of the B-Well model, alongside SFBT, helps fill this gap. Refer to the case of Karly below to see the integration of the whole person through the SFBT lens.

Applying an SFBT Perspective

SFBT focuses on finding solutions and attends only minimally to defining or understanding presenting problems. It is typically very brief—three to five sessions. Much like cognitive behavioral theory, learning the principles of classical and operant conditioning is encouraged to take place along with the use of homework. In this role, the therapist will work to support the client in changing cognitions by viewing "the existing video of life" differently.

To bring about this change, we apply the six components of SFBT. These components of SFBT are (1) developing a cooperative therapeutic alliance with the client; (2) creating a solution versus problem focus; (3) setting measurable, changeable goals; (4) focusing on the future through future-oriented questions and discussions; (5) scaling the ongoing attainment of the goals to get the client's evaluation of the progress made; and (6) focusing the conversation on exceptions to the client's problems, exceptions related to what they want different, and encouraging them to do more of what they did to make the exceptions happen. This treatment plan is not comprehensive but will give an example of how to use SFBT within the B-Well model for a holistic approach to elicit strengths and exceptions to improve thinking and doing.

TABLE 1 Recommended Goals, Objectives, and Interventions

Problem	Goal	Objective	Intervention
Anger Management	Enhance feelings of confidence and support to reduce negative emotions. *SFBT prompt: What at the end of the therapy should be achieved in order to say that the therapy has been useful?*	Objective 1 – Enhance positive interactions with co-workers and classmates. [Strength, Neighbor] *SFBT prompt: What would you rather have instead?*	• Increase opportunities for laughter when with co-workers and classmates. • Increase opportunities to engage in outdoor activities with co-workers and classmates.
		Objective 2 – Discover and construct patterns of positive thought. [Mind] *SFBT prompt: What would "better" look like?*	• Assess prior issues of stress and build on coping strategies. • Increase positive thoughts regarding self to 3-5 times daily (morning, mid-day, evening focus) using scaling, compliments, and homework.

Problem	Goal	Objective	Intervention
		Objective 3 – Find alternative positive patterns of behaviors. [Mind, Strength, Neighbor] *SFBT prompt: What experiment can you try? What would be different?*	• Consult with Karly on immediate behaviors that impact current and future vision for self. • Collaborate with Karly to enhance complimentary activities to 3-4 times a week (e.g., walking, running, outdoor campus games, devotional, weekly Bible study with friends or via app). • Experiment with sharing daily activities with close friends and family one time each week • (e.g., assessment and experimentation).

Summary

The B-Well model, combined with SFBT, provides practitioners a way to conceptualize clients holistically through a wellness lens with considerations of spiritual integration. Doing so can work to enhance overall client satisfaction in treatment and potentially enhance treatment outcomes. As you consider your future work in the field and the use of solution-focused brief therapy with any client, it is important to note considerations for when this approach may not be efficient or effective. Consider appropriate diagnostic assessment and treatment planning. Seek support when and as needed to support ethical and competent practice. Moreover, continue to engage in reading and practice that builds your understanding and competency in integration.

References

American Counseling Association (ACA). (2014). *2014 ACA code of ethics.* http://www.counseling.org/Resources/aca-code-of-ethics.pdf

Association for Spiritual, Ethical, and Religious Values in Counseling (ASERVIC). (2009). *Competencies for addressing spiritual and religious issues in counseling.* https://aservic.org/wp-content/uploads/2021/04/ASERVIC-Spiritual-Competencies_FINAL.pdf

Corey, G. (2021). *Theory and practice of counseling and psychotherapy* (10th ed.). Cengage Learning.

de Shazer, S. D. (1978). Brief therapy with couples. *American Journal of Family Therapy, 6*(1), 17-30. https://doi.org/10.1080/01926187808250271

de Shazer, S. D. (1986). *Keys to solutions in brief therapy.* W. W. Norton and Company.

English Standard Bible. (2001). ESV Online. https://esv.literalword.com/

Entwistle, D. N. (2015). *Integrative approaches to psychology and Christianity: An introduction to worldview issues, philosophical foundations, and models of integration* (3rd ed.). Wipf and Stock Publishers.

Franklin, C., Zhang, A., Froerer, A., & Johnson, S. (2017). Solution focused brief therapy: A systematic review and meta-summary of process research. *Journal of Marital and Family Therapy, 43*(1), 16–30. https://doi.org/10.1111/jmft.12193

Guiffrida, D. A. (2008). Preparing Rural Students for Large Colleges and Universities. *Journal of School Counseling,* 6(14), 1-25. http://www.jsc.montana.edu/articles/v6n14.pdf

Jones, L. J., & Butman, R. E. (2011). *Modern psychotherapies: A comprehensive Christian appraisal.* InterVarsity Press.

Joubert, J., & Guse, T. (2021). A solution-focused brief therapy (SFBT) intervention model to facilitate hope and subjective well-being among trauma survivors. *Journal of Contemporary Psychotherapy, 51,* 303-310. https://doi.org/10.1007/s10879-021-09511-w

New International Bible. (2011). The NIV Bible. https://www.thenivbible.com (Original work published 1978)

Simmons, R., Lilley, S., & Kuhnley, A. (2019). *Introduction to counseling: Integration of faith, professional identity, and clinical practice.* Kendall Hunt.

Walter, J. L., & Peller, J. E. (2000). *Recreating brief therapy: Preferences and possibilities.* W. W. Norton & Company.

CHAPTER 14

B-Well Model in Addiction Counseling Using a Multicausal Model

Brad A. Imhoff

> "Come to me, all you who are weary and burdened, and I will give you rest."
>
> — Matthew 11:28 (NIV)

Background of Addiction Counseling

The Problem of Addiction

Addiction is a complex, multi-faceted problem that significantly and negatively affects individuals, families, and society as a whole. On a societal level, the National Institute on Drug Abuse (NIDA, 2018) estimates that substance use costs the United States more than $600 billion annually. On a more personal level, 14.5% of people in the United States aged 12 or older qualified for a substance use disorder in 2020 (Substance Abuse and Mental Health Services Administration [SAMHSA], 2021a). This resulted in a historically high number of overdose deaths in the United States in 2021 at more than 104,000 people (Ahmad et al., 2021).

Despite a record number of overdose deaths in the United States, it is suggested that four out of five people in the United States who need treatment for illicit drug use do not receive it (United States Government, 2022). When individuals do receive treatment, it is professional counselors who serve the highest proportion of clients with a primary addiction diagnosis— more so than social workers, psychologists, or psychiatrists (Lee et al., 2013). Therefore, it is imperative that counselors have a way to conceptualize addiction issues in the clientele they serve.

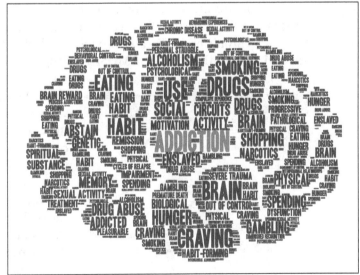

 © arloo/shutterstock.com

Models for Understanding Addiction

In addition to the theoretical models already presented in this book, addiction counselors do well to familiarize themselves with various theories of addiction, or etiological models of addiction, that attempt to explain the onset and maintenance of addictive behaviors. The models are many and a detailed discussion is beyond the scope of this chapter, but I do want to briefly review and highlight some here—especially those applicable to the case example later in the chapter. Due to the complexity of addiction, the value of many of the models, and their overlap, I will ultimately advocate for a multicausal model of addiction that is discussed at the end of this section.

Moral Model

The moral model of addiction asserts that addiction is an issue of personal choice and moral failing. Through this lens, it is believed that people who are addicted to substances are choosing to not stop their use and are simply irresponsible (Capuzzi & Stauffer, 2020). This model largely influences the legal system in the United States through which individuals are punished for "wrong" behavior when they are found to be using drugs. While it is true that individuals more often than not choose to ingest substances initially, this model undervalues biological processes occurring in the brain over time that make quitting difficult. Further, it contributes to the stigma associated with addiction by suggesting that people who struggle with it are immoral or lack the necessary character and integrity to stop using. Clients who come into our offices and report being told, "If you cared enough about your [kids, spouse, partner, job, etc.], you'd just quit," have experienced messages associated with the moral model.

Biological and Disease Models

Biological and disease models of addiction take into account genetics and processes in the brain that contribute to addiction. A thorough understanding of this is complex and research is ongoing, but family studies involving parents, siblings, twins, and adoption often demonstrate a relationship between epigenetics, genetics, and addiction (Capuzzi & Stauffer, 2020; Jones et al., 2021). This may also help explain why some people can be introduced to substances like alcohol and use it without becoming addicted, while others cannot. These models suggest that abstinence is the only option for those who struggle with addiction because of its chronic nature.

Organizations like the American Society of Addiction Medicine (ASAM), SAMHSA, and NIDA, consider addiction a chronic brain disease through which the structure and functioning of the brain is changed (ASAM, 2019; NIDA, 2005; SAMHSA, 2021b). The use of substances is associated with the release of abnormally high levels of dopamine in the brain, which results in euphoria and provides reinforcement for continued use. Further, the frontal cortex, which is responsible for self-control, becomes underactive; the amygdala, which is associated with emotions like fear and anger, becomes overactive; and the ability to control impulses or tolerate negative emotional states diminishes (SAMSHA, 2021b). Educating clients and families on the role of the brain and the changes occurring can increase understanding of addiction processes while also enhancing compassion and empathy for those who struggle with addiction.

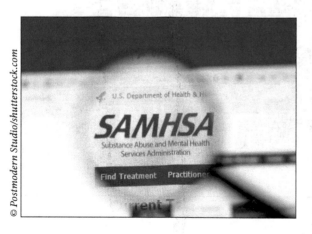

© Postmodern Studio/shutterstock.com

Psychological Models

Psychological models for understanding addiction focus on concepts like cognitions, behaviors, learning processes, and reinforcement (Capuzzi & Stauffer, 2020). Positive reinforcement would apply to the individual who consumes a substance and experiences pleasure from doing so. This person continues using that substance in the future to continue experiencing that pleasure. Unfortunately, with many substances, tolerance is developed where the typical amount no longer results in the desired effect (American Psychiatric Association [APA], 2013). This often causes the individual to increase the amount taken or to try different drugs to produce the pleasurable experience. This becomes problematic as the brain adapts to increased consumption of addictive substances, as discussed below.

Negative reinforcement would apply to the individual who uses drugs to reduce negative feelings or experiences such as boredom, anxiety, stress, sadness, or despair (Capuzzi & Stauffer, 2020). These individuals are not necessarily using for pleasure, or chasing a high, as much as they are using to rid themselves of discomfort. For example, you may have a client who experienced a significant loss or trauma. To not have to endure the ongoing cognitive and emotional discomfort associated with it, the person escapes it or numbs it by using substances.

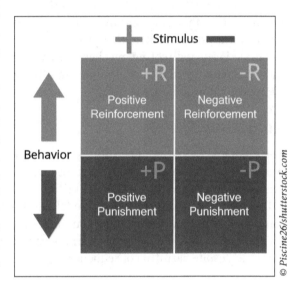

Negative reinforcement also applies to the individuals described in paragraph one of this section who initially use because of positive reinforcement (i.e., using is pleasurable). As tolerance increases, the brain adapts to the substance being present (Capuzzi & Stauffer, 2020). When the substance is not present, the individual experiences withdrawal symptoms and begins to feel sick. To avoid the discomfort associated with these symptoms, the individual ingests the substance again. This creates a cycle in which a person continues using only to avoid discomfort, despite initially doing so for pleasure.

Family Models

Capuzzi & Stauffer (2020) describe how addiction treatment historically involved only working with the individual who was addicted. Modern approaches to addiction treatment instead try to incorporate family members in treatment because of their significant influence in the process. Selbekk et al. (2015) note that treatment that involves family members of the addicted person tends to have more positive outcomes.

Some of the roles that family can play in the addiction process can include modeling, enabling, and even explicitly supporting substance use. Families sometimes model substance use as a social or celebratory necessity or as a way of coping with challenges. The child who sees alcohol at every family holiday likely associates drinking with social gatherings and grows up to expect it at most functions. The child who watches his father drink a six-pack at the end of a particularly hard day at work may associate alcohol with coping or relaxation. In these ways, substance use is modeled and learned from at an early age.

When it comes to enabling, a family member may inadvertently or advertently do so. This could be the grandparent whose pain medication is in a cabinet in the bathroom, easily accessible to a curious high school grandchild and his friends. It could be the spouse who cannot stand to see his partner experiencing withdrawal symptoms, so he picks her up a bottle of wine at the store. It could also be the parents who consistently bail a child out of jail or protect the child from other consequences of substance use because they believe they are protecting their child.

Finally, some family members explicitly support substance use. This may be the husband who thinks his wife is "more fun" when she is high or the wife who can only tolerate her husband when he is buzzed because then he is "more pleasant and not so angry." Even more shocking is the client I had who came in for addiction treatment as a young adult. During the intake process, it was revealed that the client's parents provided alcohol to the client at 10 years old and opioids as an adolescent. It was explained that they believed my client would eventually discover and use substances anyway; at least this way, they could control that process. What they believed were good intentions was actually a very misguided way of directing my client down a very destructive path. Regardless of their role in the onset and maintenance of addiction, understanding and involving family members and family dynamics in the treatment process is valuable.

Multicausal Model

The complex nature of addiction and the many processes involved makes adhering to a single model inadvisable to counselors. Each of those discussed in this section—and there are many others that exist—garners some merit and some critique as well. The very definition of addiction offered by ASAM (2019) alludes to several different models: "Addiction is a treatable, chronic medical disease involving complex interactions among brain circuits, genetics, the environment, and an individual's life experiences. People with addiction use substances or engage in behaviors that become compulsive and often continue despite harmful consequences" (p. 2).

© Sviatlana Zyhmantovic/shutterstock.com

A multicausal model encourages the application of various models discussed in this section rather than focusing on just one. The approach of taking each model into account when conceptualizing a client's addiction issues creates an individualized understanding of each client and the etiology of their addiction. For example, it may be clear for one client that elements of a family model and the moral model have played a role in the development and maintenance of addiction, while another client's story may have elements of psychological and genetic models. Often, several models will factor in for a single client, and overlap between the models can exist. Therefore, an approach that uses a multicausal model encourages the consideration of many variables and their complex interactions (Capuzzi & Stauffer, 2020). Further, a multicausal model approach can be combined with the B-Well model to view clients holistically and offer a comprehensive approach to case conceptualization and treatment.

Christian Integration Perspective

When thinking about integrating faith into counseling, I would consider myself a licensed professional counselor operating from a Christian worldview. Simmons et al. (2020) describe this as someone who obtains professional licensure as a counselor and is submitted to the requirements and ethics codes of credentialing bodies and professional organizations yet operates from a Christian worldview. More specifically, from within that worldview, I adhere to the Allies model put forth by Entwistle (2015). This model suggests that there is one sovereign God reigning over all of life and from Whom comes all truth and to Whom belongs all truth. As such, Christian theology and counseling can coexist and inform one another. As Entwistle (2015) writes, "Theological reflection typically focuses on *God's workings in the world*; psychological reflection typically focuses on *the workings of God's world*" (p. 250).

For me, this integration process begins with seeing my clients as beloved children of God. They have been created in his image (*New International Bible*, 1978/2011, Genesis 1:26), have innate value, and are worthy of love and respect. I find this mindset particularly important when working in addiction counseling where clients come in beaten down by stigma and have often lost hope for themselves. Their view of self is so often ravaged by years of struggle, and it is important that I view them as beloved and valuable and help them begin to see themselves as such, too.

In this process, I borrow from Tan's (2011) continuum of implicit/explicit integration. This model suggests that counselors operating from a Christian worldview integrate faith concepts on a continuum of implicit to explicit integration and do so in a responsible, sensitive, and ethical way. Matters of religion and spirituality are discussed in the intake process, and this will guide my approach to integrating faith on this continuum when working directly with a client. Explicit integration may occur when clients want their faith to be a part of the counseling process. With these clients, I may incorporate prayer and/or scripture into sessions, openly discuss matters of spirituality and faith, or make referrals to faith-based resources for additional support. For the client who does not want matters of faith to be a part of the counseling process, I take an implicit approach to integration. This does not involve openly discussing faith or utilizing faith-based interventions in session but may involve relying on the Holy Spirit for guidance, embodying the characteristics of Christ in my interactions with clients, showing my clients agape love, and perhaps praying for my clients on my own outside of sessions.

A Case Study: Jackson

Jackson is a 29-year-old White male. He lives in a small, rural town in the Appalachian region of the United States where he was born and raised. Jackson has been struggling with opioid addiction for about a decade and came to the treatment center of his own accord, though his mother drove him. When asked how he was doing, he fought back tears and told the counselor, "I'm so tired of this. Something's gotta change. I've lost my family. I've lost my car. I barely got my job. I can't keep livin' like this."

Intake and Assessment Instruments

During the intake interview, Jackson's appearance was disheveled, and he was wearing a sweatshirt despite sweating in the mid-afternoon heat. He later shared that he wore it because he was embarrassed about the track marks on his arms from injecting heroin. His height and weight seemed appropriate for his age, though he looked worn down and noticeably older than his stated age of 29. He was oriented times four (i.e., person, place, time, event), and while he was able to answer questions coherently throughout the intake session, his speech was a bit slurred. He also stared at the floor throughout the session. His posture was slouched in the chair, and he was notably restless.

Information from the intake interview suggested that Jackson met seven of the 11 criteria for opioid use disorder (APA, 2013). He also scored a 28 on the Leeds Dependence Questionnaire (Raistrick et al., 1994), having answered "Nearly Always" to eight out of 10 questions related to substance dependence. This included items such as, "Do you feel your need for drugs is too strong to control?" and "Do you find it difficult to cope with life without drugs?" Upon assessment for suicidal ideation, Jackson noted that he has regularly thought about what it would be like to not be alive anymore but denied any intent or plan for suicide. He stated, "I could never do that to my girls—not after what my dad did to me and my family." He exhibited some traits of major depressive disorder but did not meet the criteria for a diagnosis. This should be monitored and ruled out.

Family History

Jackson is the second born in a family of six. He grew up with his mother and father, an older brother, and younger twin sisters. He described his family as having been extremely close-knit and always looking out for one another when he was growing up. However, his father died by suicide when Jackson was 18 and enrolled in his first year at the local community college. He stated, "He was my rock, and it was like that rock just crumbled from beneath me." He said the family has never been the same since and that they all seemed to grow more distant after that.

Jackson reported that his mom and oldest brother are the only people in the family who have not struggled with substance use. He said his dad "drank like a fish" and both of his younger sisters use pills. He noted that, while he really admires and looks up to his brother, he is also envious that he has "the

perfect life," while the rest of the family struggles to keep it together. He said that, even though the family is not as close as they were before his father's suicide, they still periodically stay in touch and try to get together for holidays.

Jackson is married to his high school sweetheart and has two young daughters, two and five years old. He and his wife are currently separated. She gave him an ultimatum of stopping his drug use or being kicked out. He maintained a brief period of sobriety but has since relapsed and continued his use. He currently lives with his mother, who he claims would "do anything in the world for me and my family."

Educational & Occupational History

Jackson completed high school with a 3.2 GPA and was enrolled as a psychology major in his first year of college prior to dropping out when his dad died. He took a job as a mechanic in an auto repair shop to help his mom pay the bills. His younger sisters were still living at home and his older brother had just started a new career following his college graduation. Jackson felt responsible for assuming the role of the provider in his family in the absence of his father. He has continued his work as a mechanic and has been with the same repair shop since taking the initial job. He said he has always dreamt of going back to school and remembers "absolutely loving my psych courses."

Religiosity and Spirituality

Jackson shared that he considers himself a Christian and asked the counselor, "Am I allowed to talk about that in here?" Upon further discussion, he shared that he goes to church "wherever my mom goes." He stated that the family always went to church growing up but that they stopped a while after his dad died. He said others in the church were not very compassionate about his father's suicide or Jackson's struggle with addiction and that it drove his mother away. He vividly remembers one of the other moms in the church telling his mom, "You know he's in hell because of this, right? And your son isn't far behind."

© Nattapat.I/shutterstock.com

Though his mother found a new church to attend many years later, Jackson only went again after moving back in with her following the separation from his wife. He stated, "I still prayed and stuff—mostly when things were going bad—but I don't read the Bible anymore or anything like that."

History of Substance Use

When asked about his substance use, Jackson stated that he would occasionally drink at parties in high school but never did any of the "harder stuff." He shared that it was never even something he considered, but everything felt like a whirlwind when his dad died and that his decision to drop out of college and get a job all happened very quickly. He stated, "I just felt like I had to help my mom. She stayed at home and my dad worked. How was she supposed to keep raising my sisters with him gone?"

It was at the auto repair shop that Jackson was first introduced to opioids. He said he was not sure if anyone there *didn't* use pills. A co-worker introduced him to OxyContin when he noticed Jackson was really stressed out about everything going on in his life. Jackson shared that the pills really helped him "take the edge off" and "especially not think about my dad." He shared that he knew then he probably should not use them like he was but that they helped the workday go better and were the only thing that made him "feel content."

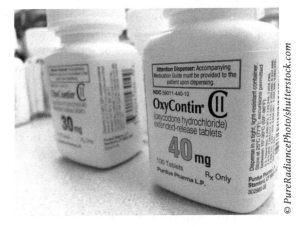

© PureRadiancePhoto/shutterstock.com

Jackson made the jump from OxyContin to heroin during a party with his coworkers. He said they were pretty much his only friends, and he would occasionally hang out with them on the weekends. After an argument with his wife, Jackson went to the party and used heroin for the first time. He shared that it was a high unlike anything he had experienced before, and it became his drug of choice. He was quick to point out that using it stopped being fun a long time ago, and now he only does it to avoid getting sick. He noted that he started using a Syringe Services Program in his town and stated, "I ain't looking to get any diseases from this crap." It was at this program that Jackson learned about this treatment center. When asked about the possibility of utilizing medication-assisted treatment to treat his opioid addiction, he said he was open to it, but he wasn't "interested in giving up one drug for another." He stated, "I traded pills for the heroin, and I ain't about to trade the heroin for another addiction."

Applying the B-Well Model Using a Multicausal Approach

The B-Well model uses six facets as a guide for understanding and working with Jackson. These include Heart, Mind, Strength, Soul, Neighbor, and Society. Each of these will be discussed in turn as we consider how they apply to Jackson's case and can be used to help him be successful in treatment. The multicausal model discussed at the beginning of the chapter, in which a variety of etiologies are considered, will also be integrated; and we will see how many are potentially influencing Jackson's addiction. This use of the B-Well model and a multicausal model helps us gain insight into Jackson's substance use and organize our conceptualization.

Heart

The Heart component of the B-Well model involves our client's emotions. In Jackson's case, there are many emotional considerations, though his use of substances has also been used to avoid or numb these emotions. This is evidenced in his comment about how the pills helped him not think so much about his dad. With Jackson describing his father as a rock and his family as having been close-knit, we can assume the relationship was mostly positive and Jackson has likely never fully processed the grief of losing his father. With suicide being the cause of death, Jackson may experience complicated emotions like anger, confusion, guilt, and rejection from this loss (Worden, 2009). Though grief experiences are individualized, Jackson has likely also felt a range of other emotions including sadness, despair, shock, and depression from this as well. Further, he may be experiencing grief because of the separation from his wife and being displaced from her and their children.

Mind

The Mind component of the B-Well model involves our client's thoughts as they pertain to self, others, and the world in general. As described in the chapters on biblical wellness and cognitive behavioral therapy, this involves quick, reactive thoughts known as automatic thoughts, which derive from deep-seated thoughts known as core beliefs. As we explore Jackson's thought processes, we want to pay special attention to those which may be maladaptive and unhelpful in his recovery process. An important aspect of this is that Jackson indicates he is to a point of only using to avoid withdrawal and feeling sick. This also ties into the aforementioned psychological model of addiction in that Jackson finds himself using to avoid unpleasant thoughts. He may also engage in catastrophizing—a cognitive distortion where he thinks to himself, "I can't stand to be sick like that." Thus, he believes he *needs* the drugs, and it reinforces and rationalizes his use.

Strength

The Strength component of the B-Well model involves the physical, physiological, and behavioral aspects of our clients. In Jackson's case, the decade of substance use has taken a toll on him. This is evidenced by his looking much older than his stated age, the track marks on his arms, slurred speech, slouched posture, and overall disheveled appearance. Jackson's behavior also involves the compulsive use of heroin despite significant consequences and wanting to change this behavior. The challenge associated with doing so relates back to biological and disease models of understanding addiction. Jackson's brain has been flooded with excessive amounts of dopamine throughout his drug use, and his brain circuitry has been rewired in a way that promotes continued use (Capuzzi & Stauffer, 2020; SAMHSA, 2021b). Jackson can begin to reverse some of these effects through changes in his behavior.

Soul

Soul in the B-Well model is the connection between the physical and spiritual world. As a counselor working through a Christian worldview, I view Jackson as an individual created in God's image (*New International Bible*, 1978/2011, Genesis 1:26) who is, therefore, inherently valuable and has meaning and purpose in his life (Jones & Butman, 2011). Though Jackson identifies as a Christian, the years of substance use, his separation from his wife, and his displacement from his kids have undoubtedly taken a toll on his view of himself, his relationship with God, and his sense of meaning. He is, however, someone who has historically prayed and gone to church—even asking in the intake process if his faith was something he was allowed to talk about in counseling. This appears to be an opportunity to reconnect Jackson with his spiritual nature and perhaps help him begin engaging in positive practices related to his faith.

Neighbor

The Neighbor component in the B-Well model relates to how the client engages, connects, and relates with others, including friends, spouses, parents, siblings, coworkers, etc. This aspect also connects to family models of understanding addiction. Selbekk et al. (2015) note that addiction has significant, adverse consequences on families, but addiction treatment that includes family members tends to be more effective. This is very true in Jackson's case as his addiction has created a lot of broken or unhealthy relationships. More positively, though, there is also the potential for reconnection in many ways. One significant connection that will deserve consideration in the treatment section is Jackson's loss of a relationship with his father. This is a person who he described as his "rock," and he has never had the opportunity to appropriately grieve this loss.

Society

The Society component of the B-Well model includes the contextual factors with which our clients interact in their communities, from local to national. One of the primary societal factors in Jackson's case is the stigma faced by those who struggle with addiction. We see in the case study that some members of Jackson's former church community were not very compassionate when it came to his father's suicide or his own struggle with addiction. As noted early in this chapter, the moral model of understanding addiction suggests that addiction is a consequence of personal choice and irresponsibility and that there is something morally wrong with people who use drugs (Capuzzi & Stauffer, 2020; Frank & Nagel, 2017). This model is especially prevalent in some religious groups and may be especially relevant in Jackson's Appalachian community where stigma related to both Syringe Services Programs and medication-assisted treatment is pervasive (Richard et al., 2020; Zeller et al., 2021).

It is noted in the case study that Jackson has engaged the services of a local Syringe Services Program where he could access sterile syringes and dispose of his used ones. In fact, it was through this program that Jackson learned of the treatment center where he is now receiving treatment. Such programs have been shown to have benefits such as reducing transmission rates of Hepatitis B and C, reducing the littering of used syringes in communities, increasing engagement in treatment, and not increasing drug use or crime in communities (Levine, et al., 2019; Marx et al., 2000; Motie et al., 2020; Surratt et al., 2020). Even so, research by Zeller et al. (2021) showed that only 49.3% of people in a rural Appalachian community supported such programs. Jackson has already faced societal challenges related to his addiction and it is likely to continue throughout his treatment process.

A Note on Jackson's Assets

The challenges associated with addiction stigma can paint a grim picture for Jackson's prognosis in treatment, but I would be remiss to conclude this section on the application of the B-Well model without focusing on client assets. It is foundational to this model, and the counseling profession in general, to focus on wellness and identify, highlight, and utilize client strengths in the counseling process.

Throughout the case study, there are many assets and resources that give us hope for Jackson's success. For example, Jackson has entered treatment voluntarily and has a desire to stop his drug use. This is significant and suggests Jackson is moving into the *action* stage of change in which individuals begin to make changes to their behaviors and experiences to overcome their problems (Prochaska & DiClemente, 1983; Prochaska & Norcross, 2001). Though separated from his wife, she wants him to be free of drug use as well. The potential opportunity to reconnect with her and his children could be an incredibly motivating factor. His mom is also a significant source of support as she allows him to live with her and has driven him to treatment. Helping educate her, and potentially Jackson's wife if she is open to it, on the effects of addiction and its course would be helpful in the treatment process.

Jackson is also altruistic and has a sense of loyalty and responsibility to care for others, as evidenced by his leaving school to help his mother pay bills. He is intelligent and passionate about learning, as evidenced by his 3.2 high school GPA and excitement for his initial psychology courses, which bodes well for the psychoeducation aspects of the treatment process. He has a faith background that he seems interested in re-engaging, which aligns well with many treatment programs and may provide additional support both through his relationship with God and potentially his church community. Though the treatment and recovery process is challenging, Jackson has many things working in his favor as well.

B-Well Treatment Plan

Before providing a specific sample treatment plan, it is worth noting some general treatment principles related to the B-Well facets described above.

Heart

Related to the Heart facet, Jackson has used substances to avoid or numb many of the emotions associated with his losses—a psychological aspect when considering a multicausal model. Jackson may confront these emotions throughout his recovery process and, as his counselor, I can help him work through these in a healthier way than he has previously done. To engage these emotions more intentionally, Jackson may benefit from doing a Loss Experience Timeline where he creates a record of the losses throughout his life and works through his emotional responses to them (Humphrey, 2009).

© DaLiu/shutterstock.com

This will allow him to reflect on each loss individually and describe how each has affected him and continues to affect him.

Mind

Pertaining to the Mind facet of the model, Jackson has had a lot of negative experiences over the past decade, and it is likely his thought processes include a lot of negativity and cognitive distortions that can be targeted in treatment. The counselor can use thought records and other cognitive restructuring activities to have Jackson monitor, identify, and begin to challenge negative self-talk and other maladaptive thoughts and beliefs. Though Jackson indicates he could never complete suicide, he does have suicidal ideation, and this should also be regularly monitored and assessed. Another aspect of the Mind as it relates to Jackson's case is his thought processes associated specifically with his substance use. A functional analysis may be useful here to further understand the driving factors of his drug use and its antecedents and consequences (Brady et al., 2021). Engagement in a medication-assisted treatment program can be useful here as well because they are known for reducing and potentially eliminating the withdrawal symptoms that so often reinforce and maintain substance use (SAMHSA, 2021b).

Strength

In the way a functional analysis intervention can lend insight into cognitive factors associated with substance use, it can do the same regarding behaviors; thus, focusing on the Strength facet of the B-Well model is beneficial. Analyzing the antecedents, drug use patterns, and consequences can help us identify meaning associated with Jackson's substance use. It can also begin the process of enhancing motivation, developing coping skills, and avoiding harmful behavior. Additionally, using medication in treatment can help stabilize abnormal brain activity and promote positive, beneficial behavior (Center for Substance Abuse Treatment, 2012). Positive behaviors related to the Strength facet of the B-Well model can also be things like getting adequate sleep and eating well-balanced meals. As his counselor, I want to assess Jackson's patterns around sleep and help him develop effective sleep hygiene. I can also help him recognize the importance of nutrition and the value of sustenance, or ingesting items that provide support and nourishment. Jackson has spent a lot of years ingesting substances that harm his body and will hopefully experience positive outcomes from engaging in healthier behaviors.

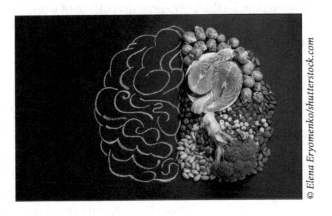
© Elena Eryomenko/shutterstock.com

Soul

Spirituality is an important aspect of substance use treatment and of the Soul facet of the B-Well model. Grim & Grim (2019) report that over 84% of scientific studies indicate faith is a positive aspect of addiction treatment and a reported 73% of programs in the United States incorporate aspects of spirituality. If Jackson is open to attending 12-step meetings, such as Narcotics Anonymous or Celebrate Recovery, as a supplement to the counseling process, he will also engage in practices there related to spirituality and a higher power. We want to help Jackson reconnect with his faith, find meaning and purpose in his existence, and return to a life of vitality and intention.

Neighbor

Related to the Neighbor facet, Jackson describes his family of origin as being very close-knit but drifting apart after his father's death. Given his drug use, Jackson has likely never appropriately grieved the death of his father. As his counselor, I want to help him do this and to keep in mind how this loss has affected him—from his rapid shift in roles as a student to a family provider a decade ago to his current role of being a husband and father himself. I also want to explore how he relates to his children and help him reconnect with them and his wife as his journey of recovery moves forward.

There are other opportunities for reconnection during the counseling process as well. Jackson could potentially be a role model of sobriety and wellness to his younger sisters who use drugs, and he might be able to reconnect with his older brother who is doing well for himself in life. Jackson's mom also serves as a significant resource throughout the recovery process because she is someone who has always been supportive of him and will, as Jackson puts it, do anything for him and his family. These positive relationships will be important, especially considering Jackson's challenging work environment. He noted that he thinks everyone who works there uses substances and maintaining sobriety in such a setting creates an exceptional challenge. His recovery process will be jeopardized by returning to the same environment in which his using habits originated, progressed, and were supported. It is likely that Jackson may have to look for other employment opportunities, if they are available, and, at minimum, develop new, healthier friendships outside of work. As his counselor, I can help him brainstorm ways in which he can develop these relationships, and a starting point may very well connect back to the Soul aspect of this model, those in his faith community.

TABLE 1 Recommended Goals, Objectives, and Interventions

Problem	Goal	Objective	Intervention
Opioid Use Disorder, severe	Accept the presence of addiction and actively participate in all aspects of the treatment program.	Participate in a full assessment and Functional Analysis to convey history of use and understand triggers and function of opioid use. [Heart, Mind, Strength, Soul, Neighbor, Society]	• Conduct a thorough assessment and Functional Analysis.
		Comply with referral for medication-assisted treatment (MAT) evaluation and follow subsequent prescription guidelines. [Mind, Strength]	• Educate the client on the benefits and effectiveness of combining MAT and counseling services. • Refer the client for evaluation for medication-assisted treatment. • Monitor medication compliance throughout the counseling relationship.

Problem	Goal	Objective	Intervention
		Attend 12-step meetings as often as necessary to support sobriety. [Neighbor, Society, Soul]	• Provide the client with a list of days and times of local and virtual Narcotics Anonymous and Celebrate Recovery meetings. • Review and process the client's experiences at the meetings.
		Develop and adhere to a Relapse Prevention Plan to include daily routines, positive self-care activities, spiritual practices, coping skills, and support people and resources. [Heart, Mind, Strength, Soul, Neighbor, Society]	• Assist the client in developing a detailed, written relapse prevention plan. • Role-play high-risk situations and help client navigate them effectively using concepts from the Relapse Prevention Plan.
	Acquire and utilize the necessary cognitive, emotional, behavioral, and relational skills to maintain sobriety.	Develop and apply coping skills to overcome cravings and unavoidable high-risk situations. [Heart, Mind, Strength]	• Educate the client on the role of coping skills in maintaining sobriety. • Brainstorm a list of coping skills individualized to the client's preferences. • Evaluate effectiveness of the coping skills and help adapt them as necessary.
		Identify, evaluate, and replace maladaptive thoughts and core beliefs that support addictive behaviors. [Mind]	• Teach the client to use thought records to identify thoughts. • Educate the client on automatic thoughts and core beliefs. • Use cognitive restructuring to help the client change maladaptive ways of thinking.
		Reengage spiritual practices and continue church attendance in support of sobriety. [Soul, Neighbor, Society]	• Assist the client in identifying spiritual practices that support his sobriety. • Process with the client the pros and cons of church attendance and its value in his life.

Problem	Goal	Objective	Intervention
		Make amends with loved ones who have been harmed by the client's addiction and participate in family and couples counseling as others are willing. [Heart, Neighbor]	• Educate the client and loved ones on the impact of substance use on the brain. • Explore with the client the need for making amends and connecting with loved ones impacted by the addiction. • Teach effective communication and problem-solving skills for couples.
		Develop and maintain new friendships that support the recovery process. [Neighbor, Society]	• Brainstorm places where the client can develop new, healthy relationships. • Assist the client in identifying characteristics of healthy friendships and positive support people.
		List significant losses from throughout his life and identify how substance use has aided in the avoidance of grieving these losses. [Heart, Soul]	• Educate the client on grief and grieving processes. • Assist the client with completing a Loss Experience Timeline. • Help the client identify and experience previously avoided emotions related to losses.

Summary

Addiction is a complex, devastating phenomenon that involves the interaction of a lot of different variables. Understanding and teasing apart these variables to best support and work with our clients can be challenging. This chapter demonstrates how using a multicausal model allows us to consider the merits of many etiological models and work to discover their role in the development and maintenance of addiction in each of our clients. From there, the B-Well model can be used to conceptualize each unique client case in a helpful way that moves us toward effective treatment. The case study of Jackson was used to provide a realistic and specific addiction-related case study for the reader to apply the concepts discussed in the chapter. Treatment considerations were offered for this case and a treatment plan with goals, objectives, and interventions was designed.

References

Ahmad, F. B., Rossen L. M., & Sutton, P. (2021) *Provisional drug overdose death counts.* National Center for Health Statistics. https://www.cdc.gov/nchs/nvss/vsrr/drug-overdose-data.htm

American Psychiatric Association (APA). (2013). *Diagnostic and statistical manual of mental disorders* (5th ed.). https://doi.org/10.1176/appi.books.9780890425596

American Society of Addiction Medicine (ASAM). (2019). *Definition of addiction.* https://www.asam.org/docs/default-source/quality-science/asam's-2019-definition-of-addiction-(1).pdf?sfvrsn=b8b64fc2_2.

Brady, K., Levin, F. R., Galanter, M., & Kleber, H. D. (2021). *The American psychiatric association publishing textbook of substance use disorder treatment.* American Psychiatric Association Publishing.

Capuzzi, D., & Stauffer, M. D. (2020). *Foundations of addictions counseling.* Pearson.

Center for Substance Abuse Treatment. (2012). *Brief interventions and brief therapies for substance abuse. Treatment Improvement Protocol (TIP) Series, No. 34.* (HHS Publication No. [SMA] 12- 3952). Substance Abuse and Mental Health Services Administration.

Entwistle, D. (2015). *Integrative approaches to psychology and Christianity* (3rd ed.) Cascade Books.

Frank, L. E., & Nagel, S. K. (2017). Addiction and moralization: The role of the underlying model of addiction. *Neuroethics, 10*(1), 129-139. https://doi.org/10.1007/s12152-017-9307-x

Grim, B. J., & Grim, M. E. (2019). Belief, behavior, and belonging: How faith is indispensable in preventing and recovering from substance abuse. *Journal of Religion and Health, 58*(5), 1713–1750. https://doi.org/10.1007/s10943-019-00876-w

Humphrey, K. M. (2009). *Counseling strategies for loss and grief.* American Counseling Association.

Jones, D. E., Park, J. S., Gamby, K., Bigelow, T. M., Mersha, T. B., & Folger, A. T. (2021). Mental health epigenetics: A primer with implications for counselors. *The Professional Counselor, 11*(1), 102–121. https://doi.org/10.15241/dej.11.1.102

Jones, S. L., & Butman, R. E. (2011). *Modern psychotherapies: A comprehensive Christian appraisal.* IVP Academic.

Lee, T. K., Craig, S. E., Fetherson, B. T., & Simpson, C. D. (2013). Addiction competencies in the 2009 CACREP clinical mental health counseling program standards. *Journal of Addictions & Offender Counseling, 34*(1), 2–15. https://doi.org/10.1002/j.2161-1874.2013.00010.x

Levine, H., Bartholomew, T. S., Rea-Wilson, V., Onugha, J., Arriola, D. J., Cardenas, G., Forrest, D. W., Kral, A. H., Metsch, L. R., Spencer, E., & Tookes, H. (2019). Syringe disposal among people who inject drugs before and after the implementation of a syringe services program. *Drug and Alcohol Dependence, 202,* 13–17. https://doi.org/10.1016/j.drugalcdep.2019.04.025

Marx, M. A., Crape, B., Brookmeyer, R. S., Junge, B., Latkin, C., Vlaohv, D., & Strathdee, S. A. (2000). Trends in crime and the introduction of a needle exchange program. *American Journal of Public Health, 90*(12), 1933-1936. https://doi.org/10.2105/ajph.90.12.1933

Motie, I., Carretta, H. J., & Beitsch, L. M. (2020). Needling policy makers and sharpening the debate: Do syringe exchange programs improve health at the population level? *Journal of Public Health Management and Practice, 26*(3), 222–226. https://doi.org/10.1097/phh.0000000000001152

National Institute on Drug Abuse (NIDA). (2005, June). *Drug abuse and addiction: One of America's most challenging public health problems.* https://archives.drugabuse.gov/publications/drug-abuse-addiction-one-americas-most-challenging-public-health-problems

National Institute on Drug Abuse (NIDA). (2018, January). *Is drug addiction treatment worth its cost?*. https://nida.nih.gov/publications/principles-drug-addiction-treatment-research-based-guide-third-edition/frequently-asked-questions/drug-addiction-treatment-worth-its-cost

New International Bible. (2011). The NIV Bible. https://www.thenivbible.com (Original work published 1978)

Prochaska, J. O., & DiClemente, C. C. (1983). Stages and processes of self-change of smoking: Toward an integrative model of change. *Journal of Consulting and Clinical Psychology, 51*(3), 390–395. https://doi.org/10.1037/0022-006x.51.3.390

Prochaska, J. O., & Norcross, J. C. (2001). Stages of change. *Psychotherapy: Theory, Research, Practice, Training, 38*(4), 443–448. https://doi.org/10.1037/0033-3204.38.4.443

Raistrick, D., Bradshaw, J., Tober, G., Weiner, J., Allison, J., & Healey, C. (1994). Development of the Leeds Dependence Questionnaire (LDQ): A questionnaire to measure alcohol and opiate dependence in the context of a treatment evaluation package. *Addiction, 89*(5), 563–572. https://doi.org/10.1111/j.1360-0443.1994.tb03332.x

Richard, E. L., Schalkoff, C. A., Piscalko, H. M., Brook, D. L., Sibley, A. L., Lancaster, K. E., Miller, W. C., & Go, V. F. (2020). "You are not clean until you're not on anything": Perceptions of medication-assisted treatment in rural Appalachia. *International Journal of Drug Policy, 85*, 102704. https://doi.org/10.1016/j.drugpo.2020.102704

Selbekk, A. S., Sagvaag, H., & Fauske, H. (2014). Addiction, families and treatment: A critical realist search for theories that can improve practice. *Addiction Research & Theory, 23*(3), 196–204. https://doi.org/10.3109/16066359.2014.954555

Simmons, R., Lilley, S., & Kuhnley, A. (2019). *Introduction to counseling: Integration of faith, professional identity, and clinical practice.* Kendall Hunt.

Substance Abuse and Mental Health Services Administration (SAMHSA). (2021a). *Key substance use and mental health indicators in the United States: Results from the 2020 national survey on drug use and health* (HHS Publication No. PEP21-07-01-003, NSDUH Series H-56). Center for Behavioral Health Statistics and Quality, Substance Abuse and Mental Health Services Administration. https://www.samhsa.gov/data/

Substance Abuse and Mental Health Services Administration (SAMHSA). (2021b). *Medications for opioid use disorder. Treatment Improvement Protocol (TIP) Series 63 Publication No. PEP21-02-01-002.* Substance Abuse and Mental Health Services Administration.

Surratt, H. L., Otachi, J. K., Williams, T., Gulley, J., Lockard, A. S., & Rains, R. (2020). Motivation to change and treatment participation among syringe service program utilizers in rural Kentucky. *The Journal of Rural Health, 36*(2), 224–233. https://doi.org/10.1111/jrh.12388

Tan, S. Y. (2011). *Counseling and psychotherapy: A Christian perspective.* Baker Academic.

United States Government (2022). *Addressing addiction and the overdose epidemic* [Fact Sheet]. https://www.whitehouse.gov/briefing-room/statements-releases/2022/03/01/fact-sheet-addressing-addiction-and-the-overdose-epidemic/

Worden, J. W. (2009). *Grief counseling and grief therapy: A handbook for the mental health practitioner* (4th ed.). Springer Publishing Co.

Zeller, T. A., Beachler, T., Diaz, L., Thomas, R. P., Heo, M., Lanzillotta-Rangeley, J., & Litwin, A. H. (2021). Attitudes toward syringe exchange programs in a rural Appalachian community. *Journal of Addictive Diseases*, 1–8. https://doi.org/10.1080/10550887.2021.1979837

CHAPTER 15
B-Well Model in Addiction Counseling Using Motivational Interviewing

Karin M. Dumont

> "So, whether you eat or drink, or whatever you do, do all to the glory of God."
>
> — 1 Corinthians 10:31 (NIV)

This chapter will focus on the application of motivational interviewing (MI) using the B-Well model. You will find a brief overview of MI, a refresher. I will offer my Christian integration approach and denominational lens. Then I will provide a case study on Max. After the case study, I will apply MI within the B-Well model to conceptualize Max's presenting problem and other clinically relevant factors. Finally, I will offer a MI/B-Well treatment plan for Max as a model.

Background of Motivational Interviewing (MI)

Origins

Addiction counseling has the unique characteristic of often treating clients who do not choose to come to counseling. They tend to come because they have been given an ultimatum by someone or something else—a spouse, their job, the criminal justice system, to keep their children, etc. Often there is already resistance to being in counseling. The therapeutic modalities and techniques that were initially used in addiction counseling frequently increased the resistance. Recidivism rates in addiction counseling are high. Individuals who relapse and return to drug and alcohol use are comparable to those with other chronic diseases, including hypertension and diabetes, with an estimated 40-60% of individuals relapsing while in recovery (National Institute on Drug Abuse [NIDA], 2020). The physical and psychological addictive properties of drugs along with therapeutic modalities that alienated clients could have a strong effect on recidivism as well as "resistance."

MI is a technique in which you become a helper in the change process and express acceptance of your client. It is a way to interact with clients, not merely as an adjunct to other therapeutic approaches, but as a style of counseling that can help resolve the ambivalence that prevents clients from realizing personal goals. It interweaves or integrates with the helping techniques to strengthen them.

When it was first created three decades ago, MI mostly focused on working with individuals dealing with addiction and the use of drugs and alcohol. It has now been applied to a variety of other areas including eating disorders, obesity, and other health issues that a person desires to change (Bonder & Mantler, 2015; Cushing et al., 2014; David et al., 2016). Research has shown that

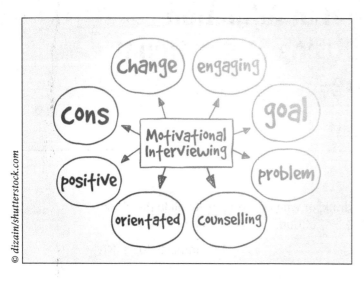

motivation-enhancing approaches that include MI are correlated with increased participation in treatment and positive treatment outcomes (Miller & Rollnick, 2013). This research has reported increased referrals to treatment, reductions in consumption and use, increased abstinence rates, and more positive social adjustment. A positive attitude toward and a commitment to change are also associated with positive treatment outcomes (Miller & Rollnick, 2004). MI's main focus is on behavioral and lifestyle change, and it works well when applied to what people value.

View of Human Nature

How and why people act the way that they do has long been an area of consideration in counseling. Understanding this construct assists in helping others to be able to change. Our reasons for acting or behaving can be located in biological origins, while others have personal, emotional, and social origins. It is an individual's instinct for survival to be motivated to obtain food, water, shelter, and procreation. An individual's behavior is also guided by a desire for social acceptance and approval, the need to succeed, and the motivation to be risk-avoidant or to take risks, to name a few (Morsella et al., 2009).

View of Change

When our behavior no longer works for us to obtain what we need to survive, or to be rewarded, we then become more motivated to make a change. In general, a person is willing to change when what they value has changed (Wagner & Sanchez, 2002), or they align their current values with their behaviors. MI is a way of understanding and conceptualizing ambivalence and motivation and facilitating behavior change to develop treatment interventions that are tailored to the needs of individual clients. All three of these (e.g., ambivalence, motivation, and facilitating behavior) need to be considered to produce an effective treatment plan for the client.

Let's start with ambivalence. Individuals with problem behaviors are usually aware of the dangers of the behavior(s) but still engage in them. They may want to stop, but at the same time, they do not want to. These conflicting emotions are characterized as ambivalence, and they are natural, regardless of a person's state of readiness. It is important to understand and accept a client's ambivalence because ambivalence is often the central problem—and lack of motivation is a manifestation of this ambivalence (Miller & Rollnick, 2013). If the counselor interprets ambivalence as denial or resistance, friction between the client and counselor tends to occur.

In MI, motivation is not defined as something that one has but rather, as something done— an action (Rollnick & Miller, 1995). Motivation is seen as purposeful, intentional, and positive. It is directed toward the best interests of the self and others. Miller and Rollnick (2013) also see motivation as an interpersonal process. They point out that this goes against the popular notion that motivation in individuals is internal, a personal characteristic or trait. Instead, it can be influenced by and developed out of interpersonal interaction and context. It has often been assumed that when individuals come into counseling that they are motivated to change. This is not always the case. It is then thought that when a client does not improve in counseling, they are not motivated. Miller and Rollnick (2013) suggest that both the difficulty and the solution for this may be in the interpersonal context between the client and counselor. Ultimately, motivation is the probability that a person will enter into, continue, and adhere to a specific change strategy.

© Trueffelpix/shutterstock.com

Finally, we consider facilitating behavior change. The heart of MI is defined by a specific clinical approach that builds this interpersonal spirit. Included in this is a collaboration between the client and counselor (partnership), evoking or drawing out the client (evocation), compassion, and acceptance of the client (Miller & Rollnick, 2013) (Figure 1).

When developing a partnership with a client, both rapport and trust are facilitated in the helping relationship (Miller & Rollnick, 2013). This does not mean that the counselor will agree with the client on the nature of the problem or the steps that the client wants to take to resolve the problem. The counselor focuses on developing the therapeutic relationship by understanding the client and seeing them as a co-expert.

FIGURE 1 The Motivational Interviewing Spirit

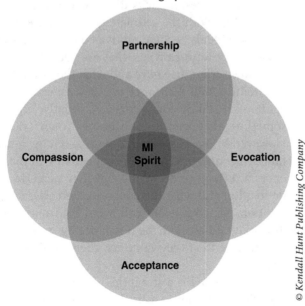

© Kendall Hunt Publishing Company

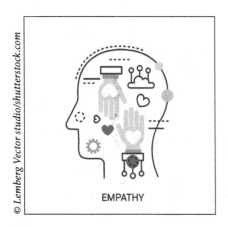

EMPATHY

Acceptance is related to partnership. Partnership recognizes the client as a co-expert while acceptance adds in the aspects of absolute worth, affirmation, autonomy, and accurate empathy (Miller & Rollnick, 2013). Absolute worth includes appreciating the worth of each individual. Accurate empathy integrates in the client's worldview. Autonomy is honoring a client's right and ability at self-direction. Affirmation recognizes the client's strengths and efforts. These all increase the client's self-efficacy, empower the client, and give the client the responsibility.

Evoking or drawing out the client includes not imposing values on the client but instead including the client's values to guide the counseling (Miller & Rollnick, 2013). In MI, the counselor draws out the client's thoughts and values instead of imposing the counselor's values or opinions on the client. Lasting change is more likely to occur when the client discovers their reasons or motivation to change. The counselor's task is to "evoke" from the client their reasons and motivation to change along with what skills the individual has to move them toward taking action.

Compassion relates to the underlying spirit of MI (Miller & Rollnick, 2013). This is described as an intentional responsibility and desire to engage in treatment for the welfare and best interests of the client.

Four General Principles of MI. Four general principles are used in MI that assist a counselor to facilitate change with their clients. These are expressing empathy, developing discrepancy, rolling with resistance, and supporting self-efficacy (Miller & Rollnick, 2013).

Being able to express empathy provides the client with the feeling that the counselor understands them. The client feels heard and understood. It is essential that the counselor expresses accurate empathy, which includes both an active interest in their client and seeking to understand the client's inner world (Miller & Rollnick, 2013). Empathy is not sympathy or merely identifying with the client's story.

Next is developing discrepancy. When hearing the client, the counselor is able to assist the client to see the difference between what they are doing and their values. By noting the difference between

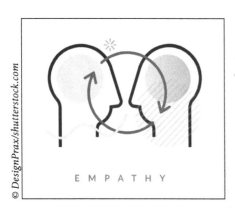

EMPATHY

action and values, it elicits discrepancy; the client's behaviors do not align with the ultimate goals that are important/valuable. Individuals become motivated to change when there is a discrepancy between where they are and where they want to be or between what they have and what they want to have.

Rolling with resistance is a key aspect of MI. Resistance is often viewed by counselors as a negative characteristic and something that needs to be squashed when it occurs in clients. However, MI harnesses this and utilizes it in counseling. Resistance in counseling generally happens when the client experiences a difference between what they perceive as the answer or solution and what the counselor perceives as the answer or solution. MI counselors will avoid confronting clients to not cause or amplify this resistance. They will work to de-escalate the resistance by "rolling" with it. Since MI focuses on having the client define the issue and what they value and then develop alternative solutions, it allows little room for the client to resist.

Finally, there is supporting self-efficacy. Because MI is a strengths-based approach, the counselor believes the client has the power to change. The counselor instills this belief in the client to increase their motivation. This is done through various techniques in MI, but the majority of these fall under the client speaking about or exploring how and why they can be successful with changing. Some of the main techniques are explained by the acronym OARS: Open Questions (asking for examples or to elaborate), Affirm (strengths and ability), Reflect (self-confidence), and Summarize (reasons for optimism of change).

Christian Integration Perspective
Christian Integration

Spiritual formation is a significant task of the Christian counselor. As a Christian counselor, I needed to have a clear understanding of how to define my identity as a Christian counselor in such a way that the two were not separate—not being a Christian *or* a counselor but being a Christian *and* a counselor.

In becoming a Christian counselor, I integrated my counseling approach with my biblical worldview. For example, the role of the Christian concept of agape love is critical in the counseling change process. This is utilized in MI through the aspect of expressed empathy (Miller & Rollnick, 2002). Similarly, the consistent concept of hope is an important biblical concept. Isaiah 30:31 states, "But those who *hope* in the LORD will renew their strength. They will soar on wings like eagles; they will run and not grow weary, they will walk and not be faint" (*New International Bible*, 1978/2011). Yahne and Miller (1999) examined the biblically consistent aspect of hope in relation to motivation and change, which are the two main components of MI. They understand that hope is a driving force for motivation and facilitating behavior change.

In reviewing scripture and applying it to counseling, I realized that, as a MI counselor, I was engaging in a deep form of empathy, or agape. This connected to 2 Corinthians 5:14-15 when Paul offered:

> For Christ's love compels us, because we are convinced that one died for all, and therefore all died. And he died for all, that those who live should no longer live for themselves but for him who died for them and was raised again. (*New International Bible*, 1978/2011)

This form of 'motivational agape love' is also affirmed in the apostle Paul's classic love pericope, 1 Corinthians 13.

Besides affirming empathy biblically, Jesus offers a potential example of the MI process when speaking with the Samaritan woman (*New International Bible*, 1978/2011, John 4:1-26). In this example, it is evident that Jesus demonstrated deep, loving acceptance and expressed empathy during their conversation. His approach was respectful, and he remained non-judgmental even when he was talking about her previous husbands. These are all traits of a good therapist and emphasize characteristics of a MI therapist. By experiencing this acceptance (agape love), she was empowered to connect on a deeper level with him, not resist him, and to see herself more clearly. Once the equivalent of a therapeutic relationship was created, Jesus developed discrepancy by mentioning what she valued in her life—ancestor Jacob, worshipping the one true God, a well

of continuous life-giving water, and eternal life. He then noted the discrepancy of her husband(s), her shameful reality, and her current problem.

This resulted in her being able to analyze for herself the discrepancy between her life predicament and her core values and goals. It is also noticeable here that she was ambivalent about changing. This may have been what caused her to move the subject of the conversation to the place of worship. Jesus could have argued with her, but he did not. Instead, he rolled with her resistance or defensiveness. He continued to be respectful. He did not force his viewpoint on her but instead invited her to consider a new perspective on life. By enhancing her confidence in her ability to handle her problems and commit to change, he supported self-efficacy. Finally, he encouraged her to turn to him as the Messiah.

To summarize, the counseling skills or characteristics seen in this biblical example that are essential for a Christian counselor are loving acceptance and respect, expressing empathy, being non-judgmental, developing discrepancy, rolling with resistance, and supporting self-efficacy. All of which are in connection with MI.

Denominational Influence

Another part of my integration approach is the influence of my specific denomination. As an evangelical Baptist, certain biblical doctrines regulate my Christian worldview. As a conservative evangelical, I hold to the following Christian beliefs: 1) All of the parts of the thirty-nine books of the Old Testament and twenty-seven books of the New Testament are the only inspired Word of God, and 2) the Bible is truth without any mixture of error. I believe that Jesus Christ is the eternal Son of God, that He was born both fully God and man, and that He came to die for the sin of the world. I also believe that salvation is the free gift of God's grace, based entirely on the merit of Christ's shed blood, and not based on human merit or works.

I also believe that Adam and Eve were created in innocence under the laws of their Maker, but by voluntary transgression, Adam fell from his sinless and happy estate. Adam represented all humanity,

and all humanity sinned in Adam. As a result, all men and women are totally depraved, are partakers of Adam's fallen nature, and are sinners by nature and conduct. Therefore, all are under just condemnation without defense or excuse.

Finally, I believe that we should display love for others. This should not only be toward fellow believers of the Lord, but also toward those who are not believers, those who oppose us, and those who engage in sinful actions and behaviors. When faced with those who oppose us, we should react graciously, gently, patiently, prayerfully, and humbly. God does not permit the stirring up of discord or conflict. He also does not sanction the taking of revenge or the threat or use of violence as a means of resolving personal conflict or obtaining personal justice. While our Lord and Savior directs us to abhor sinful behaviors, we are to pray for and love any person who participates in such sinful actions (*New International Bible*, 1978/2011, John 13:34-35; Leviticus 19:18; Luke 6:31; Matthew 5:44-48; Philippians 2:2-4; Romans 12:9-10; 17-21; 13:8-10; Titus 3:2; 1 John 3:17-18; 2 Timothy 2:24-26).

A Case Study: Max

A male client, Max, presents for addiction counseling. Max is 45 years of age and divorced. His wife left him two years ago after asking him for several years to stop drinking, and he has now been divorced for a year. Max reports that he has two children—a daughter, age 20, and a son, age 15. His wife has sole custody, but he does have visitation. His daughter is in college and his son is in high school. He reports that he has minimal contact with them. At the most, he will talk to them once or twice a month by phone, and once a month he will see them. He noted his son and his daughter offered to spend more time with him if he stopped drinking. Max offered that he thinks they are ashamed of him and that he can't blame them. He perceives himself as a failure as a husband and a father. Max desires to see his children again regularly, at least weekly, and this is a motivation for seeking counseling.

Max reports that he is drinking one and a half to two six-packs of beer a day. At least twice a week he will go out with some male friends to a sports bar and consumes a six-pack of beer and three or four shots of whiskey. He often tells himself when he goes out with his friends that he will only have a few beers, but most of the time, he drinks much more than intended. Currently, Max has to drink quite a bit more to obtain the same effect from alcohol. He also notes that he has had a desire to reduce drinking but has not been able to do this successfully. Max reports that he has tried at least four times to stop drinking but has only been able to go for one to one and a half days without drinking any alcohol. The last time he tried to stop drinking was a month ago, and when he did, he got "the shakes," which did not stop until he drank alcohol. Max also reports that when he doesn't drink, he craves or desires it and has found himself driving during a snowstorm to get alcohol.

His first alcoholic drink was at the age of 19, consuming one or two 12 oz. beers once or twice a week; but this moderation changed 8 years ago. He explained that he started drinking every day after he lost his brother, who he considered his best friend, in a car accident.

When it comes to his job as a foreman on a construction site, he reports that he has gotten to work late due to waking up hung over. Due to this, he has been written up by his boss. He also offers that since he is the foreman, he can drink some alcohol during the day as he keeps the beer in his cooler. The client shares that he never feels drunk, but it helps him to not get "the shakes." Max did report that he has operated heavy machinery after drinking. He has concerns that he may lose his job due to these issues. Max notes that this would upset him immensely because he would not be able to pay child support for his son or college tuition for his daughter. He also explains that he thinks it is irresponsible to not take care of himself and to become a burden on society. He shares that this job pays well and provides him with benefits such as health insurance.

The client appears clean but disheveled during the interview. He does not report any depressive symptoms, anxious symptoms, or homicidal or suicidal ideations. The client is alert and oriented times four (i.e., person, place, time, event). He does not appear to be intoxicated and shares that other than one beer when he woke up that morning, he has not had anything else to drink that day.

Max explains that he was brought up in church and that he is Baptist by faith. He shares that he has accepted Jesus Christ as his Savior and that this is a foundational aspect of his life. He notes that he does make it to church most Sundays, but there have been more and more misses because he is hung over. Max reports that he has support through a men's Bible study group at church and that he enjoys their company and fellowship when he is sober. He believes if the men in his group knew about his drinking problem that they would not be as accepting of him. He thinks he is a "bad" Christian because he doesn't have enough willpower to stop drinking on his own. Max notes that he has a strong desire to more fully develop his relationship with the Lord.

During the interview Max is asked about his strengths, using the lens of the B-Well model's six facets. The first strength he notes is his love for his children. He also offers that although he has lost a great deal in his life including his family, he has kept going. Max recognizes that he has been able to maintain employment and take care of his own needs up to this point. He acknowledges that his faith in God is a strength, as is having the men's group that provides positive support.

Max would meet the criteria for a diagnosis of alcohol use disorder (AUD), severe, as he meets more than six of the criteria for this disorder. Max notes that there is a persistent desire and unsuccessful efforts to cut down or control alcohol use. He also reports that he has had cravings to use alcohol. He states that his alcohol use, at times, has resulted in failure to fulfill his major obligations. Max shares that his use negatively impacts important interpersonal relationships and social activities. He reports using alcohol in situations that are physically hazardous. Both tolerance and withdrawal are noted in what he has shared.

Applying the B-Well Model Using Motivational Interviewing

As offered in Chapter 5, case conceptualization is the process of "explaining" the client's problems and offering their assets, in this case, using MI within the B-Well model. The six facets of the B-Well model (Heart, Mind, Strength, Soul, Neighbor, and Society) will be the guide in examining the factors driving Max's problems.

During the assessment, the task in MI is to help the client focus on how their behavior conflicts with their values and goals. The MI counselor assists the client to narrow their general concerns to specific changes. This is done by eliciting the client's motivation for change and by exploring the discrepancy between what the client values and his current behavior.

MI, a person-centered theory, becomes even more enhanced when fleshed out by the B-Well model. This assists in identifying the client's resources during case conceptualization and applying them in treatment planning. By utilizing this approach, we can categorize the client's values and motivating factors based on what is primary. Max has identified what he values, which will assist in motivating himself to achieve his goals. He has already begun to take action by coming in to see a counselor. Below, you will find potential problems and assets by facet.

Heart

Max noted that he becomes upset at the impact his drinking has had on his relationships with his children. He shared about fear over the possibility of losing his job due to his drinking. By integrating MI, there is a discrepancy between what the client values and his actions. While he has told the counselor that he values and is motivated by his love for his children, he has not been able to have a satisfactory relationship with them. This is something that he desires to change.

Mind

From a MI lens, Max shared that his motivation is affected by the thought that he has tried before to stop drinking but that he has not been able to do this successfully. This has affected his self-efficacy and makes him question whether he will be able to this time. He has reported that one of the reasons he wants to keep his job is to be able to care for himself and not become a burden on society. He values his ability to maintain employment and is motivated to continue this, and he is oriented times four (i.e., person, place, time, event).

 ### Strength

Max has increased his weekly consumption of alcohol to daily—at least one and a half to two six-packs a day and more on weekends. He has developed a tolerance for it and when not drinking, he has displayed some withdrawal symptoms including "the shakes." This is significant as withdrawal symptoms can be life-threatening. He is also drinking on the job and abusing his authority as a foreman. Assets for Max include that he is currently sober and is not suicidal or homicidal. Max is not currently reporting any depressive or anxious physical symptoms. He also has the physical capacity for his job as a foreman, does not have any disabilities, and is not chronically ill.

 ### Soul

He reported that he thinks he is a "bad" Christian because he does not have enough willpower to stop drinking on his own. From a MI perspective, this is another discrepancy between what he values and his behavior. He values his relationship with his Lord and Savior. Max noted that he has a strong desire to more fully develop his relationship with the Lord as accepting Jesus Christ as his Savior is a foundational part of who he is.

 ### Neighbor

AUD has affected his relationship with his children, cost him his marriage, affected his work, and potentially impacted his relationship with his men's Bible study group. He noted that he thinks the men in his Bible study group would not accept him if they knew that he drank. By applying the MI lens of what a client values, we see a discrepancy between the client's goals and his behavior. An asset is that Max has shared that he values his relationship with his children and desires to maintain his employment. Max values and is motivated by his relationships with the men in his Bible study group as well. These relationships may help Max align his behaviors with his values.

 ### Society

There are several potential Society influences. Max is a divorced man. There continues to be a societal stigma from some that divorce equates to failure. He often omits this detail about himself due to concern he will be judged. He would be considered, by many, to be "an alcoholic," which carries a potential stigma. Viewing himself as a failure and the potential stigma associated with being "an alcoholic" may affect his motivation. These factors could impact his self-efficacy. One Society aspect that is beneficial to Max is his ability to have a full-time job with benefits. Max has advantages for his position as a construction foreman based on his gender and due to his geographic location in an area that is currently experiencing a significant increase in construction.

B-Well Treatment Plan

When creating the treatment plan for Max using the B-Well model and MI, an opportunity is provided for a unique and dynamic approach to recovery. The B-Well model examines the client's values through the lens of Heart, Mind, Strength, Soul, Neighbor, and Society along with integrating key aspects of MI. By applying the B-Well model, a more dynamic, individualized, and holistic understanding of the client's problems, strengths, and assets will be developed.

In MI, the client's motivation is targeted by the counselor. When applying the spirit of MI, the counselor avoids an authoritarian stance. They will respect Max's autonomy by recognizing that the decision to change his drinking is his choice. The counselor will elicit reasons for change from Max, rather than advising or informing him of the reasons he should change his drinking. The counselor will work on understanding Max's ambivalence by exploring the pros and cons of continuing to drink alcohol. Together, Max and the counselor will then work on resolving this ambivalence by connecting his values with motivation to facilitate behavioral changes.

For example, drinking has negatively affected Max's values about being a loving father and being proud of being able to provide for his children. A discussion of how continuing to drink (maintaining the status quo) will impact his goal to have a good relationship with his children may be the focus. The counselor would emphasize that the decision to change is up to him; however, the counselor would work with Max to increase his confidence that he can change (self-efficacy).

When examining Max's presenting problem, the focus of treatment is alcohol use disorder (AUD), severe. The treatment plan (see Table 1) will be addressing this main concern using MI interventions as well as the client's values to create motivation to obtain abstinence. When creating interventions and objectives, I aim to apply, when possible, each facet of the B-Well model (Heart, Mind, Strength, Soul, Neighbor, and Society). In the treatment plan, to assist the reader, it will be noted where each facet occurs. In this plan, there will be an emphasis on the Heart facet as MI focuses on what the client values to motivate change. As Strength and Mind facets also affect this client's values, these will also be addressed in treatment.

TABLE 1 Recommended Goals, Objectives, and Interventions

Problem	Goal	Objective	Intervention
Alcohol Use Disorder, Severe	The client will increase days of abstinence from 0 per week to 3 per week.	Objective 1 – The client, in session, will identify triggers and strategies for avoiding or coping based on values. [Heart]	• Psychoeducation • Enhancing efficacy • Positive affirmations • Eliciting change talk • Values assessment • Open-ended questions
		Objective 2 – The client will explore motivators for change and identify areas of increased confidence for change. [Heart]	• Enhancing efficacy • Rolling with resistance • Positive affirmations • Open-ended questions
		Objective 3 – The client will develop skills for emotional regulation and healthy coping. [Heart]	• Skills coaching • Role-playing
		Objective 4 – The client, in session, will develop a schedule to support sobriety. [Mind and Strength]	• Eliciting change talk • Rolling with resistance • Pros and cons list

Problem	Goal	Objective	Intervention
		Objective 5 – The client will identify barriers to sobriety and problem-solving solutions for these. [Mind]	• Thought log • Journaling • Open-ended questions
		Objective 6 – The client will be referred and evaluated for alcohol detoxification. [Strength]	• Referral to Detoxification Center
		Objective 7 – The client will identify, reach out to, and interact with key individuals for social support aiding in the improvement of self-efficacy and abstinence. [Social, Neighbor]	• Small group Bible study • Alcoholics Anonymous
		Objective 8 – The client will identify and continue to develop key spiritual disciplines based on his understanding of his Christian beliefs as an aid to remaining abstinent. [Soul]	• Bible • Prayer • Silence • Solitude • Pastoral care • Bible study

Summary

This chapter provided an overview of how to meld the B-Well model with Motivational Interviewing (MI) to create a robust modality for an individual dealing with an addiction. It integrates the Mind, Heart, Strength, Soul, Neighbor, and Society with the main concepts of MI, which include what a client values, what motivates them, and facilitating behavior changes. From this, a therapist can assess, diagnose, develop a case conceptualization, and create a treatment plan that is holistic and individualized.

References

Bonder, R., & Mantler, T. (2015). The efficacy of motivational interviewing and adapted motivational interviewing as an eating disorder intervention: A scoping review. *Western Undergraduate Research Journal: Health and Natural Sciences, 5*. 1-10. https://doi.org/10.5206/wurjhns.2014-15.8

Cushing, C. C., Jensen, C. D., Miller, M. B., & Leffingwell, T. R. (2014). Meta-analysis of motivational interviewing for adolescent health behavior: Efficacy beyond substance use. *Journal of Consulting and Clinical Psychology, 82*(6), 1212-1218. https://doi.org/10.1037/a0036912

David, L. A., Sockalingam, S., Wnuk, S., & Cassin, S. E. (2016). A pilot randomized controlled trial examining the feasibility, acceptability, and efficacy of adapted motivational interviewing for post-operative bariatric surgery patients. *Eating Behaviors, 22*, 87-92. https://doi.org/10.1016/j.eatbeh.2016.03.030

Miller, W. R., & Rollnick, S. (2002). *Preparing people for change* (2nd ed.). Guilford Press.

Miller, W. R., & Rollnick, S. (2004). Talking oneself into change: Motivational interviewing, stages of change, and therapeutic process. *Journal of Cognitive Psychotherapy: An International Quarterly, 18*(4), 299-308. https://doi.org/10.1891/jcop.18.4.299.64003

Miller, W. R., & Rollnick, S. (2013). *Helping people change* (3rd ed.). Guilford Press.

Morsella, E., Bargh, J. A., & Gollwitzer, P. M. (Eds.). (2009). *Oxford handbook of human action.* Oxford University Press.

National Institute on Drug Abuse (NIDA). (2020, June). *Drugs, brains, and behavior: The science of addiction.* U.S. Department of Health and Human Services. https://nida.nih.gov/sites/default/files/soa.pdf

New International Bible. (2011). The NIV Bible. https://www.thenivbible.com (Original work published 1978)

Rollnick, S., & Miller, W. R. (1995). What is motivational interviewing? *Behavioural and Cognitive Psychotherapy, 23*, 325-334. https://doi.org/10.1017/S135246580001643X

Wagner, C. C., & Sanchez, F. P. (2002). The role of values in motivational interviewing.

In W. R. Miller & S. Rollnick's (Eds.), *Motivational interviewing: Preparing people for change* (2nd ed., pp. 284-298). The Guilford Press.

Yahne, C. E., & Miller, W. R. (1999). Evoking hope. In W. R. Miller (Ed.), *Integrating spirituality into treatment: Resources for practitioners* (pp. 217-233). American Psychological Association.

CHAPTER 16

B-Well Model in Pastoral Counseling

John A. King

> "The thief comes only to steal and kill and destroy; I have come that they may have life, and have it to the full."
>
> — John 10:10 (NIV)

As we begin this chapter, it is important to note that for many professing Christians, faith in Christ often meant being saved from something, or at least having their sins forgiven and saved from eternal punishment. While this is true, the saving work of Jesus is much, much more than a simple sacrificial transaction. This passage from John 10:10b shows that Jesus came to not only deliver us into heaven but also to "give them a rich and satisfying life" (*New Living Translation*, 1996/2015). It is reasonable that this kind of life that Jesus offers is not just for tomorrow (eternity) but also for today. The B-Well model gives all of us who walk alongside broken and hurting people a model for healing and hope. It is with this backdrop that we look at how pastoral counseling can use this model to help others experience a more fully abundant life.

Background of Pastoral Counseling

Pastoral counseling is a form of counseling that has its roots in Christian thought. Hunter (2005) writes that the distinguishing feature between pastoral counseling and more traditional psychotherapy is the role and understanding of the counselor and their expression of the pastoral relationship. In other words, pastoral counselors generally have a dual identity of both pastoral and counselor roles.

Most pastoral counselors often have specialized training in both counseling and theology/ministry. Because of the need for pastors to more effectively shepherd and care for their congregations well, professionals in church ministry contexts and psychology circles began to discuss and research ways to integrate. Because of this need, a few organizations have sprung up in the past few decades that have focused on the integration of Christian theology/faith and counseling, including the American Association of Christian Counseling (AACC) and the Christian Association for Psychological Studies (CAPS). These organizations are friendly to pastoral counselors who work in settings both inside and outside the church.

© MIA Studio/shutterstock.com

One of the significant influences in pastoral counseling occurred in the latter part of the 20th century by such noted authors, pastors, and psychologists as Gary Collins (2006), Jay Adams (1986), James Dobson (1970), David Benner (2003), Larry Crab (1975), and Neil T. Anderson (2019). Many of these Christian authors and pastors had many points of disagreement, yet the one thing that tied these people together was that they found ways of relating the disciplines of counseling, theology, and pastoral care together. One of the outgrowths of this integration resulted in the proliferation of counseling training programs that were centered in seminaries that traditionally prepared pastors and missionaries. The idea of Christian counseling became much more acceptable in the Church because of the work of these early leaders. From my perspective, this has been good for the counseling profession because it helped to change the function of practical ministry in the local church. With the expansion of counselor licensure laws in every state in the U.S., and as the counseling profession has grown and matured, there is still much room for pastoral counselors and their meaningful service both inside and outside the church walls.

Christian Integration Perspective

My Christian Integration Approach

As a pastor for over two decades, and as a mental health counselor and counselor educator, I operate out of a background of many authors and influences. I am deeply committed to the integration of Christian faith and theology in counseling. While I am committed to finding several ways to express this integration approach (Entwistle, 2015; Hawkins & Clinton, 2015; Neff & McMinn, 2020; Wardle, 2003), the bottom line for me is that I see how Christ offers hope for a broken world. He is first in my mind

as I care for people in a congregational setting. At the same time, I see the benefit of operating under a model of the integration of Christian theology and counseling. I have found that the Allies model from Entwistle (2015) is the most helpful. Entwistle provides a good and helpful balance of incorporating the best counseling theories with solid Christian theology. The overarching idea of this model of integration is that God is sovereign over all things and that He is the source of all Truth. According to Entwistle (2015), this truth can be found in studying and understanding the Word of God and the Works of God, much in the way a Christian physician can see their role as an agent of healing.

In one of the most poignant scenes of Jesus' life, he entered the local synagogue in Nazareth where he was brought up as a boy. The scroll of the prophet Isaiah was handed to him to read, and he started reading the following words that were 600-700 years old at the time:

> The Spirit of the Sovereign Lord is on me,
> because the Lord has anointed me to proclaim good news to the poor.
> He has sent me to bind up the brokenhearted,
> to proclaim freedom for the captives and release from darkness for the prisoners,
> to proclaim the year of the Lord's favor and the day of vengeance of our God,
> to comfort all who mourn, and provide for those who grieve in Zion—
> to bestow on them a crown of beauty instead of ashes,
> the oil of joy instead of mourning, and a garment of praise instead of a spirit of despair.
> They will be called oaks of righteousness, a planting of the Lord for the display of his splendor.
> (*New International Bible*, 1978/2011, Isaiah 61:1-3)

Luke 4 then records that he rolled up the scroll and sat down. Everyone's eyes were fixed upon him, and he said, "Today this scripture is fulfilled in your hearing" (Luke 4:21). As we look at those powerful words that were written many, many centuries ago, we see the mission of Jesus more clearly in how he lived his earthly life. These are, after all, the very first words he is recorded as saying in his three years of ministry; and if we accept Jesus' mission from Isaiah 61 as our mission, then we can focus on bringing good news to those who are poor in spirit. We can comfort people who mourn; we can bind up the brokenhearted and bring freedom to the captives and those in prison.

This is the Church's calling.

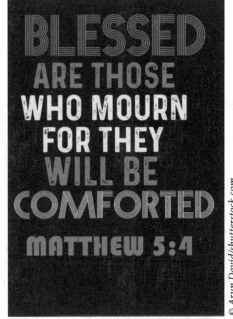

Denominational Influence

The next logical question is, "How can pastors and pastoral counselors live out these words?" In the Anabaptist/Mennonite background of my childhood, I learned that to follow Christ, we need to do what he did. We need to follow the words of the Sermon on the Mount (*New International Bible*, 1978/2011, Matthew 5-7) literally. We follow Jesus and look to his example. So, we feed people; we love enemies; we bring hope to broken people; we pray for and encourage those who are in need; and we view the whole person rather than just focusing on right thinking and right theology. The book of James (*New International Bible*, 1978/2011) was a favorite epistle in the New Testament in my church. In Chapter 2, we read:

> What good is it, my brothers and sisters, if someone claims to have faith but has no deeds? Can such faith save them? Suppose a brother or a sister is without clothes and daily food. If one of you says to them, "Go in peace; keep warm and well fed," but does nothing about their physical needs, what good is it? In the same way, faith by itself, if it is not accompanied by action, is dead. (James 2:14-17)

In this vein, the B-Well model is helpful in that it focuses on the whole of a person, rather than just right thinking or saying a prayer and accepting Jesus. While having the right theology and praying is important, it is not all that is important. God has so much more for us. Jesus has come so that we might live a full and abundant life (*New International Bible*, 1978/2011, John 10:10). So, to think more holistically, and to help facilitate lasting change in people, we can find ways of incorporating help and support in each of these six ways (Heart, Mind, Strength, Soul, Neighbor, and Society). Below is one example among many of how pastors and pastoral counselors can competently put together a game plan for people in the church who are struggling. For those of you who are pastors or pastoral counselors, perhaps you, too, could think about someone you are working with that could benefit from these six areas of focus.

A Case Study: Joe and Kristen

Joe (32) and Kristen (30) are a Caucasian couple that has been married for five years and have two young children: a three-year-old son, James, and a newborn little girl, Kylie, who is less than three months old. They come to you as a pastor/pastoral counselor because Kristen recently found some information on

her husband's cell phone that led her to believe that Joe was involved with another woman. Upon significant questioning, he finally came out and confessed to her that he was sending pictures to another woman (sexting) and that he had an ongoing struggle with pornography use since he was 12 years old.

Joe and Kristen are college educated. He has a degree in finance and accounting and is a CPA at a large firm in a neighboring city, while Kristen has a degree in elementary education and taught for a few years before she met and married Joe. When their first child was born three and a half years ago, she initially experienced some postpartum depression, but then she went back to teaching full-time after three months of maternity leave. Now that their second child has come, Joe and Kristen both agreed that it would be best for their family if she stayed home for a few years while their young children grow, and then, when they are both in elementary school, she would go back to teaching.

Joe and Kristen are both Christians. Kristen is the daughter of a pastor, and her childhood years were filled with attending church events and getting involved in the life of the church community. There was a season of pastoral ministry that was difficult for Kristen's family in her middle school years when the church board asked her father to leave. She was deeply hurt because of all the significant changes that happened in her life at that time. Five months later, her father found a new church at which to serve as pastor, and after a move during her eighth-grade year, she spent the next four years at a new church in a neighboring state. She was involved in youth ministry, and she had great friendships with people with whom she stays connected to this day.

Joe started to attend church in high school because some friends initially asked him to come to a youth event. Through the loving mentorship of some adult volunteers, Joe became a follower of Jesus and was baptized when he was a junior in high school. It was during his later high school years that he and Kristen started spending more time together, and they eventually started dating during his senior year of high school and her 10th-grade year. They continued their relationship through his first year of college but grew apart because his focus in life changed while she continued her high school experience. It was through a church service when they both were home during the holidays that they started dating again. She was 24, and he was 26. They were married a year later.

Kristen is now deeply wounded emotionally because of the recent revelation of his unfaithfulness to her. She is still suffering the effects of post-partum depression, and this revelation of her husband's secret behavior drives her into a deeper depression and pendulum swing of emotions. Sometimes she screams at him. Sometimes she cries, and sometimes she withdraws. She exhibits many of the stages of grief (Kübler-Ross & Kessler, 2005) in one conversation: shock, denial, anger, bargaining, and depression. She threatens to leave the marriage, and she has made plans for moving out with the two children to live at her parent's house. The only thing that is stopping her is how her meetings with you as the pastoral counselor go for the next two weeks. They both do not believe in doing secular counseling, but they are at the stage in their relationship where they do not see any hope for their marriage.

Applying the B-Well Model as a Pastoral Counselor

A lot is riding on this counseling work with Joe and Kristen: two young children need both of their parents, and there is a church community that looks up to them because of their involvement in the life of the church. If their marriage breaks apart, it could significantly impact the youth ministry where they are volunteers. It would also be significant emotionally for Kristen's father and mother because it would impact them on many levels including emotionally, spiritually, and relationally. So, as we navigate these issues in Joe and Kristen's marriage, let's think through the B-Well model's six facets to conceptualize what is happening here with this dear couple.

Heart

Proverbs 4:23 says, "Above all else, guard your heart, for everything you do flows from it" (*New International Bible*, 1978/2011). Our emotions, often referred to in scripture as the heart, play a big role in how we process information, as well as how we act and behave. As we look at the Heart of Joe and Kristen's situation, see if you can identify some ways how both process their feelings in healthy, and especially unhealthy, ways.

Joe undoubtedly feels a deep level of shame because of being caught in his addictive behavior. In the same way, Joe confesses to you as the counselor in an individual meeting that he almost feels relieved that he was finally caught by his wife. He had been struggling with his pornography addiction for many years, and until recently he was battling this addiction on his own, praying that God would deliver him. This recent battle was like other times in his past when he would engage in this battle on his own, only to relapse and go back to where he was after being clean for four or five months. The relief that Joe experienced follows in many ways what the Psalmist wrote:

> Blessed is the one whose transgressions are forgiven, whose sins are covered.
> Blessed is the one whose sin the LORD does not count against them and in whose spirit is no deceit. When I kept silent, my bones wasted away through my groaning all day long. For day and night your hand was heavy on me; my strength was sapped as in the heat of summer. Then I acknowledged my sin to you and did not cover up my iniquity. I said, "I will confess my transgressions to the LORD." And you forgave the guilt of my sin. (*New International Bible*, 1978/2011, Psalm 32:1-5)

Someone who is now in active recovery from pornography addiction once defined shame for me with an acronym: *Some Harmful, Awful Memories Emerge.* Brene Brown (2013) says this about shame: "I define shame as the intensely painful feeling or experience of believing that we are flawed and therefore unworthy of love and belonging—something

© Boris15/shutterstock.com

we've experienced, done, or failed to do makes us unworthy of connection" (para. 2). This describes Joe's feelings very accurately.

In a one-on-one meeting with you as a pastoral counselor, he divulges that when he was five years old, there were a series of incidents with an older neighbor that involved "sexual touching" that he only later found troublesome. You are the only person with whom he has ever shared this. The catalyst for his sexual addiction came when he was introduced to pornography by a friend at 12 years of age. His behavior triggered shameful memories of his past, and this paved the way for a full-fledged addiction to pornography, masturbation, and sexual experimentation. After struggling with his sexuality through his late teen years and into his early twenties, he thought that when he finally reconnected with Kristen that this was an opportunity for him to finally "get better" sexually. However, his shameful past and subsequent hiding kept him from honesty, vulnerability, and accountability with others.

Kristen also has some of her own heart issues. While she generally had an emotionally and spiritually healthy childhood, she shares with you individually that the incident where her dad got fired during her eighth-grade year was very traumatic for her. She would overhear her parents talking about how her dad and mom's minor personality deficits were singled out by the church leadership as inappropriate, which is what caused her dad to be fired from his position. She later learned that two subsequent pastors were let go after two or three years of service in that church congregation. Nevertheless, Kristen made a vow to herself during those days that she would never divulge any personal information to people in the church because they would likely turn on her.

This environment of secrecy continued into her adult years. There were a few incidents where she dated other young men in her college years, only to push away from them because they got too close to her emotional issues. When she met Joe again, he seemed like a perfect match. However, now that his sexual addiction has come to light, it not only threatens to tear apart their marriage, but it also threatens to cause their private life to become more public.

One more issue should be mentioned here in conceptualizing Kristen's situation, and that is the issue of postpartum depression. The depression that Kristen is experiencing seems to have come from a more organic/physical ailment, and so I will address this issue more in the Strength section. For now, suffice it to say that Kristen's postpartum depression could be impacting her overall outlook on her life situation. It is likely a lens that she is looking through in all aspects of her life.

As we think about Joe and Kristen and how they relate to one another, we can see how Joe's fear and shame interacted with Kristen's desire to control and make sure that her family maintained a good public persona. Everything in their home was fine on the surface if secrets were kept from one another. Unfortunately for them, their conflict now threatens their marriage. However, on the other hand, the revelation of this truth in their marriage can become an opportunity for both, if they decide to engage in pursuing health in their relationship with one another.

Mind

Romans 12:1-2 says,

> Therefore, I urge you, brothers and sisters, in view of God's mercy, to offer your bodies as a living sacrifice, holy and pleasing to God—this is your true and proper worship. Do not conform to the pattern of this world, *but be transformed by the renewing of your mind.* Then you will be able to test and approve what God's will is—his good, pleasing and perfect will. (*New International Bible*, 1978/2011, italics mine)

As we think about the minds of both Joe and Kristen, we encounter several false beliefs that they are carrying with them. Dr. Terry Wardle (2003) shares that people develop false beliefs out of wounding events in their lives. For example, the traumatic experiences they encounter in their childhood—if left unprocessed—can fester and develop into internalized belief patterns that contribute to significant emotional upheaval and dysfunctional behavior. To heal emotionally and spiritually, it is important to identify these faulty belief patterns and allow the presence of Christ into those harmful and wounding memories.

This is the case with both Joe and Kristen. Joe's internalized thought patterns can be described this way:

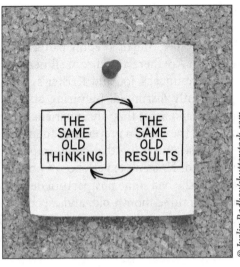

1. I can never share my struggles with others.
2. If I share my struggles with others, people will see me as weak.
3. My wife is not an emotionally safe person.
4. God disapproves of me and is looking over my shoulder to punish me.
5. I am damaged goods.

If you look at each of these false beliefs that Joe has internalized, we can see that they have come from deep wounds that he has experienced (Wardle, 2003). With #1 and #2, not only was the sexual abuse as a five-year-old painful, but he recalls in a meeting with you that when he talked about what he experienced with his mom, he remembers that his mom stopped him from talking about it. With thought pattern #3, early on in his second dating experience with Kristen, he remembers bringing up something personal to her that was unrelated to his sexual struggles. However, as she responded to him by making light of the issue, he had an internal emotional reaction that reminded him of his mother's reaction when he was five. Thought pattern #4, relates to the hiding of his struggles with pornography and how he remembered a time when his youth pastor spoke about the sinful behavior of pornography use but did not provide a way out for people who were struggling. Finally, thought pattern #5 was an all-encompassing view of himself based on all the other thought patterns; this one zapped him of all hope of ever getting better.

For Kristen, her primary false beliefs are as follows. Notice how her thought patterns compliment his:

1. Do not share your personal struggles because people will reject you or turn on you.
2. Keep family secrets within the family.
3. You need to go to church because that is what good Christians do.
4. The church is an emotionally unsafe place.

We will stop there, but I think you can get the idea. These four false beliefs have most of their origins within her childhood experiences as a pastor's daughter, particularly from all that happened in her eighth-grade year. The result is that she has enabled and created a family dynamic of secrecy and hiding, where no one is allowed to express weakness.

While we do not want to jump too far ahead in terms of Joe and Kristen's plan for treatment, we can understandably conceptualize their faulty thought patterns in light of scripture. In the Romans 12 passage mentioned above, Paul admonished the Church in Rome to be transformed by renewing their minds (*New International Bible*, 1978/2011, Romans 12:1-2). A significant part of their transformation will revolve around a change in the way they think. There will be more on that later, but suffice it to say for now that faulty thought patterns abound in each of them individually, as well as in their marriage.

Strength

As we think about and conceptualize Joe and Kristen's physiological health, we may be quick to dismiss this as not necessarily relevant to their situation. However, there are two things that would help a pastoral counselor as they use the B-Well model. First, Joe and Kristen are in crisis, and with any emotional and spiritual crisis, it is important to check in and ask some questions for each of them: 1) How are you feeling physically? 2) How many hours of sleep are you getting per night on average in the past week? 3) Have your eating or sleeping patterns changed recently? 4) How is this crisis impacting your physical health? 5) Are there any chronic illnesses that are contributing?

As we unpack Joe and Kristen's situation, one consideration is that their sleep patterns could be significantly disrupted. Inquiring about their sleep patterns, especially during a time of emotional upheaval like what they are experiencing, will aid in assessing their physical health. It is also very helpful to ask the Lord in prayer with them for good sleep in the midst of all that is happening in their lives.

The second thing that could impact Joe and Kristen's sense of wellness is to investigate the brief mention of Kristen's experience of postpartum depression. As her pastoral counselor, she shares with you that she had some postpartum depression after their first child was born. However, now that she is nursing a three-month-old, and especially since this sexual addiction has come out, it has exacerbated her depression to the point where it is mildly debilitating. A referral to a family physician or even a psychiatrist could be helpful for a season of time.

 Soul

Hebrews 13:4a says, "Marriage should be honored by all, and the marriage bed kept pure" (*New International Bible*, 1978/2011). It is important to address the area of spirituality for Joe and Kristen and how they would view their relationship with God and with each other. Joe and Kristen have attended their church congregation together since they got married, and though her father is the pastor of the church they attend, in many ways they have functioned as their own family unit. While many of the more senior members of the church know the relationship between Kristen and Joe and her parents, many of the newer attendees of the church are not acutely aware of this relationship. Kristen and Joe are actively involved in youth ministry while serving with the youth pastor in the church. They are also involved with a small group of youth leaders that meets on a regular basis. They have found a good, solid group of people with whom to do life. In many ways, there is a solid base of friendships through the youth ministry.

Now that Joe's struggles with sexuality have come out, this not only threatens to destroy their marriage, but also threatens to separate them from serving in youth ministry, and consequently, the small group they love. Upon further investigation, Kristen and Joe generally take time to read the Bible on a regular basis separately, but they don't often pray together, other than at mealtimes. Since Joe's addiction has come to light a week ago, both have been praying and spending a lot of time with the Lord in prayer and scripture reading.

So, to summarize, Joe and Kristen's spirituality is focused on the life of their church community, but their personal relationship with God has been somewhat stagnant since they were married. This lack of spiritual depth makes sense considering the secret sin that Joe has been struggling with for years. The Apostle Paul points us to the significance of sexual sin above all other sins when Paul writes: "Flee from sexual immorality. All other sins a person commits are outside the body, but whoever sins sexually, sins against their own body" (*New International Bible*, 1978/2011, 1 Corinthians 6:18). For a long time, Joe's relationship with God was distant because of his persistent sin, and the consequences were devastating for his soul. Psalm 32, which was previously mentioned in this chapter, highlights the distance from God that someone caught in the grips of sin experiences, particularly with sexual sin:

> Blessed is the one whose transgressions are forgiven, whose sins are covered.
> Blessed is the one whose sin the LORD does not count against them and in whose spirit is no deceit. When I kept silent, my bones wasted away through my groaning all day long. For day and night your hand was heavy on me; my strength was sapped as in the heat of summer (1978/2011, v. 1-4).

What scripture speaks to numerous times in both the Old and New Testaments is that faith in God is lived out in community where there is accountability, vulnerability, and transparency around issues of sin. This brings us to the next section of Neighbor.

Neighbor

"Brothers and sisters, if someone is caught in a sin, you who live by the Spirit should restore that person gently. But watch yourselves, or you also may be tempted. Carry each other's burdens, and in this way you will fulfill the law of Christ" (*New International Bible*, 1978/2011, Galatians 6:1-2). In the spirit of this passage from Galatians, followers of Jesus Christ form spirit-filled communities where there is meaningful fellowship and support. As mentioned in the Soul section, Kristen and Joe have significant friendship assets with people in the church. Most of their relationships are based in their church, but as mentioned previously, they do not have a lot of strong and deep accountability, vulnerability, and transparency in their lives. This carries into the relationships that they have with their friends. Much of this community involvement is focused on their volunteer youth ministry work. While youth work is good, the work itself has provided an opportunity to stay clear of other more personal issues.

This is similarly played out with their extended families. Joe's parents have been married for 30 years, and he has two other siblings—a brother and his wife and family who live two hours away in the same town as his parents and a sister who lives one time zone away. He recently reached out to his sister to tell her what happened, and she was much more gracious to him than he thought she would be. Kristen has a younger brother who moved away to college when he was 18, and now that he is 22 and graduating, he secured a job out of state. In short, all that is left for Joe and Kristen as family nearby are her parents.

Society

According to Proverbs 11:14, "Without good direction, people lose their way; the more wise counsel you follow, the better your chances" (*The Message Bible*, 2002). There are a lot of things going for Kristen and Joe in terms of the Society aspect of the B-Well model. Because of Joe's accounting job, he earns enough money for Kristen to not worry about finances. The downside of this is that she is home all day with the children, which can be frustrating for someone who was used to having adult conversations throughout the day. As far as opportunities for Joe and Kristen to get help, there are a few recovery support groups in the community, including a Celebrate Recovery group (https://www.

celebraterecovery.com/crgroups) that meets at a church on the other side of town. There is also a non-profit Christian counseling agency in the next town 20 minutes away that specializes in helping people with sexual addictions.

B-Well Action Plan

It should be noted that most pastoral counselors who work in a church setting do not necessarily develop a treatment plan for the parishioners they serve. Nevertheless, in situations like this, which can become very relationally complicated because of the potential for others to be involved and take sides, it is important to develop a plan for both the husband and the wife to be clear about the path forward. It is also wise for pastors and pastoral counselors to keep confidential notes of parishioners to keep a continuity of care. Kristen and Joe are experiencing significantly raw emotions, and in this case, the pastoral counselor's role is to help provide hope and a working plan. Fortunately, the B-Well model provides a good template for them to walk through. What follows is a working game plan for Kristen and Joe, covering all six areas where they can begin to reorient their lives.

1. Joe and Kristen will meet initially for a few weeks to establish boundaries for their marriage relationship, including living arrangements, cell phone usage, finances, care for the children, etc. (Heart, Mind, Soul)
2. Kristen and Joe will each find someone with whom they can connect as their primary counselor, whether it is a pastoral counselor or a licensed professional counselor. In this case, Joe is referred to the Christian counseling practice 20 minutes away that specializes in sexual addiction. Kristen will meet one-on-one with a pastor in the church who is skilled in supporting women who have been sexually betrayed. Joe and Kristen meet weekly with you for the first two months, and then step the marriage counseling back to once every two weeks while they continue their individual counseling. (Heart, Mind, Neighbor) Bear in mind that for people struggling with sexual addiction, the recovery process can take two years or longer (Carnes, 2001). For this reason, an outside referral might be necessary, depending on your time commitments.
3. As a pastoral counselor, you work with them to find an addiction recovery community that is very supportive of their Christian faith. They settle on attending a Celebrate Recovery (CR) group where each of them has a small group that supports them. (Society)
4. You work with Joe and Kristen to find three other men or women each who are emotionally healthy and understanding of the struggles of pornography addiction. (Neighbor) For Joe, one of these people is Tim, who attends the church and has had his own journey of emotional healing for the past 10 years, while the other two are part of the weekly CR group. For Kristen, one of the women is an older person in the church, Nancy, who walked through some marriage struggles in her earlier years; she was widowed a year ago after 52 years of marriage. One of the other two women she met at the CR small group, and the final person is a very close college friend who was in her wedding party. Joe has great respect for her. They start reaching out to these people when they struggle emotionally, rather than dumping their raw emotions onto their spouse.
5. You refer Kristen to a physician who prescribes a mild antidepressant for her postpartum depression as well as a prescription for a sleep aid to use only as needed. Both Joe and Kristen consulted with a nutritionist/wellness consultant who helped them find a natural sleep aid that they found helpful. (Strength)
6. They continue to attend church together, and at the conclusion of nearly every Sunday service for the next three months, they meet with you, Tim, and Nancy while you all pray together for the Lord to continue to heal their marriage. (Neighbor, Soul)

TABLE 1 Recommended Goals, Objectives, and Interventions

Problem	Goal	Objective	Intervention
Joe's struggle with pornography and personal wounds	Joe will stop/decrease pornography use.	Increase Accountability [Neighbor]	• Referral to an addiction recovery ministry • Referral to a counselor who specializes in sexual addiction
Marriage conflict	The couple will increase intimacy and trust in the marital relationship.	Establish healthy boundaries in their relationship [Neighbor]	• Couples counseling with you • Regular church attendance and prayer with mentors
Kristen's past individual struggles and postpartum depression	Kristen will gain clarity and healing from her past emotional wounds and decrease depressive symptoms.	Increase emotional and spiritual healing; Decrease postpartum depression symptoms [Heart, Soul, Mind, Strength]	• Individual counseling with pastor in the church • Referral to doctor to treat postpartum depression symptoms

Summary

Pastors and pastoral counselors are often the first lines of defense when Christian couples are in crisis. Couples are much more likely to seek out a pastor when they are struggling, as opposed to a licensed professional counselor or a marriage and family therapist. What is important to know is that for these couples and families, a pastor or pastoral counselor can make a significant difference in the trajectory of a marriage and family for generations. Their calming presence during a marriage crisis or in the presence of someone having a breakdown of some kind can be a difference-maker for the trajectory not only of that person's life but also for the lives of the children who are often caught in the crosshairs.

For pastors and pastoral counselors, the B-Well model offers a helpful guide for thinking through the various areas of a person's life. This model is especially helpful in that it keeps us from narrowly focusing on the spiritual and emotional aspects of a person's life only; it finds a way for the pastor/counselor to be a change agent for the person or the couple. From my perspective, the B-Well model is a great model to find ways of incorporating the person or couple into the life of the church, rather than ostracizing a person in their greatest moment of need. It takes a lot of emotional, spiritual, and relational health for a church to operate this way, but if the spiritual leaders are committed to walking with people caught in sin and brokenness, rather than ostracizing them, it allows for the Kingdom of God to expand in that congregation's community through the stories of changed lives.

References

Adams, J. (1986). *Competent to counsel*. Zondervan.

Anderson, N. T. (2019). *The bondage breaker: Overcoming negative thoughts, irrational feelings, habitual sins*. Harvest House Publishers.

Benner, D. (2003). *Strategic pastoral counseling: A short-term structured model* (2nd ed.). Baker Books.

Brown, B. (2013, January 15). *Shame vs. guilt*. Brene Brown. https://brenebrown.com/articles/2013/01/15/shame-v-guilt/#:~:text=I%20define%20shame%20as%20the,makes%20us%20unworthy%20of%20connection.

Carnes, P. (2001). *Out of the shadows: Understanding sexual addiction* (3rd ed.). Hazelden Publishing.

Collins, G. (2006). *Christian counseling, revised and updated* (3rd ed.). Thomas Nelson.

Crabb, L. (1975). *Basic principles of biblical counseling*. Faithwords.

Dobson, J. (1970). *Dare to discipline*. Tyndale House.

Entwistle, D. N. (2015). *Integrative approaches to psychology and Christianity: An introduction to worldview issues, philosophical foundations, and models of integration*. Cascade Books.

Hawkins, R., & Clinton, T. (2015). *The new Christian counselor: A fresh biblical & transformational approach*. Harvest House.

Hunter, R. J. (2005). *Pastoral counseling. Dictionary of pastoral care and counseling*. Abingdon Press.

Kübler-Ross, E., & Kessler, D. (2005). *On grief and grieving: Finding the meaning of grief through the five stages of loss*. Simon and Schuster.

Neff, M. A., & McMinn, M. (2020). *Embodying integration: A fresh look at Christianity in the therapy room*. InterVarsity Press.

New International Bible. (2011). The NIV Bible. https://www.thenivbible.com (Original work published 1978)

New Living Translation. (2015). New Living Translation. https://www.tyndale.com/nlt/ (Original work published 1996)

The Message Bible. (2002). The Message Bible Online. https://messagebible.com/read-the-message/
Wardle, T. (2003). *Healing care, healing prayer*. Leafwood Publishers.

CHAPTER 17

B-Well Model in Marriage and Family Counseling Using Structural Family Therapy

Shannon P. Warden

> "Let us not become weary in doing good, for at the proper time we will reap a harvest if we do not give up."
>
> — Galatians 6:9 (NIV)
>
> "Many families are discouraged and doubt their potential for change. But this is where you have to decide: 'Do I do nothing? Or do I do something?' Doing something—even making the smallest effort—is progress."
>
> — Gary Chapman & Shannon Warden

Structural Family Therapy (SFT) is a prominent, practical family systems approach to counseling with families. This chapter explores SFT's core tenets and interweaves principles from the B-Well model. My application of both SFT and B-Well is heavily influenced by my Christian worldview, and thus, I will share briefly about my religious affiliation and how I integrate Christian beliefs into my work as a counselor. Finally, an integrated application of SFT and B-Well will be demonstrated through the conceptualization of and treatment planning for the fictional Leone family.

Background of Structural Family Therapy (SFT)

Origins

In the 1960s, Salvador Minuchin and his psychiatry and social work colleagues at Wiltwyck School in New York recognized that traditional mental health therapies were ineffective with the school's residents (inner-city, poor, delinquent boys). Traditional psychotherapy focused solely on the individual client and often failed to take into account the client's social context. Out of context, a client's behavior tended to be misunderstood and pathologized. However, the Wiltwyck team's observations affirmed that the boys' behaviors, though socially problematic, made sense against the backdrop of their family subcultures

(Minuchin et al., 1967). Helping the boys change required that their families were helped to change. These discoveries and resulting strategies led to the development of SFT, which is an action-oriented, practical family systems approach that reflects its founder's (Minuchin) commitment to engaging families in meaningful ways that help raise their awareness of their ineffective patterns and replace those patterns with new, more effective ways of relating to one another.

Since the 1960s, like other leading family systems theories, SFT has flourished. Minuchin himself was an active practitioner and thought leader until his death in 2017 at age 97. A team of dedicated structural family therapists (SFTs) carries on his work and SFT training through the Minuchin Center for the Family. Researchers also continue to explore and advance the practice of SFT (Jimenez et al., 2019; Ma et al., 2020; Negash & Morgan, 2016; Tadros & Finney, 2018; Weaver et al., 2019).

View of Human Nature

The concept of structure is paramount when approaching family therapy from an SFT perspective. According to Napier and Whitaker (1978):

> Families come into therapy with their own structure, and tone, and rules. Their organization, their pattern, has been established over years of living, and it is extremely meaningful and very painful for them. They would not be in therapy if they were happy with it. (p. 11)

Minuchin said of families in therapy "… they've gotten stuck—stuck with a structure whose time has passed, and stuck with a story that doesn't work" (Minuchin & Nichols, 1993, p. 43).

Structure, as referred to in SFT, is more than the composition of a family; structure is how the family organizes itself and relates to one another in subsystems that comprise the whole family system. Among the possible subsystems are spouse, parent, sibling, parent-child, extended family, and blended family subsystems. "Subsystems in a family are aggregates of particular members who are in close relationship with each other … The affiliations can be both a source of strength and a generator of stress …" (Minuchin et al., 2014, p. 50). Ideally, to function optimally, family members should be valued and feel that they belong in the family; they should be supported in working through and adjusting to problems that naturally arise in life. The parents or parent (if a single parent) should lead by establishing and maintaining clear and appropriately flexible boundaries (not rigid or diffuse) between them and their children, such that children are supported in growing toward maturity with increasingly developmentally reasonable freedom but are not allowed to lead the family in place of the parent(s). If married or partnered, couples should attend to their spouse subsystem in healthy ways that allow it to be a source of refuge and strength against the many forces that naturally attack the family (Minuchin, 1974; Sells & Yarhouse, 2011). The same is true for single parents; they, too, should strive for health and wholeness so that they are best able to lead their family.

View of Change

From the start of counseling, SFTs observe key patterns in individual family members' ways of being, how members' ways of being influence and are influenced by other members' ways of being, and the overall sense of acceptance, or belongingness, that the family seems to feel together. In terms of observation, Minuchin said, "What I am always looking for is flexibility, complementarity, competition, empathy, hierarchy, chaos. Who starts talking? Is this the authority delegated to function in relation to outsiders? Who agrees with whom? Is there more support or more argument?" (Minuchin & Nichols, 1993, p. 45). These and many other patterns emerge quickly in therapy as SFTs actively engage with the family through genuine curiosity and transparent conversation about their interpersonal dynamics that are playing out in real time in a session. Whatever patterns manifest in a session are believed to be the family's typical "dance," or way of interacting with one another (Minuchin & Fishman, 1981). SFTs challenge the family system's established perspective of each family member's ways of being by observing and questioning the positive and negative effects of their patterns. In this way, SFT is not focused on individual behaviors but on the clarity, rigidity, or diffuseness of subsystem boundaries and the family system's overall verbal and nonverbal behaviors (Umbarger, 1983).

A common test of a family's boundaries and communication patterns happens as children age, requiring the various subsystems (i.e., spouse, parent, parent-child, sibling) to adapt accordingly (Fishman, 1993). One reason adapting is difficult can be that parents may not have prepared their children or otherwise may be reluctant to allow their children to take responsibility typical of the next stage of development. Children want and need to be able to step up to that next level of maturity, but they and their parents can become stuck in unhealthy battles for healthy control. Another of many reasons adapting to expected developmental changes can be difficult is that parents may see

in their children's behaviors their own negative characteristics (Chapman, 2010; Chapman & Warden, 2016) or past negative behaviors (Taibbi, 2015). Through SFT, families can gain clarity about how they are presently stuck, and rather than over-interpreting the past (Minuchin, 1974), SFTs can help them to engage with one another in new ways that open new possibilities for change.

Allowing an outsider access to their private family dance can be a vulnerable act for many families. An ongoing activity that helps reassure families and build trust in their therapist is the therapist's ongoing effort at joining with the family (Minuchin & Fishman, 1981). Joining means "tuning in to people and responding to the way they move you" (Minuchin & Nichols, 1993, p. 42). "One of our major tasks in therapy is to pay attention to our immediate feelings—they represent precious data" (Yalom, 2002, p. 65). We must

be able to be objective in our awareness and analysis of our feelings, but there is a strong possibility that what we sense about family members in the office is a snapshot of their patterns at home. By tuning in to a family's patterns and naturally and carefully engaging in and challenging the family's conversations, SFTs join with their client, the family, "... not to educate or socialize it, but rather to repair or modify the family's ability to support, regulate, nurture, and socialize" (Minuchin, 1974, p. 14).

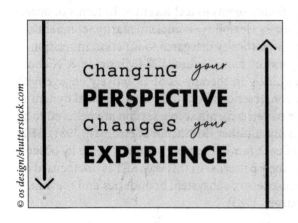

In addition to joining with families, complimenting their positive patterns, and challenging their negative patterns, SFTs also attempt to help families change through enactments (Minuchin, 1974; Minuchin et al., 2014). This technique is one in which the counselor asks an unexpected question or prompts the family or a subsystem of the family to engage in an unexpected conversation. For example, in the case of an adolescent child desiring more freedom to make his own choices, the counselor might instruct the parents to answer aloud between themselves the question, "How do we already see him making good choices?" The family's pattern thus far has been to stay stuck in their normal conversation—the adolescent child wants more freedom but is inconsistent in handling responsibility; parents are mad that he pleads for more freedom and nag him with, "When you're more responsible, we'll allow you more freedom." To challenge and disrupt that normal conversation, the counselor uses enactment to direct the parents to have a different conversation—this one about examples of when their son actually does demonstrate responsibility. Through such a conversation, the parent subsystem and the family system as a whole may take on a new perspective, "gain[ing] control over behaviors they insist are beyond their control" (Gladding, 2015, p. 306), and, thus, opening new possible solutions to their present problems.

Christian Integration Perspective

Christian Integration

As someone who trained in secular (non-Christian) universities but who has worked in church counseling ministries for many years, I sometimes explain to Christian clients that I am not a Bible scholar or theologian but incorporate scripture and prayer into my counseling as led by the Holy Spirit. Additionally, my Southern Baptist influences and personal interpretation of the Bible lead me to believe that God desires that all people would be saved (*New International Bible*, 1978/2011, John 3:16); that Jesus modeled humility and grace in His approach with all people; that it is the Holy Spirit's role to convict people of their sins; and that hardships and trials are not always because of someone's sin but can serve to glorify God (John 9:3). These Truths not only guide me in my client interactions but also help me to successfully balance such that I honor both the American Counseling Association's Code of Ethics (ACA, 2014) and my Christian moral convictions.

In addition to being firmly anchored in God's Word (the Bible) and committed to providing ethically-sound, effective counseling, I am mindful of and intentional about my integration of spirituality, counseling, and theology. As cautioned by McMinn (2012), I avoid "resort[ing] to haphazard means of relating psychology, theology and spirituality, drawing on Christian and psychological resources whenever one or the other seems most convenient, popular or pragmatic" (p. 84-85). By God's grace, and after many years of clinical practice, spiritual integration is more automatic for me, meaning I sense when to shift my focus and intervention based on what clients' spiritual, clinical, and combined (spiritual and clinical) needs seem to be in any given moment. This is true with my Christian and non-Christian clients alike. With Christian clients, of course, I tend to draw from the Bible or other trusted Christian resources. With non-Christian clients, I tend to approach spirituality more from a general standpoint of what gives their life purpose and meaning. At all times, however, I am attentive to clients' unique treatment goals and am always aiming to meet those goals.

A specific spiritual integration model of which I am a fan is called "grace-based counseling" (Fowler & Ford, 2021). This simple and clear model is built on the inerrancy of the Holy Scriptures and explained through the acronym GRACE: (G) God's image, (R) rebellion, (A) altruism, (C) connection, (E) empowerment. In short, all people are created in (G) God's image and are worthy of respect. We should recognize but not hold against our clients their (R) rebellious nature; instead, we can help them to take responsibility for past mistakes. Counselors are to care deeply about our clients' welfare and serve them with Christ-like (A) altruism. Further, grace-based counselors seek to cultivate humility within themselves and approach clients with humility. This helps to establish

a trusting (C) connection between the two so that the counselor can better speak grace and truth (*New International Bible*, 1978/2011, Ephesians 4:15; John 1:17) into a client's life, and the client may potentially be more open to receiving that grace-and-truth combination. Finally, whether counseling with Christian or non-Christian clients, we should continually draw from biblical wisdom; God's wisdom at work in us (E) empowers us to encourage and empower our clients so that they might change for the better.

Denominational Influence

Having already mentioned my Southern Baptist heritage, I will add here that I feel fortunate to not have been raised in legalistic churches or by legalistic parents. By God's grace, I grew up being taught, "All have sinned and fall short of the glory of God" (*New International Bible*, 1978/2011, Romans 3:23). As a result, I do not have unnecessary guilt or fear of judgment with which so many people wrestle. I guess, maybe, it was always clear to me that I was a sinner, "saved by grace, through faith," which is "the gift of God" (Ephesians 2:8-9). All I needed to do was accept the gift, which I did by accepting Jesus as my personal Savior. My parents and my church families did a great service to me by not making my value and my salvation about "how good I was" or "how well I did." They told me the truth, and I believed it; they modeled grace, and I received it. I still believe and receive the good news of God's Truth today, even more strongly than ever, and I say, "Thanks be to God for his indescribable gift" (2 Corinthians 9:15). His unmerited gift of salvation through his son—Jesus' death and resurrection and the resulting promise of eternal life in Heaven—produces an emotional and spiritual freedom within me, as well as a deep desire to honor and serve God in every aspect of my life, including in my work as a professional counselor.

A Case Study: The Leone Family

Cindy Leone submitted a request for counseling through our church's counseling ministry website. This is a short-term service through which we offer a limited number of sessions at no cost for both church members and non-church members. More chronic or severe mental health issues are referred out. Our ministry is best suited for less severe relational and mental health issues.

In her request form, Cindy indicated that she and her family are not church members. She shared that the counseling request was for her 15-year-old son, Noah, who had become increasingly belligerent and disrespectful toward her and his father (Cindy's husband, Vincent). I followed up with a brief phone call to Cindy to explain how our church counseling ministry operates and to rule out for Noah any suicidal ideation or other severe mental health issues. I explained that I would require her and Vincent to participate in family counseling with Noah versus me doing individual counseling with Noah alone. This is fairly typical of family counselors, especially for SFTs.

Like Minuchin, I did not do a structured family history of the Leone family in our initial meeting because I anticipated that their interactions in the meeting would tell me much of what I needed to know about their family dynamics (Minuchin & Nichols, 1993). I did, of course, explain the specifics of confidentiality and how counseling works, and I asked a few "get-to-know-you" questions, such as asking the parents where they work and asking Noah what grade he was in and where he went to school. I then explained that families often seek out counseling when they are stuck and need to figure out new solutions for new problems (Minuchin & Fishman, 1981). Using metaphor, I likened how families are constantly aging and "growing up" to how we grow out of our old clothes. Like old clothes, old solutions do not quite fit, or work, anymore. Further, I shared that I am particularly interested in their communication patterns, as "it often takes someone outside the family drawing the communication pattern to our attention to help us understand why the pattern needs to be changed" (Chapman, 2010, p. 36).

Before launching more fully into the session and having heard Vincent and Cindy say that they were Christians (Noah said he believes in God but is not a Christian), I explained that I believe that our struggles are purposeful (*New International Bible*, 1978/2011, Romans 8:28). I view the family through a strengths-based perspective, trusting that God has already equipped them in many ways for success as a team. Further, I trust that God will guide me and the family in identifying new possibilities for how they might work through the current challenges they are facing. I then asked who would like to be the family spokesperson and share with me how they thought counseling might help the family. Noah shrugged his shoulders and stared at his shoes. Vincent looked at Cindy. Cindy proceeded to report the family's issues, which can be summarized as follows:

- She and Vincent have to tell Noah several times before he finally does as he is told. They end up yelling. He responds angrily. They end up arguing with each other. He ends up losing privileges.
- Noah picks on his sister and gets into arguments with her.
- Noah does not have many friends at school, and Cindy and Vincent do not trust the friends he does have. They worry that they are bad influences on Noah.
- Noah's grades have gone down a bit, and he does not seem to care.
- In recent months, Noah has said things like, "I wish I wasn't part of this family."

Following Cindy's five-minute report, I looked at Vincent, who appeared annoyed even though he had his hands behind his head and sat in a relaxed posture on the couch. Cindy also appeared relaxed and had reported in a fairly calm, matter-of-fact way. Vincent almost immediately responded, "Noah wouldn't be having problems if you (Cindy) would let me discipline him. If it was up to me, he would lose everything—all his games, all his tech—until he finally got the point." Vincent's intensity rose as he shared that he "just doesn't want problems;" that he does not know why "Noah has to make it so difficult on the family;" and that had he talked to his parents like Noah talks to them, he would have gotten "way worse punishment." Adding to Vincent's intensity was his use of lots of curse words. He did

not apologize for his language, nor did I edit him; I was learning a lot about him and the family dynamics as he spoke in his natural manner.

Having heard from the parents (the parent subsystem), I next checked in with Noah and asked for his thoughts on all that his parents had shared. His response was somewhat nonchalant, as evidenced by a slight grin and slouched body language. He said, "It's not as bad as they say." He looked at Cindy and Vincent and said, "You guys overreact. And, why don't you get on Sidney? She's always starting stuff with me, but you don't ever punish her." Cindy answered, "You start way more stuff than Sidney does, and that's not even the main problem anyway. The main problem is that you need to listen more and start being more respectful toward all of us." Vincent then gave a long, impassioned speech about how it is so important to him that he has a good relationship with his kids and that he would be willing to do almost anything they asked if they would just listen and "stop with all the drama."

By the end of that first session, my primary observations of the Leone family were these:

- Cindy and Vincent's spouse subsystem is one of complementarity in that they seem comfortable with one another and mostly accepting of the roles they play (i.e., Vincent as the enforcer of rules, Cindy as the family comforter).
- Cindy and Vincent's parent subsystem is conflicted, with Vincent tending toward rigid boundaries and Cindy tending toward diffuse boundaries.
- Cindy and Noah are in danger of forming a cross-generational coalition as they, at times, seem to triangulate, or work against, Vincent. (Healthy parent-child subsystems are normal and good in families; what is problematic is when those subsystems threaten the rightful leadership of the spouse and parent subsystems.)
- Sidney (the 13-year-old sister) was not present in the session but is clearly part of a conflictual sibling subsystem with Noah.
- V.J. (Vincent Jr., the 19-year-old son who was barely mentioned by the family) was not present in the session and apparently, in relation to Noah, is in a more nonconflictual sibling subsystem with Noah and Sidney.
- Noah is neither clinically depressed nor suicidal but is negatively impacted by his parents' inconsistent boundaries with him, their diffuse boundaries with his sister, and their clear boundaries with his brother.

Applying the B-Well Model Using SFT

SFT and the B-Well model both focus on the whole—SFT on the whole family (Minuchin, 1984) and B-Well on the whole person. Further, both SFT and B-Well are strengths-focused, meaning counselors recognize and build on clients' strengths, or assets, while also working to repair and improve clients' problems, or deficits. Building on these shared principles and on their shared value for the health and healing of families (as a Bible-based model, B-Well is naturally pro-family), B-Well can be applied to the Leone family as indicated within each facet below.

Heart

The Leone family is not as emotionally well as they would like to be. Among their Heart strengths (assets), Vincent and Cindy are loyal to each other and want to be successful as a couple and as parents. Yet, a key concern and point of need for Vincent and Cindy is their increasing emotional disconnection. After 22 years of marriage and with many parenting and work responsibilities, they are on autopilot (Chapman & Warden, 2019) and drifting toward discord. They are drawn together in their shared desire for the emotional closeness of their family, but they are not on the same page in terms of how to accomplish that goal.

Noah said he knows his parents love him and want the best for him (assets). However, he feels discouraged about his place in the family and is angry, both about his perceived lack of freedom and the lack of fairness in contrast to how his sister is treated. He is confused by his parents' inconsistency around the rules and subsequent punishments. That leaves him often feeling like he cannot win with them and that they see him as a failure. This also contributes to his conflicted sibling subsystem with Sidney. These problems signal Heart needs for the Leone family.

Mind

Vincent's emphasis on wanting to be close to his children and his willingness "to do almost anything they ask" (assets) suggest that he thinks closeness means "no drama." He also apparently believes in a *quid pro quo* system, in which he gives back to others what they give to or do for him. This is a works-based rather than a grace-based economy and, thus, problematic when family members cannot live up to Vincent's expectations.

Cindy quietly dismisses some of Vincent's rigid rules and dismisses Noah's anger at being treated differently than Sidney. She seems to do this for peace-keeping purposes, which can be considered an asset. After all, Matthew 5:9 (*New International Bible*, 1978/2011) says, "Blessed are the peacemakers …" Unfortunately, Cindy's good peacemaking intentions sometimes contribute to Vincent and Noah's feeling disrespected and angry. A change of perspective for Cindy may help her to discover new possible solutions for co-creating peace with Vincent first, as the parent subsystem, but then with Noah as well, in a healthy, or balanced, parent-child subsystem.

Strength

Vincent and Cindy hold leadership positions within their companies and have leadership skills that can be helpful to them in their home life (asset). Their jobs afford them some flexibility in their work schedules, which is another asset. Nonetheless, they still often work 50 to 60 hours each week, which takes a toll on their physical health. Furthermore, they are in their mid-40s and beginning to feel the effects of age, which impede their energy and endurance and add to their stress. From an SFT standpoint, their spouse subsystem is strained. From a B-Well standpoint, they do not regularly honor the Sabbath (*New International Bible*, 1978/2011, Exodus 20:8), and they are not always operating with as much unity and power as they could if they made more time for rest and togetherness (Ecclesiastes 4:8-12).

Related to Vincent and Cindy's busy work lives and to the busyness of being a family with three active teenagers, the Leones want to spend more time relaxing together as a family (asset) but do not follow through as often as they could. This lack of quality time together detracts from emotional closeness and contributes to conflict in the family (Chapman & Warden, 2019).

Soul

Vincent and Cindy both identify as Christians (asset). Cindy is more active in attending church and growing her Christian faith than Vincent, who tends to think, "Once saved, always saved; no need to do more than that." They admitted to thinking that part of their family issues relates to their inconsistency in their Christian walk (i.e., prayer, Bible reading, church involvement).

Noah has attended church with Cindy at times but also, as a teenager, is heavily influenced by his peer group and social media. This, in part, has played into his believing in God (asset) but not identifying as a Christian. Forcing Christianity on him would be unethical and unwise, but from a B-Well model, his parents and the counselor are wise to model Christian behaviors such as justice, mercy, and humility (*New International Bible*, 1978/2011, Micah 6:8). This also is an opportunity to extend compassion and love such as that described in Romans 5:8— "But God demonstrates his own love for us in this: While we were still sinners, Christ died for us."

 Neighbor

The Neighbor facet of the B-Well model is another natural fit with SFT in that both target connection and belongingness in families. All the Leones could be helped by growing more of an "us" and "we" mentality (Chapman & Warden, 2019; Sells & Yarhouse, 2011). This "us" and "we" mentality is important in family therapy. The family therapist, somewhat like a director or coach, carefully observes, supports, challenges, and guides the family through the therapy process with the goal of improved family dynamics. From a biblical standpoint, the Leones could also be helped by reestablishing their focus on love for one another (*New International Bible*, 1978/2011, 1 Corinthians 13:1-13; John 13:34). The counselor may complement the family's effort at establishing more loving dialogue with one another. As it is currently, they often sarcastically refer to their love for one another. Their family humor is an asset, but their empathy and tenderness toward each other need improvement.

 Society

Despite not conducting a structured family history with the Leones, Vincent and Cindy's obviously different interpersonal styles led to discussions about their families of origin and cultural backgrounds. Vincent is from an Italian background; his paternal grandparents were first-generation immigrants to the United States. Cindy's ancestry is largely of English descent. She is less sure of when her family moved to America, but she thinks it was sometime in the early- to mid-1800s. Vincent considers his Italian origins an important part of his identity and says he is not "angry" but instead opinionated and loud because that is how he was raised. Cindy, on the other hand, is softer-spoken and says she grew up in a calm, "hippie" home in the southwest United States. They are like-minded in their religious and political affiliations (asset), but their culturally influenced interpersonal styles contribute to their marital and parental conflicts and assist in maintaining negative patterns in the family system.

Another Society challenge Vincent and Cindy face, and one that many parents face, is that of allowing and supporting healthy individuation of their teenage children. This is a complicated process and is uniquely specific to each individual family. Vincent and Cindy love their children and want the best for them (assets) but are not comfortable with some of Noah's choices in friends, attitude, language, social media usage, school performance, and spiritual health. Noah also feels the pressure of making good choices (asset) but is understandably both positively and negatively influenced by a myriad of social, cultural, religious, and political factors. He does not consciously wish to upset or offend his parents (asset), but he also wishes they would trust him more and give him credit for the good choices that he makes.

B-Well Treatment Plan

With SFT's emphasis on clarifying boundaries and strengthening family relationships, and with B-Well's emphasis on holistic, Bible-based wellness (i.e., Heart, Mind, Strength, Soul, Neighbor, Society), a practical treatment plan for the Leone family would include the following: 1) increased closeness in the spouse subsystem; 2) increased unity and clearer boundaries in the parent subsystem; 3) increased parent-child subsystems [Vincent and Noah; Cindy and Noah]; and 4) increased family system connection. These goals are conducive given the Leones' specific needs and the time-limited structure in which the Leones' case study takes place. However, this treatment plan could also be expanded upon to include additional goals and greater inclusion of the siblings in family therapy. Finally, while much of SFT's emphasis is on in-session interactions with the family and restructuring of their family dynamics, it would be permissible, and in some settings necessary, to include homework goals as part of the treatment as well.

TABLE 1 Recommended Goals, Objectives, and Interventions

Problem	Goal	Objective	Intervention
Discord in the spouse subsystem	Goal (1) – Increased closeness in the spouse subsystem	Objective (1a) – Vincent (V) and Cindy (C) will be gracious toward each other in session. [Mind, Heart, Neighbor]	• Joining • Compliments (positive reinforcement) • Enactments
		Objective (1b) – (V) and (C) will follow through with a weekly "date night." [Mind, Heart, Neighbor]	• V and C may want to keep record of success as a source of positive reinforcement.
		Objective (1c) – V and C will do a simple devotion together at least two times per week. [Heart, Soul, Neighbor]	• Recommend possibilities
Conflicting boundaries in parent subsystem	Goal (2) – Clearer boundaries and consistent follow-through with family rules	Objective (2a) – V and C will check in with each other in session to ensure they maintain a mutually-agreeable approach to boundaries and rules. [Mind, Heart, Neighbor]	• Joining • Compliments (positive reinforcement) • Enactments
		Objective (2b) – V and C will identify two family rules, establish a mutually-agreeable boundary, and follow through with related rewards and consequences as planned. [Mind, Heart, Neighbor]	• V and C may want to keep record of success as a source of positive reinforcement.
		Objective (2c) – V and C will check in with each other at least once per week to process parenting issues and ensure ongoing teamwork. [Mind, Heart, Neighbor]	• V and C may want to keep record of success as a source of positive reinforcement.

Problem	Goal	Objective	Intervention
Parent-child discord for father and son	Goal (3) – Repair and build V and Noah's (N) relationship	Objective (3a) – V and N will speak respectfully to each other in session. [Mind, Heart, Neighbor]	• Joining • Compliments (positive reinforcement) • Enactments
		Objective (3b) – V and N will spend one hour weekly doing something mutually enjoyable together. [Mind, Heart, Strength, Neighbor]	• V and N may want to keep record of success as a source of positive reinforcement.
		Objective (3c) – V will affirm N at least three times weekly for responsible behavior. [Mind, Heart, Neighbor]	• V and N may want to keep record of success as a source of positive reinforcement.
Parent-child discord for mother and son	Goal (4) – Repair and build C and N's relationship	Objective (4a) – C and N will speak respectfully to each other in session. [Mind, Heart, Neighbor]	• Joining • Compliments (positive reinforcement) • Enactments
		Objective (4b) – C and N will spend one hour weekly doing something mutually enjoyable together. [Mind, Heart, Strength, Neighbor]	• C and N may want to keep record of success as a source of positive reinforcement.
		Objective (4c) – C will affirm N at least three times weekly for responsible behavior. [Mind, Heart, Neighbor]	• C and N may want to keep record of success as a source of positive reinforcement.
Discord in the family system	Goal (5) – Repair and build Leone family's relationship.	Objective (5a) – Leone family will engage in at least one fun, family activity per week. [Heart, Neighbor]	• V and C may want to keep record of success as a source of positive reinforcement.
		Objective (5b) – The Leone family will calmly discuss cultural and social influences at least once weekly to build understanding of and compassion toward each other. [Society]	• Joining • Compliments (positive reinforcement) • Enactments

Summary

Individuals are "like chips in a kaleidoscope, always part of patterns that are larger than ourselves and somehow more than the sum of their parts" (Minuchin, 1984, p. 3). For the family counselor attempting to explore and understand an individual client's narrative in context, it is essential to consider and engage with the "kaleidoscope" from which the "chip" comes. It is through that larger family scope that the individual client's narrative makes more sense and, likewise, can be better resolved. In this way, the family becomes "the client," and when the family as a whole changes, the individual family members change.

The B-Well model shares a similar premise—to be wholly well, we must look at all the aspects that make us well. B-Well builds on existing wellness models to provide counselors with a Bible-based wellness model that speaks to all facets of our spiritual, psychological, and physical selves. Through this model, SFTs and counselors from all theoretical orientations can better encourage our Christian and non-Christian clients alike in the wellness facets of Heart, Mind, Strength, Soul, Neighbor, and Society. Certainly, in the case of the fictional Leone family, SFT and B-Well integrate well for a holistic, practical approach to encouraging the family in all areas of family and individual wellness.

References

American Counseling Association (ACA). (2014). *2014 ACA code of ethics.* https://www.counseling.org/knowledge-center

Chapman, G. (2010). *Things I wish I'd known before we got married.* Northfield Publishing.

Chapman, G., & Warden, S. (2016). *Things I wish I'd known before we became parents.* Northfield Publishing.

Chapman, G., & Warden, S. (2019). *The DIY guide to building a family that lasts: 12 tools for improving your home life.* Northfield Publishing.

Fishman, H. C. (1993). *Intensive structural therapy: Treating families in their social context.* Basic Books.

Fowler, R. A., & Ford, N. (2021). *Grace-based counseling: An effective new biblical model.* Moody Publishers.

Gladding, S. T. (2015). *Family therapy: History, theory, and practice* (6th ed.). Pearson.

Jimenez, L., Hidalgo, V., Baena, S., Leon, A., & Lorence, B. (2019). Effectiveness of structural-strategic family therapy in the treatment of adolescents with mental health problems and their families. *International Journal of Environmental Research and Public Health, 16,* 1-14. https://doi.org/10.3390%2Fijerph16071255

Ma, J. L. C., Wong, C., & Xia, L. L. L. (2020). Helping a depressed Chinese adult with high functioning autism reconnect with his family through structural family therapy. *Journal of Family Therapy, 42,* 518-535. https://doi.org/10.1111/1467-6427.12281

McMinn, M. (2012). An integration approach. In S. Greggo & T. A. Sisemore (Eds.), *Counseling and Christianity: Five approaches* (pp. 84-109). IVP Academic.

Minuchin, S. (1974). *Families and family therapy.* Harvard University Press.

Minuchin, S. (1984). *Family kaleidoscope.* Harvard University Press.

Minuchin, S., & Fishman, H. C. (1981). *Family therapy techniques.* Harvard University Press.

Minuchin, S., & Nichols, M. P. (1993). *Family healing: Strategies for hope and understanding.* Free Press.

Minuchin, S., Montalvo, B., Guerney Jr., B. G., Rosman, B. L., & Schumer, F. (1967). *Families of the slums: An exploration of their structure and treatment.* Basic Books.

Minuchin, S., Reiter, M. D., & Borda, C. (2014). *The craft of family therapy: Challenging certainties.* Routledge.

Napier, A. Y., & Whitaker, C. (1978). *The family crucible: The intense experience of family therapy.* Harper Perennial.

Negash, S., & Morgan, M. L. (2016). A family affair: Examining the impact of parental infidelity on children using a structural family therapy framework. *Contemporary Family Therapy, 38,* 198-209. https://doi.org/10.1007/s10591-015-9364-4

New International Bible. (2011). The NIV Bible. https://www.thenivbible.com (Original work published 1978)

Sells, J. N., & Yarhouse, M. A. (2011). *Counseling couples in conflict: A relational restoration model.* IVP Academic.

Tadros, E., & Finney, N. (2018). Structural family therapy with incarcerated families: A clinical case study. *The Family Journal: Counseling and Therapy for Couples and Families, 26*(2), 253-261. https://doi.org/10.1177%2F1066480718777409

Taibbi, R. (2015). *Doing family therapy: Craft and creativity in clinical practice* (3rd ed.). Guilford Press.

Umbarger, C. C. (1983). *Structural family therapy.* Grune & Stratton.

Weaver, A., Greeno, C., Fusco, R., Zimmerman, T., & Anderson, C. M. (2019). Not just one, it's both of us: Low-income mothers' perceptions of structural family therapy delivered in a semi-rural community mental health center. *Community Mental Health Journal, 55*, 1152-1164. https://doi.org/10.1007/s10597-019-00444-2

Yalom, I. D. (2002). *The gift of therapy: An open letter to a new generation of therapists and their patients.* Harper Perennial.

CHAPTER 18

B-Well Model in Couples Counseling Using Emotionally Focused Couples Therapy

Laura Daniel

"The harvest is plentiful, but the workers are few. Ask the Lord of the harvest, therefore, to send out workers into his harvest field."

— Matthew 9:37-38 (NIV)

This chapter will focus on the application of emotionally focused couples therapy (EFCT) using the B-well model. In this chapter, you will find a brief overview of EFCT, a case study, an application of EFCT within the B-Well model to conceptualize the couple's presenting problem along with assets, and a treatment plan, which will be offered as an illustration of therapy using this approach.

Background of Emotionally Focused Couples Therapy (EFCT)

Origins

EFCT, pioneered by Susan Johnson and Leslie Greenberg, is an experimental approach to couples therapy that emphasizes client awareness of inner experiences translating to emotional engagement between partners (Goldenberg & Goldenberg, 2013). Johnson and Greenberg posit that "emotion organizes attachment responses and serves a communicative function in relationships" (Nichols & Schwartz, 2005, p. 151). EFCT places the therapist as an active participant with the couple through the change process. Couples are guided toward using feelings

© pixelheadphoto digitalskillet/shutterstock.com

to create secure attachment bonds within their relationship, improving the reported overall relationship satisfaction. In this way, EFCT views couples both from the intrapersonal and interpersonal lens, helping them to identify their own emotionally significant values and then share that with their partner (Goldenberg & Goldenberg, 2013). Individual experience is the building block toward understanding the couple's dynamic more powerfully. The effectiveness of EFCT has been measured in various outcome studies with diverse samples (Greenberg & Goldman, 2008; Greenberg et al., 2010; Johnson et al., 1999). Based on the abundance of research efforts toward evaluating this approach, EFCT is one of the most empirically validated couple's interventions available as counselors guide couples to share their primary emotions with one another to create a more secure attachment bond (Goldenberg & Goldenberg, 2013).

View of Human Nature

As a hopeful and empowering approach, therapists using an EFCT orientation believe that humans are self-actualizing and driven to reach their full potential (Goldenberg and Goldenberg, 2013). We use our most important intimate relationships to drive this change toward achievement and make sense of our experiences. Importantly, our emotional states provide the primary lens through which we organize and understand our lives. Further, our previous and current attachments inform our emotional state, providing either a safe, secure space to bond or leading to fear of loss and negative emotional intensity.

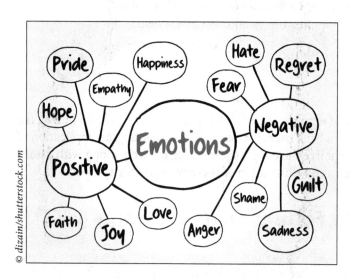

Attachment theory provides a central explanation for how couple relationships can become dysfunctional. Specifically, if the relationship does not provide a sense of security, trust, and safety, emotional engagement decreases, and both parties are left with negative emotions such as anger and frustration (Goldenberg and Goldenberg, 2013). Marital distress results from the "failure of an attachment relationship to provide security, protection, or closeness, resulting in anxiety and a sense of vulnerability in one or both partners" (p. 270). From this perspective, emotions reflect attachment needs where primary emotions (i.e., fear of rejection) are expressed through secondary emotions (i.e., anger), leading to negative interactions where partners do not reveal their primary emotions. EFCT counselors guide couples to share their primary emotions with one another to create a more secure attachment bond.

View of Change

In EFCT, change happens through several theoretical models. One of the foundations of EFCT is humanistic therapy and the work of Carl Rogers, which emphasizes creating a safe, therapeutic environment and counselor/client relationship. In this way, counselors using an EFCT approach collaborate and partner with couples in a non-judgmental stance (Goldenberg & Goldenberg, 2013). EFCT also applies John Bowlby's attachment theory to the bonds in adult love relationships. Gestalt therapy influences EFCT through the role of the counselor as an active, directive agent of change.

Change happens through restructuring negative emotional patterns so that couples can become more responsive, attuned, and bonded to one another (Johnson et al., 2001). In order to meet this goal, couples must first recognize or identify these negative interaction patterns. Instead of taking a problem-specific focus (content), counselors help the couple to find the underlying emotional themes that dominate their interaction (process). Greenberg and Johnson (1988) believe that change is unlocked when couples first recognize their own emotional experiences and then share them with one another, creating more positive and meaningful interactions.

Negative interaction patterns such as "attacking-withdrawing" become habitual for couples, leading to distress and a lack of emotional connection. The EFCT therapist works actively with couples through activities to modify the emotional experiences of both partners and the roles they take in their relationship dance to improve the quality of attachment and build a stronger emotional bond (Johnson & Greenberg, 1995). EFCT "provides a process for both partners ... to communicate and to cope with the emotional mechanics of relating to one another, thus providing emotional and behavioral change that is sustainable" (Brigance et al., 2021, p. 74).

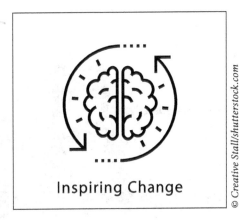
Inspiring Change
© Creative Stall/shutterstock.com

Christian Integration Perspective

The model that drives my approach to counseling is the integration approach developed by McMinn (2012), which guides counselors to draw on the "rich theoretical and scientific tradition of psychology" while being led by "biblical revelation and theological wisdom" in a way that is intentional and thoughtful and honors the ethical guidelines of our profession (p. 84). Counselors draw from the three primary perspectives of psychology, theology, and spirituality to conceptualize and form effective treatment plans unique to each client. Integrative counseling calls for "adaptability, fluidity, and sensitivity ... to see different realms of authority in relation to the particular situation being faced" (p. 84). To ascertain the best approach, counselors must ask themselves to consider the setting, the client, the presenting concern, and the treatment plan. For example, in supporting a couple who is struggling with the mental illness of one or both partners, the psychological perspective may be most relevant. The psychological perspective will allow the counselor to utilize research-based treatment approaches to help educate the client and alleviate suffering. Incorporating theology is another approach for a couple who has requested direct integration. As a treatment goal, counselors may help the couple to increase connection with their spiritual community to provide support and growth in faith. Finally, spirituality may be most helpful in guiding my self-care as I complete spiritual practices of renewal and strength.

The guiding scriptures of the B-Well model outlined in Chapter 4 are foundational for my belief system related to faithfulness to God and one another, allowing these to drive all of our interactions. My educational background is secular, and my clinical experiences have been in school settings. This integration approach allows me to use theology and spirituality for case conceptualization, integration with client consent, and as a tool for my own self-care and strength base. Conceptualizing the client through a multicultural assessment lens, including the client's religious and spiritual beliefs, is an important component and honors the ACA code of ethics to recognize the client's support community (American Counseling Association [ACA], 2014, A.1.d). Further, failure to include religious and spiritual beliefs in our conceptualization fails to respect the diversity of our clients (A.4.b). This is consistent with the B-Well model of wellness incorporating mind, body, and spirit leading to enhanced development across the lifespan. Further, with client request and consent, I can incorporate religious and spiritual resources into the counseling session to enhance counseling goals and treatment outcomes. In summary, it allows for implicit application to my work with clients and explicit application when ethically appropriate.

A Case Study: Elena and Sam

Elena and Sam have been married for 16 years. They both have advanced graduate degrees. Elena is a 42-year-old Mexican American female who works as a dental hygienist. Sam is a 45-year-old White male who works as a corporate attorney; his professional travel often takes him away from the family. The family owns a home in the urban area of Phoenix, Arizona. They both ascribe to the Catholic faith and attend Mass regularly at their local Catholic church. They are self-referred to couples counseling to cope with stress related to their 14-year-old daughter, Maria, who is currently being treated in a residential mental health program. The couple is in a higher socioeconomic bracket. They both report good physical health and enjoy exercising regularly. Both are under the regular care of a physician. The family enjoys traveling together and spending time outdoors.

The couple presents to counseling as they would like to improve the quality of their relationship, strengthen their parenting skills, and process the difficulty in supporting their daughter struggling with mental health challenges. The couple describes their marital distress specifically as engaging in frequent, volatile arguments and blaming one another, resulting in a pattern of withdrawal by Sam that leaves Elena feeling abandoned. The couple exemplifies the pursuer (Elena) and withdrawer (Sam) dynamic in their arguments. She responds to the threat of conflict by pursuing, attacking, and moving toward Sam while he hides and seeks safety outside the conflict. Further, they both report feelings of guilt and shame related to their daughter's struggles, as well as grief at her absence while in treatment.

The content of their argument is in two areas: (1) how to best parent Maria and (2) Elena's discontent with Sam's ability to be present and supportive in their relationship. The couple reports their interaction patterns to follow a common theme of Elena becoming angry and hurt and expressing herself loudly and in an animated manner to gain Sam's attention. Sam feels overwhelmed and flooded by her strong emotion. In response, Sam protects himself from Elena's anger by staying distant and avoiding her, which he often accomplishes by spending many hours on his career.

Maria's struggles with mental illness began at age nine when she was referred to the school psychologist for testing related to withdrawal in the classroom, underperformance academically, and isolation from peers. While Elena and Sam noticed her sadness at home, it seemed most pronounced in the school setting. Unfortunately, Maria had a shift from confiding in her parents, especially Elena, to withdrawing and refusing to share. This scared Elena and resulted in her becoming more and more demanding toward her daughter. Upon comprehensive testing to evaluate both academic and cognitive functioning, the school psychologist diagnosed Maria with attention deficit hyperactivity disorder, inattentive type, unspecified depressive disorder, and unspecified anxiety disorder. Results of the assessment were shared with Maria's parents and school with recommendations for academic accommodations and counseling support. Since that time, despite following the psychologist's recommendations, Maria's overall functioning has declined, resulting in her withdrawal from traditional school and enrolling in a residential, therapeutic program that focuses on supporting girls struggling with depression and anxiety. The physical absence from Maria has heightened Elena's distress and need for support from Sam, who has coped with their daughter's absence by further withdrawing into his career.

Applying the B-Well Model Using EFCT

There is a conceptual overlap between EFCT and the B-Well model as both approaches view the client from a holistic lens, knowing that all influences in a couple's life, both internal and external, have an important role in their health and challenges. Further, it is important for counselors to view the couple from this vantage point to provide effective treatment that leads to long-

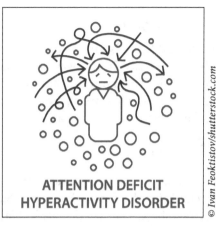

ATTENTION DEFICIT HYPERACTIVITY DISORDER

© Ivan Feoktistov/shutterstock.com

term change. When applying the B-Well model to the couple, the model's six facets (Heart, Mind, Strength, Soul, Neighbor, and Society) are the guide.

Heart

The Heart facet is the most central feature of EFCT as it applies to the B-Well model. Emotions drive the therapeutic process—first, in developing a strong and safe rapport with the counselor; then, recognizing the client's emotional health; and finally, sharing and accepting their partner's emotional experience. The attachment bond that is central to the concept of EFCT is an extension of the Heart facet with the B-Well model. In the case of Elena and Sam, we can conceptualize their primary challenge in the Heart facet and will allow that knowledge to guide intervention. Elena and Sam report feeling lonely and isolated within their relationship; neither member knows how to best serve as a support system for the other, especially during this time of difficult emotion with their daughter's crisis. Elena is exhibiting an anxious-insecure attachment pattern in her marriage; she feels she cannot trust Sam as a safe and constant presence in her life and, as such, clings to him and becomes more demanding. Sam is exhibiting an avoidant-insecure attachment bond towards Elena; he rejects her need for attention, shutting down his own emotional experience and diminishing her feelings.

Mind

The Mind is the facet that is a source of strength for both Elena and Sam and an area in which they can bond as a couple. They both have achieved advanced educational degrees and report that their love of continued learning and professional growth is an area that brought them together as a couple. Elena and Sam have related to one another from an intellectual level, with their interactions dominated by cognition more than emotion. Another reason the Mind facet is an asset is that they will be willing and eager to learn more about human development, parenting skills, and mental illness, allowing them to support their daughter in a healthier way (one of their presenting concerns).

In terms of challenges for the couple, their unique cultural backgrounds influence their expectations of one another and can come into conflict. Elena was raised in a collectivist culture with the expectation that couples and families cling to one another in times of distress. Her belief system does not include divorce as a viable option, and when Sam withdraws, it scares her even more. Sam, being raised in a family that embraces the traditional U.S. value of individualism, does not appreciate the way in which Elena's culture influences her to lean on him and their marriage as a source of strength. For Sam, divorce is normalized in his own background and family experience, and while he does not wish for that to be an outcome of their marriage, he does not respond in a way that is reassuring and comforting to Elena. Her emotionality and fear of losing him cause him to pull further away.

Strength

Elena and Sam also prioritize their physical wellness through preventative medical care and ongoing physical activity. In this way, the Strength facet bonds them together and helps them relate as a couple and family. The family, including Maria, enjoys spending time outdoors, engaging in hiking, fishing, and camping. They are also members of their local YMCA and participate in physical fitness training and exercise on a regular basis.

 ## Soul

The Soul facet, which connects the physical and spiritual world, is another source of connection and strength for the family. Elena and Sam report regular attendance at the Catholic church where they are members. They participate in Mass and all activities related to Mass, as well as volunteer their time toward service projects initiated by their priest and congregation.

While they both report a strong connection to their faith, they generally talk about church participation in more of an individual way instead of as a place of community worship and connection to other people in their faith community. Mass serves as a time of quiet reflection and looking inward. Their faith experiences are powerful, and the couple may benefit from ways to share insights from these meaningful experiences more with one another. The values of their Roman Catholic faith related to collectivism and respect for authority mirror Elena's Mexican American heritage and tie them together as a couple in these shared goals.

 ## Neighbor

The dyad's conflict can also be conceptualized through the Neighbor facet, which addresses relational or interpersonal wellness. As a strength, they do have close friendships with other Mexican American families who share their value system and can offer support and encouragement. They derive social fun and enjoyment from time spent with these friends. Further, they both have professional careers, regular church attendance, and are active at the YMCA. However, their feelings of guilt and shame prevent them from sharing with others in their community their true struggles related to their daughter. While they struggle to make sense of their experiences together, they are "not ready" to share them with others. This leaves them with feelings of loneliness outside of one another. They report sharing time and activities with others but not the emotional closeness that would lead to feelings of support and encouragement by their community. While Maria is participating in a residential community and receiving a strong level of support in the Neighbor facet, her parents cling to one another without outside support. At the time of counseling, Sam and Elena are lacking support in their faith community, friendship community, and marital relationship. This leads to feelings of sadness and isolation because the stigma of mental health services within their cultural community prevents them from sharing fully with others.

 ## Society

Elena identifies her cultural background and identity most strongly as a Mexican American, in which family collectivism and inclusiveness are central components. While Elena was raised to rely on extended family members to provide social support, she and Sam feel isolated in this regard as she immigrated to the United States with her parents, who are now deceased. There is a persistent stigma present in the Latino community related to mental health treatment ("Overcoming mental health stigma in the Latino community," 2017). While Elena understands that her daughter needs the support of mental health professionals, she feels isolated in sharing this with members of her extended family and friends who believe that mental illness is a sign of weakness and should not be addressed outside of the family and faith communities. While her cultural background is a central component of her identity, not being able to garner support in this way leads to her feelings of sadness and loneliness.

B-Well Treatment Plan

According to EFCT theory, when couples express vulnerability, their partner is likely to respond compassionately. On the other hand, when partners are insecurely attached, they fear vulnerability will lead to rejection and turn to anger instead. In our couple, Sam's withdrawal is a sign of insecure attachment. He is pushing away Elena even though he longs for love and to be close to her. Our primary goal, then, is to help Elena and Sam to share fears, increase vulnerability, and allow genuine emotions to emerge. The couple "learns the skills critical to regulating the individual emotions as well as hearing the emotional response of the partner, thus leading to better communication cycles and a more secure attachment within the relationship" (Brigance et al., 2021, p. 74). The inclusion of the B-Well model along with EFCT allows for a more robust treatment approach with the couple as it helps the counselor to highlight areas of strength and use those toward building the therapeutic alliance and a safe environment to share vulnerable emotions.

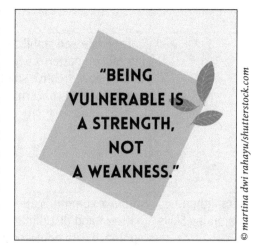

"BEING VULNERABLE IS A STRENGTH, NOT A WEAKNESS."

© martina dwi rahayu/shutterstock.com

Treatment Plan

Since the Heart is the most central feature for EFCT as it applies to the B-Well model, conceptualizing this couple's primary challenge in the Heart facet will guide intervention and the development of a treatment plan. Additionally, Elena and Sam report feeling isolated, and the Neighbor facet is weak for them. While they both have professional careers and regular church attendance, their feelings of guilt and shame prevent them from sharing with others in their community. While they struggle to make sense of their experiences together and their struggles related to their daughter, they are "not ready" to share them with others. This leaves them with feelings of loneliness outside of one another. Interventions targeted at both understanding mental illness and connecting them to other parents with similar concerns could be transformative in this regard.

TABLE 1 Recommended Goals, Objectives, and Interventions

Problem	Goal	Objective	Intervention
Volatile argument pattern resulting in both members feeling abandoned	Identify problematic interaction cycle that maintains attachment insecurity and relationship distress. Assessment. Identify negative interaction patterns. Reframe the problem in terms of the cycle/process and unmet attachment needs.	Objective 1 – The couple will have a clear understanding of their interaction patterns. [Mind] Objective 2 – The couple will uncover and share emotions that underlie interaction patterns. [Heart]	**Stage One: De-escalation** • Reflection of the emotional experience • Clarifying experience for the couple • Validation • Reframing • Externalizing • Reflecting and replaying of interactions • Restructuring and shaping interaction cycles

Problem	Goal	Objective	Intervention
	Express unmet attachment needs for each partner and promote acceptance of new ways of relating, resulting in healing and emotional engagement.	Objective 3 – The couple will facilitate new interaction patterns with honest expressions of attachment needs. [Heart, Neighbor]	**Stage Two: Bonding**
	Consolidate and stabilize new interaction patterns while finding new, creative solutions to relationship concerns.	Objective 4 – Solidify new interaction patterns by having the couple support a healthier attachment style with one another through open communication. [Mind, Heart, Spirit]	**Stage Three: Consolidation of Change**
Strengthen Parenting Skills	Improve communication patterns and disciplinary approach with adolescent daughter.	Objective 5 – Provide education on normal developmental tasks for adolescent females. [Mind] Objective 6 – Provide education on active listening strategies. [Mind]	• Psychoeducation • Role-play
Grief	Cope with daughter's absence while in treatment and improve understanding of mental illness.	Objective 7 –The couple will join a local National Alliance of Mental Illness (NAMI) support group for family members to provide education and support. [Neighbor, Society] Objective 8 – The couple will experience support from other parents to combat feelings of isolation due to stigma of mental health care in the Latino community. [Soul]	• Referral to community-based NAMI support group

Problem	Goal	Objective	Intervention
	Increase spiritual connection with supportive faith community.	Objective 9 – Help the couple to find ways to connect with their faith community that allow them to share more of their struggles and receive support. [Soul]	• Psychoeducation • Role-play new communication patterns/ ways of interacting with faith members

Summary

Conceptualizing Elena and Sam within the framework of EFCT and the B-Well model allows the counselor to draw from areas of strength—Mind, Strength, and Soul—to support areas that are causing turmoil within their marriage—Heart and Neighbor. Focusing on the strengths is an empowering and hopeful way in which to build rapport and engage the couple. This approach also allows them to view one another from a more positive standpoint, giving confidence in their ability to make long-lasting changes to their interaction patterns that have become painful and negative. One of the primary goals of EFCT is to help couples view one another in a more understanding and compassionate way as they share their primary emotions and attachment needs with one another. A natural overlap exists in these approaches conceptually to aid counselors in working with couples like Elena and Sam.

References

American Counseling Association (ACA). (2014). *2014 ACA code of ethics.* https://www.counseling.org/ docs/default-source/default-document-library/2014-code-of-ethics-finaladdress.pdf

Brigance, C. A., Brown, E. C., & Cottone, R. R. (2021). Therapeutic interventions for couples experiencing infertility: An emotionally focused couples therapy approach. *The Family Journal, 29*(1), 72-79. https://doi.org/10.1177/1066480720973420

Goldenberg, H., & Goldenberg, I. (2013). *Family therapy: An overview* (8th ed.). Cengage Learning.

Greenberg, L. S., & Goldman, R. N. (2008). *Emotion-focused couples therapy: The dynamics of emotion, love, and power.* American Psychological Association.

Greenberg, L. S., & Johnson, S. M. (1988). *Emotionally focused therapy for couples.* Guilford Press.

Greenberg, L., Warwar, S., & Malcolm, W. (2010). Emotion-focused couples therapy and the facilitation of forgiveness. *Journal of Marital and Family Therapy, 36*(1), 28-42. https://doi.org/10.1111/j.1752-0606.2009.00185.x

Johnson, S. M., Hunsley, J., Greenberg, L., & Schindler, D. (1999). Emotionally focused couples therapy: Status and challenges. *Clinical Psychology: Science and Practice, 6*(1), 67-79. https://doi.org/10.1093/clipsy.6.1.67

Johnson, S. M., & Greenberg, L. S. (1995). The emotionally focused approach to problems in adult attachment. In N. S. Jacobson & A. S. Gurman (Eds.), *Clinical handbook of couple therapy* (pp. 121–141). The Guilford Press.

Johnson, S. M., Makinen, J. A., & Millikin, J. W. (2001). Attachment injuries in couple relationships: A new perspective on impasses in couples therapy. *Journal of Marital and Family Therapy, 27*(2), 145–155. https://doi.org/10.1111/j.1752-0606.2001.tb01152.x

McMinn, M. (2012). An integration approach. In S. Greggo & T. A. Sisemore (Eds.), *Counseling and Christianity: Five approaches* (pp. 84-109). IVP Academic.

New International Bible. (2011). The NIV Bible. https://www.thenivbible.com (Original work published 1978)

Nichols, M. P., & Schwartz, R. C. (2005). *The essentials of family therapy* (2nd ed.). Pearson.

Overcoming mental health stigma in the Latino community. (2017, November 21). Consult QD Cleveland Clinic. Retrieved June 30, 2022 from https://consultqd.clevelandclinic.org/overcoming-mental-health-stigma-in-the-latino-community/

CHAPTER 19

B-Well Model with Children Using Child-Centered Play Therapy

Kevin B. Hull

>
>
> "Take care that you do not despise one of these little ones; for, I tell you, in heaven their angels continually see the face of my Father in heaven."
>
> — Matthew 18:10 (NRSV)

This chapter will focus on the application of child-centered play therapy (CCPT) using the B-Well model. I will review the basic tenets of CCPT and present the case of Michael. I then discuss the theological application of the B-Well model with Michael's case and demonstrate the integration of theology and theory. Finally, a treatment plan is presented as a model for applying the B-Well model.

Background of Play Therapy

Play therapy has a rich history, evolving from divergent sources and branching into several variations, all of which spring from the idea that a child granted the freedom and safety for self-expression and exploration through play will emerge from the process as a healthier and adaptive person (Hull, 2009). The roots of play therapy spring from the psychoanalytic approach beginning in the 1920s with Hermine von Hug-

© Prostock-studio/shutterstock.com

Hellmuth, a retired teacher who included play with children to better understand their emotional experiences. This resulted in Hug-Hellmuth realizing an easier pathway for children to express internalized material. Later in the same decade, Melanie Klein further advanced the use of play in relieving anxiety and unconscious fears. She created a room completely devoted to play that provided a safe, neutral place for self-expression and self-discovery. Virginia Axline further developed play therapy and ushered it into the mainstream clinical culture of the 1960s and 1970s, creating an approach known as non-directive or child-centered play therapy, following the tenets of Carl Roger's approach consisting of unconditional positive regard. This approach granted children full freedom and autonomy in play, with little involvement of the play therapist other than to affirm the child's worth and reflect upon what the child was doing. The goal is that through full acceptance of the child through the warm environment of safety created by the therapeutic relationship with the therapist, the child will solve problems while becoming self-actualized. We will be examining child-centered play therapy (CCPT) in this chapter.

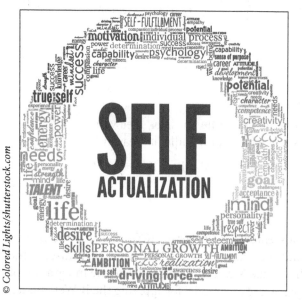

© Colored Lights/shutterstock.com

Origins

CCPT was born in Carl Roger's ideology of non-directive therapy. Rogers maintained that people have a natural tendency to grow and learn when provided with a safe and affirming environment created by a warm and nurturing relationship with another human being. Virginia Axline adapted and applied Roger's approach in play therapy with children, viewing the relationship with the child as a major component in the change process (Bratton et al., 2009). Axline, like Rogers, was convinced that safety in the therapeutic relationship translated to pathways for growth and overcoming in the child and that the warmth and acceptance of the therapist would allow the child to develop in a healthy way. Self-actualization is the ultimate goal, otherwise known as the realization of the self, which is the result of the individual developing adequate self-confidence achieved through the process of self-acceptance and self-discovery. Many research studies have supported the efficacy of CCPT (Ray, 2008), and variations of CCPT have been adapted for use with special populations such as autism spectrum disorders (Hull, 2015).

© Natata/shutterstock.com

View of Human Nature

CCPT views the personality as consisting of three concepts: the person, the phenomenal field, and the self (Landreth, 2012). The person, a conglomeration of the child's thoughts, feelings, behaviors, and physical being, is constantly shifting as the child reacts to their environment. As one part of the child adapts and changes, the other parts of the self also change. CCPT particularly focuses on a child's development from the ages of two through 10, although it holds the view that CCPT is applicable to populations across all age groups. CCPT views development from the principles of Jean Piaget, Erik Erikson, and Lev Vygotsky, all of which support the powerful element of play, particularly make-believe play, in understanding the self and the surrounding world (Glover & Landreth, 2016).

© Natata/shutterstock.com

The phenomenal field consists of the internal and external experiences of the child and is through the relationship with the play therapist who is completely accepting of the child's view of the world and does not judge or question. The self is how the child sees themselves in light of the world around them. This "me" adapts and changes as the world around the child changes, and growth is contingent on relationships with others. Self-realization is the ultimate goal, resulting from a reflective process of the child interacting with the world around them and changing behavior as the world changes, thus

© Natata/shutterstock.com

influencing how the child develops internally. Therefore, children in environments and relationships that are accepting and affirming are more likely to produce a "self-directed, congruent, healthy individual" (Glover & Landreth, 2016, p. 95).

View of Change

CCPT regards therapeutic change as coming from within the child once the environment is one of safety and that those who have a relationship with the child communicate messages of empathy, compassion, and acceptance. Therefore, the play therapist creates a warm and accepting environment, complete with empathy and understanding. CCPT is child-directed, with the child free to explore and learn without judgment or questioning from the play therapist so that the child may engage in free play. This engagement in free play with an affirming therapist is where emotional, cognitive, and relational growth occurs, result-

ing in the child engaging in self-evaluation and, eventually, self-directing toward new ways of thinking and behaving. Ultimately, the child's self-acceptance translates into self-confidence that results in overcoming challenges and adapting across every part of the child's life, such as home, school, or other social situations; the child reaches developmental milestones and has a "positive quality of life" (Glover & Landreth, 2016, p. 95).

Therapeutic Powers of Play and Therapist Skills. Embedded within the change process of CCPT are the therapeutic powers of play and the play therapist's strategic skills, which are the ingredients that create the environment necessary for growth and insight to occur. Twenty therapeutic powers of play currently exist and span four major areas in which play "initiates, facilitates, or strengthens their therapeutic effect" (Drewes & Schaefer, 2016, p. 38). These four areas are facilitating communication, fostering emotional wellness, enhancing social relationships, and increasing personal strengths. While an in-depth analysis of these therapeutic powers is beyond the scope of this chapter, it is worthy to note some specific powers of play, such as self-regulation, empathy, access to the unconscious, and resiliency. It is important to note that CCPT does not see play as an adjunct to the therapeutic process but rather as the most important and powerful element of the therapeutic process, from which all growth and coping skills emerge.

The play therapist's strategic skills are useful in creating a warm and accepting relationship with the child and encouraging the child to engage in free play to achieve therapeutic outcomes. One of the strategies employed in CCPT is tracking, which involves verbally stating what the child is doing out loud. This lets the child know they are seen and noticed (e.g., "Now you are building a house with the Lincoln Logs."). Reflection of feelings is another important strategy that helps the child feel validated and increases self-knowledge (e.g., "When the blocks fell, you felt frustrated, but you figured out how to stack

them; now you are glad that you got them to stay."). Reflection of content lets the child know that the play therapist perceives what is happening (e.g., "You are very angry with your mom right now.") as well as facilitates creativity (e.g., "You can build with the LEGO however you want.") and facilitates decision-making (e.g., "You get to decide where you want the minifigures to go."). A strategy employed for self-worth and self-acceptance is encouraging the child (e.g., "You worked really hard to get that to open."), while fostering the relationship is done through acknowledging the child's behavior toward the play therapist (e.g., "You want to make sure that I'm a safe person."). Limit setting is also included in CCPT to let the child know what is and is not acceptable (e.g., "The sand isn't for throwing.") and provides alternatives when the child wants to do something not allowed in the playroom. Limit setting creates important boundaries for the child, protects the therapeutic alliance, and creates the opportunity for the play therapist to provide alternatives with empathy.

Christian Integration Perspective

Other chapters of this book explain how integrating scripture with a counseling approach provides a powerful foundation for change and growth. Similarly, this author ascribes to the Integrative/Allies model (Entwistle, 2015), which demonstrates working within both aspects of faith and science that provide a foundation for theory and practice. For example, there is much to support the importance of

© Rachata Sinthopachakul/shutterstock.com

children in both God's view as well as directly from the words and example of Christ. God is a "father to the fatherless" (*New International Bible*, 1978/2011, Psalm 68:5) and compares His love for His people to a mother's love for her child (Isaiah 66:13). Scripture makes several references to the importance of parents' teaching, love, and guidance for their children (Isaiah 54:13; Proverbs 1:8-9; 22:6). Jesus modeled and taught the importance of loving children and emphasized protection and valuing when "He said to them, 'Let the little children come unto Me' ... And He took the little children into His arms, placed His hands on them, and blessed them" (Mark 10:13-16). Jesus specifically emphasized valuing and respecting children, even to the point of comparing the heart of a child with entering Heaven (Matthew 19:14), and he associates the welcoming of a child with welcoming Christ Himself (Matthew 18:2-6). Jesus also teaches that children occupy a special place in the spiritual realm when He stated, "See that you do not despise one of these little ones. For I tell you that their angels in Heaven always see the face of my Father in heaven" (Matthew 18:10). Scripture repeatedly compares believers to children and emphasizes God's caring for us through His Spirit as the ultimate comfort and hope (Romans 8:16).

A Case Study: Michael

Michael is an 8-year-old African American male in the second grade referred for play therapy due to impulse control problems and abandonment issues due to an absent father. The play therapist, Stephen, met with Michael's mother at the first session to gather history and background information and to provide her with resources related to the issues that were happening at home. Michael's mother reports that the onset of these problems began at the beginning of first grade. She reports that Michael is angry and acts out at school and home, is tearful and lethargic at times, and has made comments about hurting himself. She states that Michael isolates himself from peers and other family members and appears to be sad most of the time. Michael's mother reports that Michael likes sports, playing outdoors, and video games. She states she punishes Michael for misbehaving at school and takes away his outside play time, sports, and video games, hoping to motivate him to change, but it seems to make things worse.

Michael's mother reports no developmental delays or conditions and that he is in overall good health. Michael's mother reports being a Christian. She and Michael attend church regularly, and he enjoys Sunday school and learning about the Bible. She says that Michael's father abandoned the family when Michael was just an infant. However, in the last year and a half, Michael has become aware of his father's absence and has been vocal about feeling "different" due to his father not being in his life.

Applying the B-Well Model Using Child-Centered Play Therapy

In our application of the B-Well model using CCPT, it is important to remember that CCPT is theoretically rooted in person-centered theory and thus is not viewed as a grouping of techniques but rather as an entire therapeutic process. This means that the process of trust, safety, and exploration results in the child being able to heal and grow in a "self-directing" manner. (Landreth, 2012, p. 53). With this in mind, we will examine the facets of the B-Well model through the CCPT lens.

Heart

Michael's heart is hurting. He has voiced sadness and feelings of self-harm, and his anger indicates that he is likely feeling wounded by the absence of his father. Because of the hurt in his heart, he is lashing out at the world around him, which ultimately brings more pain, rejection, and a crashing in on the self. It is likely that Michael is feeling internalized shame resulting in self-rejection, which, in turn, drives his feelings of anger.

Mind

Michael's mind is consumed with thoughts of his father's absence, and at this developmental stage, he does not have the capacity to process the thoughts related to his experience of loss and pain. The inability to make sense of this loss leaves Michael at the mercy of his emotions, resulting in his acting out at school and isolating behavior at home.

Strength

Michael likes to play video games, is involved in sports, and likes being outside. He is physically healthy overall, and while he is struggling in school currently, he is still willing to go. He enjoys church and Sunday school and continues to want to learn new things. It is evident that while he is suffering, he continues to have at least some interest and motivation to keep going.

Soul

Regarding Michael and the Soul aspect, we see that his mother has raised him to attend church and that he likes learning about God. She specifically stated that Sunday school is one of Michael's favorite parts of church, and he has not wanted to stop attending despite his recent struggles. As previously stated, Michael comes from a Christian background, and his mother is raising him through Christian principles and values. One of Michael's main struggles is his awareness of his absent father and the emotions that come from feeling abandoned and lost at this stage of development. Being in church and having his soul nourished with the knowledge that God is Michael's heavenly father provides a sense of stability. Thus, Michael works through the pain of acceptance regarding the reality of his earthly father's absence while self-development continues in a normal and progressive manner.

 ## Neighbor

Michael struggles in social situations and has been lashing out at classmates in school. This represents an outward direction of energy based on his lack of ability to process the intense emotions of grief related to his realization of the absence of his father.

 ## Society

From a cultural lens, it is important to examine further the impact of being an African American male and the societal norms around being "abandoned" by a father. There is a stereotype that African American fathers are usually absent. How does this mythos indirectly influence Michael's view of self, others, and the world? Does it indirectly influence his acting out and isolating behaviors? There are also potential resources within the Society facet that can help Michael, such as school personnel and community supports, once his view shifts from potential threat to supportive and nurturing.

B-Well Treatment Plan

The focus of CCPT is on the development of the child (self, person) rather than focusing on the elimination of the problem. Strengthening the child's sense of self through self-confidence and self-acceptance promotes the child's ability to solve problems and become a self-advocate while also promoting the ability of the child to communicate and reach out to trustworthy caregivers. This results in the child being socially healthy. Glover and Landreth (2016, p. 105) state the following broad treatment goals for CCPT:

- Develop a more positive self-concept;
- Assume greater self-responsibility;
- Become more self-directing;
- Become more self-accepting;
- Become more self-reliant;
- Engage in self-determining decision-making;
- Experience a feeling of control;
- Become sensitive to the process of coping;
- Develop an internal source of evaluation; and
- Become more trusting of self.

We can see that all these apply to the case of Michael and that through the course of CCPT sessions, all of these were developed or manifested during treatment.

Application

Stephen will observe Michael through the lens of the B-Well model and bear in mind all of the components, including the Soul component. However, in keeping with the principles of CCPT, Stephen will not influence Michael in any way with questions or leading statements that might influence Michael's exploration and play. Instead, he will reflect themes in Michael's play that align with the Christian teachings and Bible stories with which Michael is likely to be familiar. For example, when Michael was playing out the theme of abandonment with the LEGO minifigures, Stephen reflected that it looked like the group of people were without their leader and were angry because they were all alone. Michael nodded and added, "Just like the people of Israel got scared when Moses went away on the mountain," while moving to a large mound he created earlier in the sandbox. He moved some of the minifigures to the bottom of the mound, stating, "We're scared; oh no!" Stephen reflected, "They were scared because Moses didn't seem like he was coming back." Michael replied, "Yeah, but God told them He wasn't going to leave them alone, even if it felt like He wasn't there." Stephen reflected, "So even when it feels like we're alone, we're really not because God promises to always be with us," and Michael nodded in agreement. This exchange demonstrates Michael leading the play with a familiar Bible story that obviously brings him some sense of comfort through playing it out, helps him make sense of his own feeling alone, and shows how play can be self-nurturing and self-comforting. Stephen's reflections simply expand the ideas that Michael has played out and provide affirmation of understanding of Michael's thoughts and feelings.

The playroom was designed in the typical CCPT style, complete with toys that allowed for expression, interaction, soothing, and imaginative/creative activity. For a complete review of a typical setup and toys for the CCPT approach, please see Glover & Landreth (2016, p. 101-103). The course of treatment was designed for 16 sessions, with one session per week. At the first play session, Michael was hesitant upon entering the playroom; however, rapport with Stephen was quickly established, and upon seeing the toys, Michael appeared comfortable. Michael initially gravitated to LEGO and LEGO minifigures in particular, as well as anything related to superheroes. For example, he found an Ironman minifigure and kept it with him during the entire first session. It turned out to be a constant throughout the play therapy sessions, and Michael used the figure in most of his play each week.

© NOTE OMG/shutterstock.com

To assess progress, four markers were used in the format addressed by Josefi & Ryan (2004, pp. 537-538):

1. *Attachment:* How would Michael connect and bond with the play therapist, and would the relationship improve through increased interest sharing as the course of treatment continued?
2. *Autonomy:* How would Michael demonstrate self-initiated choices, behaviors, and mastery over the toys and activities in the playroom?
3. *Symbolic play development:* How would Michael's play display enjoyment as well as the emergence of social play evolving out of solitary play?
4. *Nurturing:* How would Michael demonstrate self-nurturing behaviors, and would there be evidence of symbolic play involving nurturing themes?

The theme of abandonment quickly emerged as Michael played out a scene with the LEGO minifigures in which the leader of the group (Captain America) simply disappeared with no reason or explanation. Stephen tracked this with a reflective statement, "He is gone now, and the others don't know where he is." Upon saying this, Stephen received eye contact and a head nod from Michael. Michael played out many abandonment scenarios throughout treatment, often by burying the significant figure of his story in the sandbox. The theme of anger also surfaced soon after the initial scenario of abandonment, in which Michael had the Ironman minifigure destroy the house made of LEGO upon Captain America's abandonment of the group. Stephen reflected to Michael, "It feels scary when someone leaves

us alone, and we don't know where they are." Anger was also expressed when Michael had some of the minifigures fight with each other. Each time, the Ironman minifigure, with whom Michael identified the most, was always the winner. Each time Michael displayed anger, the play therapist reflected on it. Over the course of treatment, Michael's play went from a solitary nature to involving Stephen in the play, telling him what parts to play or asking Stephen to help build a structure. Most of Michael's play involved LEGO and the minifigures, but he also used the sandbox in which he set up and played out many battles.

At the latter end of treatment, Michael used the markers and drawing paper and spent the last two sessions drawing out scenes from his favorite movies, school events such as spending time with friends, and family scenarios.

Overall, the outcome of CCPT with Michael was successful. Regarding the four themes mentioned above, Michael showed the ability for attachment and connected with the therapist, as evidenced by his moving from solitary play to inviting Stephen into his play. Michael demonstrated autonomy in his play, moving confidently in the playroom and adopting a directive, masterful style in choosing toys and creating stories through his play. Michael showed evidence of symbolic play development through his body language of joy when he played and emotional expression through scenarios in which he expressed anger, satisfaction, and sadness. Michael expressed his anger about his father's abandonment and not being present through the symbolic representation of certain powerful characters disappearing and then destroying something or leaving a scene where play had occurred with objects strewn about in a chaotic manner. Play allowed Michael to look at this horrific experience and all the complicated facets at a safe, controlled distance where he was in control of the pace and level of intensity. When emotions surfaced, the playroom was a sanctuary of self-expression, and Michael was free to express those physically and symbolically. All the while, Stephen affirmed his value and worth through an honoring and accepting presence.

Regarding the nurturing element, Michael demonstrated self-nurturing through the strength of self that emerged in later sessions where his specified character (Ironman) recovered from being abandoned and helped others in need. At one key moment, while playing out a battle scene, Michael commented as Ironman swooped in to aid the helpless victims, "I'm here now, and I'm not going to leave until you guys are okay!" In later sessions, Michael also drew himself at school and home, where he was a protector and helper. He told Stephen that he was like Ironman and that he could help others who were not doing very well. Michael's mother reported that Michael's behavior at school and home improved and that he no longer made comments about hurting himself. His grades went up, and his teacher noted his increased ability to concentrate and that Michael resumed his helpful and happy attitude. Michael's mother reported that when Michael did need correction, he responded appropriately, made an apology, and accepted his consequence.

TABLE 1 Recommended Goals, Objectives, and Interventions

Problem	Goal	Objective	Intervention
Impulse control problems that result in getting in trouble at school and missing out on activities he loves, such as outside play, sports, and video games [Strength]	Michael will assume greater responsibility and become more self-directing.	Autonomy development and Nurturing	Non-directive play with affirming, empathic responses from the play therapist, allowing Michael to express his energy within the limits of the playroom
Father's absence and feelings of abandonment [Heart, Mind]	Michael will become more self-reliant and become more trusting of self.	Attachment and Nurturing	Non-directive play with affirming, empathic responses from the play therapist while Michael is free to create and express himself through play
Feelings of sadness [Heart]	Michael will develop a more positive self-concept and develop an internal source of evaluation.	Autonomy	Non-directive, exploratory play with the freedom to express his thoughts and feelings
Anger/Lashing out at others [Heart, Neighbor]	Michael will engage in self-determining decision-making and become more self-directing.	Autonomy and Symbolic play development	Non-directive play with affirming, empathic responses from the play therapist, providing Michael with a reference point of an accepting relationship as he works to accept himself

Summary

This chapter demonstrates the application of the B-Well model to CCPT. Due to the theoretical components of CCPT, this chapter described modifications that can be made to apply the B-Well model through the lens of CCPT. While this chapter serves as a guide, it should be remembered that CCPT is a "complete therapeutic system" (Glover & Landreth, 2016, p. 96). It is not focused on a regimen of techniques. Instead, CCPT rests on the bedrock of play as the catalyst for insight and healing, coupled with an atmosphere of safety and affirmation from the play therapist. The B-Well model, with its many facets, is an appropriate fit with CCPT and, as demonstrated through the case of Michael, proved to be an all-encompassing approach that yielded growth and healing.

References

Bratton, S. C., Ray, D. C., Edwards, N. A., & Landreth, G. (2009). Child-centered play therapy (CCPT): Theory, research, and practice / kindzentrierte spieltherapie (CCPT): Theorie, forschung, praxis / terapia de juego centrada en el niño (TJCN): Teoría, investigación y práctica / la thérapie par le jeu centrée sur l'enfant: Théorie, recherche et pratique / ludoterapia centrada na criança (LTCC): Teoria, investigação e prática. *Person-Centered & Experiential Psychotherapies, 8*(4), 266-281. https://doi.org/10.1080/14779757.2009.9688493

Drewes, A. A., & Schaefer, C. E. (2016). The therapeutic powers of play. In K. J. O'Conner, C. Schaefer, & L. D. Braverman (Eds.), *Handbook of play therapy* (2nd ed., pp. 35-60). John Wiley and Sons.

Entwistle, D. (2015). *Integrative approaches to psychology and Christianity* (3rd ed.). Cascade Books.

Glover, G., & Landreth, G. (2016). Child centered play therapy. In K. J. O'Conner, C. Schaefer, & L. D. Braverman (Eds.), *Handbook of play therapy* (2nd ed., pp. 93-118). John Wiley and Sons.

Hull, K. (2009). *Computer/video games as a play therapy tool in reducing emotional disturbances in children* (Publication no. 3380362) [Doctoral dissertation, Liberty University]. ProQuest Dissertations & Theses Global. (305247135). http://ezproxy.liberty.edu/login?qurl=https%3A%2F%2Fwww.proquest.com%2Fdissertations-theses%2Fcomputer-video-games-as-play-therapy-tool%2Fdocview%2F305247135%2Fse-2%3Faccountid%3D12085

Hull, K. (2015). Play therapy with children on the autism spectrum. In D. A. Crenshaw, & A. L. Stewart (Eds.), *Play therapy: A comprehensive guide to theory and practice* (pp. 400-414). Guilford.

Josefi, O., & Ryan, V. (2004). Non-directive play therapy for young children with autism: A case study. *Clinical Child Psychology and Psychiatry, 9*(4), 533-551. https://doi.org/10.1177/1359104504046158

Landreth, G. L. (2012). *Play therapy: The art of the relationship* (3rd ed.). Taylor and Francis.

New International Bible. (2011). The NIV Bible. https://www.thenivbible.com (Original work published 1978)

New Revised Standard Version. (2021). Division of Christian Education of the National Council of the Churches of Christ in the USA. (Original work published 1989)

Ray, D. (2008). Impact of play therapy on parent-child relationship stress at a mental health training setting. *British Journal of Guidance & Counselling, 36*(2), 165-187. https://doi.org/10.1080/03069880801926434

B-Well Model, Reminiscence Therapy, and Counseling People with Neurocognitive Disorders

CHAPTER 20

Stephanie JW Ford

> *This chapter is written in the loving memory of my mother, Audrey ML Walton.*
>
> "May the God of hope fill you with joy and peace as you trust in him, so that you may overflow with hope by the power of the Holy Spirit."
>
> — Romans 15:13 (NIV)

The Alzheimer's Association (2022) reports that 6.5 million individuals in the United States of America are living with Alzheimer's Disease (AD). The organization provides yearly reports on the impact of AD on individuals, families/caregivers, and communities. According to the Alzheimer's Association, 13 million individuals will be diagnosed and live with AD by 2050. Mental health professionals and those entering the profession must obtain the skills and knowledge to support individuals diagnosed with AD and their caregivers. The

© Pintau Studio/shutterstock.com

B-Well model provides a framework to integrate Christianity along with the use of Reminiscence Therapy (RT), an evidence-based practice to treat and support individuals diagnosed with AD. The remaining content of this chapter will aid individuals with understanding how to integrate spirituality in counseling by pairing the B-Well model with RT to illustrate how individuals can serve and support people who desire a joyful and abundant life while living with AD.

Background of Reminiscence Therapy (RT)

Origins

Reminiscence in late adulthood has been considered in the following ways: beyond a person's control, unsolicited, pleasurable, aimless, and inquisitiveness of the mind (Westerholf & Bolhmeifer, 2014). Purposive reminiscence is interpreted as helping an individual fill a void in later life and assists with understanding their lived experiences (Butler, 1963). In his writing, Butler acknowledged

Aristotle's comment about people living by memory rather than by hope because the future of life is little compared to one's long past. He believed people reflect on their lived experiences and enjoy sharing allegories of the past. Subsequently, Butler created a construct known as the "life review" to aid with purposive reminiscence.

Butler (1963) published his seminal article about the life review and the benefits of reminiscence in late adulthood. He distinguished reminiscence from solely being about an individual's personal memories. More fully, it is the ability of one to recollect memories to review experiences and beliefs in one's life while evaluating life's events and conflicts (Westerhof & Bohlmeijer, 2014). A life review is a naturally occurring process. Humans return to consciousness, past experiences, and unresolved conflicts to review and reintegrate (Butler, 1963). He noted this process occurs as one approaches terminations and closures. Butler explained life reviews as occurring as one approaches death and when individuals realize their vulnerability, and it is marked by synchronous experiences.

In reminiscence therapy, the life review is a complex process with three broad functions (Westerhof & Bohlmeijer, 2014). The social function focuses on sharing personal memories to foster bonds between people. The instrumental function is the recollection of earlier coping strategies to assist with managing current challenges. Lastly, integrative functions allow people to reflect on the past to aid with being flexible and adjusting one's identity. The outcomes of lived experiences are often associated with an individual's self-identification of their lifelong character.

© absolut/shutterstock.com

View of Human Nature

The key tenant of reminiscence therapy is that people reflect on their lives. The ability to be reflective is a person's process of looking forward toward death, allowing one the potential to proceed toward personality reorganization (Butler, 1963). Researchers later found that people can engage in reminiscence throughout the lifespan (Westerhof & Bohlmeijer, 2014). Humans use past experiences and thoughts to aid with managing current experiences, thoughts, and interpersonal relationships while striving for self-identified wellness.

View of Change

The life review is a universal and normative process (Butler, 1963). The process may have varied manifestations and outcomes. As individuals reflect on their lives, people remember the significance of life events and their thoughts. With the life review process, people can reintegrate and reorganize their events as well as thoughts into various levels of their awareness. People can process their thoughts and their life events to identify meaning, how their character is developing, and how to continue to live a life aligned with their desires and goals (Redulla, 2020).

Reminiscence aids with clinical change by allowing people to share their personal memories and to teach and inform others about past experiences (Westerhof & Bohlmeijer, 2014). While individuals are sharing their memories, the process allows a person to recall coping strategies used in the past and how one may apply successful strategies to current problems as well as lived experiences. Reminiscence therapy allows grants individuals the opportunity to remember previous relationships and reflect on implement effective coping strategies. Previous interpersonal relationships can be used to identify symbolic bonds. Reflecting on symbolic bonds aids people with the identification of healthy interpersonal relationships, which can assist with current interpersonal relationships. The identification of effective coping strategies and symbolic bonds aids individuals with the regulation of emotions. It is essential for clinicians to be aware of the client's overreliance on past coping strategies and previous symbolic bonds because this can be maladaptive if they are trying to avoid current lived experiences.

Reminiscence therapy and autobiographical memories have been identified as key developmental skills across the lifespan (Westerhof & Bohlmeijer, 2014). Autobiographical memories contain a person's recall of significant events in their life. In reminiscence therapy, autobiographical memories are retrieved when people share memories that were significant to them throughout the course of their lives. Recalling autobiographical memories in remi-

niscence therapy allows a person to create meaning and understanding of significant events in one's life, which can assist with wellness and clinical change.

Christian Integration Perspective

In the case study presented below, Kalida uses Entwistle's (2015) Allies model when working with Nicole. The Allies model embraces psychology as God-given and integrates Christianity with psychological research and interventions. The Allies model allows Kalida to integrate Christianity into therapy if the client chooses. Using the B-Well model, evidence-based practices, and interventions, Kalida will gain insights into Nicole's intrapersonal processes, relationships, physical and emotional health, and work experiences using reminiscence therapy and the B-Well model. The Allies model is a framework for understanding how counseling and Christianity can be integrated. The B-Well model allows Kalida to operationalize the Allies model in the therapeutic process.

A Case Study: Nicole

Nicole has been an active member of her city since she moved to the community at age 32 with her family of three, including her husband, Gregg, and her daughter, Celia Beth. Nicole and Gregg decided to leave one of the largest cities in the U.S. to return to a smaller Midwestern city to be closer to their families, as they wanted Celia Beth to have close relationships with her extended family. Gregg and Nicole planned to use their knowledge and skills to create programs to assist individuals in late adolescence and early adulthood who were reared in foster care. These programs assist with enrollment in

vocational and academic post-secondary educational training. Through the programs participants are prepared to enter the workforce and supported while learning how to live independently.

Nicole is currently 63, and has recently been diagnosed with neurocognitive disorder due to Alzheimer's disease, mild. Nicole has already begun to reduce her involvement with family and community activities. Nicole thought her work and community involvement needed to decrease because she would forget important dates and information she had recently learned. These were new behaviors because she was often described as "having the memory of an elephant" and was a walking, talking, living calendar of events for her family (immediate and extended). Gregg (64) recalled a recent situation where she kept asking for the new garage code because she was unable to recall it when she had to use a ride-share service for a week while her car was being repaired.

While being assessed for the changes in her behavior, Nicole reported that she often had to retrace her steps because she would misplace items. Nicole shared, "I was often misplacing things. This was not uncommon for me because I occasionally misplace my car keys; however, misplacing things became a regular part of my daily activities. I would also find myself at a loss for words or searching to try to recall the word I wanted to say when interacting with others at work." She also reported noticing differences in her vision, particularly depth perception, when working in her flower and vegetable gardens (her favorite self and soul care activity). Due to the frequency of these behaviors, her mood became melancholy. Gregg and Nicole spoke with Celia Beth (32) and their parents, informing the family that Nicole would schedule an appointment with her physician for assistance.

Her extended family, which includes her parents in their mid-80s and her siblings, have no known medical conditions. She has a paternal aunt with high cholesterol, a maternal uncle with diabetes, and her paternal grandfather (currently 90 years old) was diagnosed with neurocognitive disorder due to Alzheimer's disease, moderate, at age 87.

Nicole's physician referred her to the local hospital for testing and additional assessments. With care and empathy, Nicole was informed that she has neurocognitive disorder due to Alzheimer's disease, mild. Nicole and her family went to the city where they previously lived for a second opinion, and the results were the same.

With the support of their large African American family, the congregation at Heights United Church of Christ, and the love from friends and colleagues, Nicole and Gregg have decided she will live her best life and incorporate all of the necessary mental and physical health practices to ensure she has quality of life while living with a neurocognitive disorder. Nicole has decided to attend individual counseling to aid with her wellness plan for optimal living.

Applying the B-Well Model Using Reminiscence Theory

The B-Well model is incorporated with RT because it is grounded in humans' innate ability (based upon God's creation) for people to have interconnectedness with one another. Kalida, the therapist, used the B-Well heuristic for treatment planning to aid Nicole with incorporating her Christian faith in the case conceptualization and treatment planning to create the wellness she desired. Provided are examples of how the B-Well model can be used in counseling individuals diagnosed with neurocognitive disorder due to Alzheimer's disease.

Heart

According to the B-Well model, the heart is where the client's emotions are housed. Nicole shared that her emotions ranged from sadness and to feeling depressed when she received her AD diagnosis. Now she describes herself as feeling peaceful. A major tenant of RT is the reviewing of one's past. An individual's past has an adaptive role when conceptualizing and accepting the finality of one's life (Butler, 1963). Kalida will use this key concept in RT and combine this with the B-Well model's heart facet.

While conceptualizing Nicole's case, Kalida is mindful that one of Nicole's strengths is her willingness to be actively involved in the therapeutic process. An aspect of Kalida's case conceptualization of Nicole includes continuously assessing Nicole's mood as she learns more about AD and lives with the disease. Kalida has Nicole focus on managing her emotions as she is accepting the diagnosis, engaging in emotional regulation, and processing her feelings regarding the disease in sessions and with her family.

Mind

The B-Well model recognizes the Mind facet as the seat of cognitions and the role of one's thoughts on the self, others, and the world. Nicole acknowledges she may currently have challenges with her short-term memory and confusion (e.g., loss of words, misplacing items). Kalida is conceptualizing how Nicole's short-term memory impacts her perceptions of herself, others, and the world in which she currently resides while living with AD.

Strength

In the B-Well model, the Strength facet includes the client's physical, physiological, and behavioral aspects. Kalida understands the salience of physical health on mental health, especially for clients with chronic health conditions or diseases. Kalida is aware of the threat to Nicole's vision, as well as other potential future physical concerns to monitor and adapt to, such as loss of balance, difficulty walking, fatigue, sleep disturbances, and bladder/bowel impacts.

Nicole reports eating a well-balanced diet as recommended by her nutritionist, checking her physical activities off the list daily, and engaging in her heart, mind, and soul check-ins daily to create a life of optimal health. Kalida recognizes the importance of physical health in Nicole's life. After completing her intake assessment, she recognizes acknowledges that being physically healthy has been a priority for Nicole since she was in the late stages of emerging adulthood.

Soul

The B-Well model describes the Soul facet as a place of connection between the physical and spiritual world. While Kalida has been working with Nicole, she is aware that Nicole's relationship with God positively influences her life, despite the obstacles and hardships she has faced in her lifetime. Kalida acknowledges that Nicole's relationship with God and her faith are protective factors that increase her resilience while living with AD. Using RT, Kalida is aware that Nicole's spirituality is applied daily to all her lived experiences and that Nicole has learned to rely on God. Nicole disclosed that she understood at an early age that one would have troubles in this life due to the fallen world in which we live. She also learned at an early age to expect the unexpected and to never stop having joy, no matter how hard life becomes. An example of a time in her life when she wrestled with the hardships of life and learned to have joy, these concepts to learn these lessons occurred when she was an adolescent. One of her close female friends was abducted at age 16, and her disappearance remains unsolved. At 17 years old, Nicole memorized John 16:33 "I have told you these things, so that in me you may have peace. In this world you will have trouble. But take heart! I have overcome the world."

As Kalida evaluates the positive variables and barriers to treatment, she notes Nicole's ability to recall God's Word and her reliance on one of her favorite sections of the Holy Bible, the fruit of the Spirit (*New International Bible*, 1978/2011, Galatians 5:22-23), are incorporated into Nicole's life daily. Kalida is aware of her ability to apply the fruit of the Spirit to aid Nicole with recalling God's compassion and unfailing love toward her throughout the treatment process. Kalida recognizes that Nicole has identified soul care and her time with the Lord as her sustaining force; therefore, Kalida will incorporate this into the treatment plan.

Neighbor

The B-Well model's concept of Neighbor addresses how individuals engage, connect, and relate to others. The focus is on the interpersonal process. Historically, Nicole has had healthy relationships. She shares stories of challenges in some interpersonal relationships in her youth and young adulthood. However, she does not currently have challenges like she had in the past.

Her primary trepidation is her relationship with her immediate family. She is concerned that she may forget her husband, daughter, and grandbabies. She loves the life she has created with Gregg and her family, and she does not want to be a burden to him if her health worsens. She has also decreased her involvement in her community due to her cognitive impairment (Mind). This illustrates how her Mind is influencing her social ties and the risk of further disconnection in the short and long term.

Society

Society is the concept in the B-Well model that clinicians use to explore indirect, contextual factors that are resources and threats in prevention and recovery. This facet addresses circumstances and events on society's local, state, regional, and national levels, which indirectly impact clinical outcomes. The B-Well model describes Society as the contextual factors that influence the client, which includes the indirect impact of discrimination based on age, race, ethnicity, gender, etc., that influence the other facets in addition to problems and assets.

Kalida is mindful of the perceptions of African American women in the United States. In keeping with the B-Well model, the Society facet applies to Kalida's conceptualization of Nicole's case by understanding societal circumstances and how Nicole is and may be indirectly impacted by gender, sex, race, and ethnicity. Nicole has shared with Kalida the unique and challenging circumstances she has faced as an African American woman. Her awareness of her physical appearance, size, and stereotypes like (i.e., Mammy, Jezebel, Sapphire, and Strong Black Woman (West, 1995), along with discriminative practices she has faced in the workplace or while shopping in a store (i.e., being followed by the salesperson), have shaped her perceptions of what it means to be Black in this country.

B-Well Treatment Plan

Nicole's treatment plan includes goals, objectives, and interventions to aid her with fulfilling her desire to be well, including accepting her diagnosis, learning how to live with AD, maintaining and cultivating healthy relationships, and being a supporting member of her community. Nicole's therapeutic goals align with the B-Well model. Kalida has identified how Nicole's treatment plan will incorporate the B-Well model and RT.

Heart

While conceptualizing Nicole's case, Kalida is mindful of the shift in emotional responses that happens when clients with AD forget their diagnosis and experience memory loss and confusion. Kalida is using RT to facilitate Nicole's life review and will identify events (data) from her past to demonstrate how Nicole is/was able to adapt to stressors previously and apply these strategies to her acceptance of AD and the finality of her life (Butler, 1963).

Nicole's childhood experiences with a food allergy taught her not to be afraid to let people know of her health condition and how to manage her emotions when she feared certain foods making her ill and/or being life-threatening. At a young age, Nicole realized this was a little different than most of her peers, but it was okay. She also learned how to use her decision-making skills to maintain her health and well-being.

Currently, she is working with Kalida to identify strategies and interventions from the past and present to address her fears and anxiety when her emotions plague her about her AD or when she forgets something, in addition to working on managing her emotions. Nicole shared stories in counseling about how her emotions did not always allow her to make the best decisions. She once heard Pastor Loritz say, "Emotions make good passengers, but bad drivers." Nicole has decided to focus on having joy and enjoying life as she did in her youth despite her food allergy. Kalida and Nicole are focusing on learning and implementing coping strategies and interventions to have a good quality of life with this disease.

Mind

While working with Nicole to learn about her adaptive strategies used in the past, Kalida becomes aware of other health conditions Nicole has addressed in her lifetime. Kalida is mindful of the times when Nicole recalled personal memories of tenacity, learning to be an advocate for herself, and the challenges she faced as a child and adolescent living with a food allergy during a time when people did not understand food allergies. As a school aged child, she could not benefit from the medications and advancements of health care as it is today. After several sessions of reflecting on her ability to survive amid the daily risk to her health, she was able to identify how she (with her family) developed healthy coping strategies. She learned to have a "voice" to ensure she maintained her health. Nicole is currently managing her thoughts about living with AD by relying on the skills she learned as a child and remembering she still has a "voice." Kalida is also mindful that one of Nicole's strengths is her willingness to be actively involved in the therapeutic process. Kalida will work with Nicole on a continual review of the diagnosis and acceptance of her memory in each phase of the disease. Kalida is aware of the prognosis, and if Nicole begins to have difficulty recalling her past, the two will rely on previously- acquired coping strategies and new ones to support Nicole. One new strategy Nicole is doing with her family is getting involved with their local AD association to increase their knowledge and expand on the resources they currently have to support her.

Strength

Part of Kalida's assessment of Nicole's health includes checking in to ensure she is maintaining her physical health regimen and learning how she sleeping and her eating habits. Kalida receives updates from Nicole Nicole, her family, and during individual and family counseling. her family during individual and family counseling. Kalida has recommended that Nicole use an activities chart to aid her with recording her activities and strength-promoting behaviors. Therefore, Nicole uses her Pleasant and Helpful Physical Activities chart as a part of her treatment plan.

Soul

Kalida acknowledges Nicole's understanding that life is unpredictable. Using RT in treatment has allowed Kalida to discover and process with Nicole her loss of her beloved friend during adolescence as a traumatic life event. This horrific life event will be addressed through the incorporation of the B-Well model's Soul facet. Nicole has been able to have grace for the adults in her life who did not discuss the emotions and hurt people felt when her friend was never found. She knows that when she was a child, people did not discuss the loss of life in childhood and adolescence like people do today. Through the counseling process, the treatment plan will focus on healing from the trauma of this adverse childhood experience, and it will rely on Nicole's relationship with God, her faith, and a strengths-based approach to reframe the tragedy of the loss of her friend as a call to live to the fullest as she has done. The Soul facet of the B-Well model, along with RT, is also used to aid Nicole in applying verses and allegories from the Holy Bible to address what Nicole refers to as her current "pitfall" of living with AD.

The treatment plan will include the RT life review. Specifically, Nicole recalls autobiographical memories of the salience of gardening and how she has used being in the yard—which she expressed through her favorite saying: "working her land"—as a time to be centered, breathe, and reflect on life. She shares how God uses this time to speak to her and gives her magnificent ideas for herself, her family, and her community.

Before concluding one of the sessions, Nicole stated, "I have known since middle school that God had a call on my life. Although there are numerous challenges in our world, personal hardships, and losses, and my health is not what I thought it would be at this age, I stand on Psalm 46:5—'God *is* in the midst of her, she shall not be moved; God shall help her, just at the break of dawn.' I will continue to run my race, like Paul!" Nicole departs every session stating, "It is well with my soul!"

Neighbor

Nicole's treatment plan includes incorporating her interpersonal relationships— her immediate family—as a part of the treatment process. Nicole and Gregg have worked with Kalida to identify prosocial and effective behaviors to support her wellness. While engaging in her daily gardening activities alone, with her family, and/or friends, Nicole enjoys listening to Biblical parables. Nicole loves working in the garden and listening to the allegories Jesus shared about agriculture and scriptures that remind her of God's faithfulness and the need not to be anxious or sad about her and/or her family's future. Nicole has identified Joel 2:23-25 as one of her daily scriptures:

> Be glad, people of Zion, rejoice in the LORD YOUR GOD,
> For he has given you the autumn rains because he is faithful.
> He sends you abundant showers, both autumn and spring rains, as before.
> The threshing floors will be filled with grain; the vats will overflow with new wine and oil.
> I will repay you for the years the locusts have eaten—the great locust and the young locust, the other locusts and the locust swarm—my great army that I sent among you.
> (*New International Bible*, 1978/2011)

Nicole and Gregg are committed to having a healthy marriage and enjoying one another. The two participate in a community health and wellness program, eat a balanced diet, and leave room for a daily dessert because she wants to enjoy the life God has given her. She describes a slice of Tres Leche cake with a seasonal fruit compote as tantalizing to her taste buds. In addition, the two walk three miles per day together and lift weights three times per week. On the weekends, the two swim at the local community center.

Nicole reports enjoying each time of engagement with her family and community members. She continues to volunteer at the local food bank disseminating food and is now serving as a consultant/

volunteer in their adolescent and young adult support program. She is also actively involved with her grandchildren and her daughter's lives. Their families have meals together on Friday evenings and Sundays after church.

Society

Throughout the therapeutic process, Kalida has used RT and the Society facet of the B-Well model to aid Nicole with recalling how societal events and personal experiences have shaped who she is and how she makes meaning of life. Nicole describes being aware of what it means for her to be a member of the Baby Boomer Generation. Her development has been marked by being reared after the U.S. Civil Rights Movement, the Los Angeles race riots when she was in the early middle adulthood phase of life, along with numerous incidents of social and racial injustice (in recent years the death of George Floyd and others). These events have influenced the perceptions and strategies used by herself, family, and community members to have a good quality of life.

In the therapeutic process, Nicole reflects on the hardships people of African descent have faced in the U.S. United States of America (if using an abbreviation, it should be U.S.A.) and her personal lived experiences. Kalida shares data and information from peer-reviewed research on adverse experiences people of color face and their correlation with AD. This validates the impact of lived experiences, and Nicole is motivated to continue to serve her community and have a positive impact, making life better for future generations.

Clinician Insights on the Treatment Process

After completing Nicole's intake assessment, meeting Gregg and Celia Beth. Kalida learned, learning of Nicole's counseling goals, and Kalida explained how she will utilize reminiscence therapy (RT), an evidence-based treatment (Westerhof & Bohlmeijer, 2014), and the B-Well model to support Nicole with the obtainment of her goals. It is important that for Kalida to be cognizant of evaluate how she shares information about the therapeutic process and continuously assess Nicole's ability to recall the parameters around the therapeutic process. Kalida informed Nicole every counseling session may not be easy. However, Kalida reinforced her commitment to be a compassionate, competent, ethical, culturally attentive, and humble counselor throughout their counseling process. Kalida also informed Nicole that sessions may occur outside her office if this is something Nicole desireds. Additionally, there might be sessions when her loved ones—family (Noted as biological relatives and close and friends. The collectivist culture of African Americans defines close friends as family.). The two agreed on the locations where sessions would take place and the involvement of loved ones.

Implementing the B-Well model requires Kalida to be aware of the diverse methods used to practice Christianity. When planning to use the B-Well model, Kalida is aware of her own Christian, Non-Denominational values, belief system, how her understanding of the Holy Bible and religious practices may differ from Nicole's. Kalida is willing to learn how Nicole operationalizes her faith and demonstrates an openness to Nicole's beliefs by allowing her to share her faith, scriptures, and her understanding of Biblical principles. She allows for space in the counseling sessions for Nicole to describe and/or demonstrate various religious practices in which she engages.

Kalida has viewed and listened to several sermons to aid her with understanding Nicole's perspectives and how she practices her religion to assist with the development a therapeutic alliance with Nicole.

Throughout the therapeutic process, Nicole has shared information from several books and various sermons she enjoys on YouTube. Kalida has reviewed and read some of the books. One includes a devotion that the two discuss briefly at the start of each counseling session. Kalida has viewed and listened to several sermons to aid her with understanding Nicole's perspectives and how she practices her

TABLE 1 Recommended Goals, Objectives, and Interventions

Problem	Goal	Objective	Intervention
Lack of understanding of neurocognitive disorder due to Alzheimer's disease	Learn more about Alzheimer's disease.	Objective 1 – The client will commit to learning and implementing a proactive approach to managing the challenges of living with AD (Jogsma et al., 2021). [Mind, Strength] Objective 2 – The client will join the local Alzheimer's Disease Association. [Heart, Mind, Social] Objective 3 – The client will increase her ability to use metacognitive strategies to process her thoughts about living with AD. [Mind] Objective 4 – The client will commit to acknowledging her feelings while living with AD. [Heart]	• Assess the level of insight about the disease. • Provide psychoeducation on neuro-cognitive disorders and Alzheimer's disease. • Use Stress Inoculation Training to help develop knowledge, self-management, and skills to understand and manage AD (Jogsma et al., 2021). • Include family and friends to reinforce social support (Jogsma et al., 2021). • Verbalize acceptance of the medical conditions; explore the client's emotions associated with the diagnosis; and use personal memories to aid with the identification of coping strategies (Jogsma et al., 2021; Westerhof & Bohlmeijer, 2014).
How to maintain and improve her physical fitness level	Engage in recreational activities that are enjoyable and helpful for her medical diagnosis.	Objective 5 – The client will identify and complete activities for physical health to maintain and/or increase her strength. [Strength]	• Schedule and engage in Pleasant and Helpful Physical Activities (Jogsma et al., 2021). • Continue to participate in community activities. • Assess ability to maintain physical and community activities and the need to implement new activities.
Identify methods to improve the quality of interpersonal relationships	Increase the healthy variables in interpersonal relationships.	Objective 6 – The client will strengthen current relationships. [Social] Objective 7 – The client will identify the changing dynamics in relationships, in addition to the challenges and victories in relationships, while living with AD. [Neighbor]	• Strengthen powerful relationship factors, such as empathy and working collaboratively (including engagement in community service activities while continuously adjusting to personal and interpersonal changes while living with AD) (Jogsma et al., 2021).

Problem	Goal	Objective	Intervention
How to maintain spiritual wellbeing while living with a neurocognitive disorder due to Alzheimer's disease	Continue and enhance daily time with the Lord.	Objective 8 – The client will increase knowledge and understanding of God. [Soul] Objective 9 – The client will main and work to increase faith for God to continue to sustain her while living with AD. [Soul]	• Implement daily devotional time with the Lord, which includes reading and/or listening to the Holy Bible and listening to worship music (Jogsma et al., 2021). • Include biblical scriptures (Jogsma et al., 2021) on her notes to maintain her recollection of items and regulate her emotions.

religion and to develop a therapeutic alliance with Nicole. Kalida has also consulted with Reverends Houston and Lassiter, members of the United Church of Christ, to learn how the community aids members who are ill and to obtain additional resources to aid her in supporting people who are members of the United Church of Christ.

According to RT, cultural context has a role in social functions, and there is a stronger social function among members of the African American community (Shellman et al., 2011). African Americans in the United States have a rich oral tradition. Stories have been passed down from generation to generation to main the cultural heritage of families and enslaved Africans; therefore, sharing personal memories is something Nicole may enjoy in the therapeutic process. Kalida aims to learn more in order to gain insight into how Nicole has made meaning of her life and how she addresses conflicts and victories while helping her adjust to living with a neurocognitive disorder. Kalida utilized RT to allow Nicole to share personal memories regarding daily activities, conversations, and to learn about her past as well as current social functions. Nicole used her personal memories to share past experiences and teach the insights she has learned along her life journey thus far. Nicole enjoys sharing her lived experiences and the lessons she has learned, often referring to these experiences as her "pearls of wisdom." Kalida reflects on the time Nicole talked about an instance in her undergraduate studies when she learned about group think and how silence negatively impacted her life. She stressed learning the importance of having a voice and speaking up, especially as an African American woman. Nicole also shared how the undergraduate experience of being silent taught her to speak up for herself and others.

Nicole expressed that she has learned she is powerful because the Holy Spirit lives in her. Nicole shared that she accepted Jesus Christ as her Lord and Savior in childhood and rededicated her life as a sophomore in college. She recalled one of her favorite scriptures, Isaiah 54:17, "'No weapon formed against you shall prosper, and every tongue which rises against you in judgment you shall condemn. This is the heritage of the servants of the LORD, AND THEIR RIGHTEOUSNESS IS FROM ME,' SAYS THE LORD" (*New King James Bible*, 1982). After quoting the verse and telling her narrative, she said: "No weapon formed against me will prosper, not a one! Yes! That's it! Just like I used the Word of God

FOR THE WORD OF GOD IS ALIVE AND ACTIVE

Hebrews 4:12

© Borsuk Renat/shutterstock.com

to help me in tough times, I will not be moved. I am going to keep using them to help me with Alzheimer's disease! I know how to fight my battles with the Word of God. God is faithful!" She chuckled and said, "The Word of God is alive and active; I do not have any problem recalling scriptures I memorized before my memory began to change. When I feel down, I need to recall this because telling you that story gave me a boost in my energy and zeal in my spirit. God has this!" She then sat back in her chair with a bright smile on her face.

The narrative about Nicole's undergraduate experience along with her intrapersonal and interpersonal insights allowed Kalida to learn how Nicole used coping strategies when facing a challenging situation in early adulthood. Reflecting on her undergraduate experience supported Nicole in identifying a healthy coping strategy—reliance on the Word of God. This also helps with emotion regulation because Nicole described her mood changing from being down to experiencing joy and peace.

After identifying strategies together in previous sessions to assist with locating her phone, Kalida proposed how they could work together to create screen savers on her phone to remind her of scriptures that encourage her. These can be used as a coping strategy when she is feeling down. Throughout the therapeutic process, Nicole has shared how colors like yellow, bright pink, and orange bring her joy when she sees them. Since colors are important to Nicole, the two discussed typing scriptures in difference colors and posting them in her home and garden.

Throughout the therapeutic process, Nicole and her family focused on the changes that life is bringing due to her diagnosis. There have been sessions in the family home, in her gardens, and with her parents in a private room at their church. Kalida engages Nicole and her family in meaningful settings that are identified as safe and comforting as a method of providing additional support throughout the therapeutic process.

Kalida's use of the B-Well model and RT creates an opportunity for Nicole to form an identity of living a life of wellness and having meaningful relationships with family as well as friends while living with a neurocognitive disorder due to Alzheimer's disease.

Kalida: A Self-Reflective Scholar-Practitioner

From the start, Kalida is attentive to how the two would interact with one another and others who may be involved in the therapeutic process. Kalida and Nicole are both African American women, Kalida is aware of the similarities and differences of the identities they share regarding race and sex. Kalida is also mindful of generational differences. On occasion, Nicole has stated, "Well in my generation …" and acknowledges her perspectives could be different from Kalida's due to their age difference. Kalida is respectful and open to Nicole's diverse opinions resulting from their generational differences. Often Kalida reflects and processes their interactions in her personal therapy notes to aid her with increasing her awareness of viewing Nicole the way she presents as opposed to adhering to the stereotypical perspective in the U.S. of African American women (West, 1995) in the later stage of middle adulthood.

Initially, Kalida had a heightened awareness of Nicole's age and that she is her elder. Kalida works to ensure that she demonstrates professionalism when implementing basic counseling skills (e.g., eye contact) and advanced counseling skills (e.g., challenging) in a culturally sensitive manner to aid Nicole in perceiving her as respectful and supportive of Nicole's counseling goals. Kalida is committed to being a scholar-practitioner and reviews current research to aid with being an ethical and competent professional. Kalida relies on the counseling skill of immediacy as well as the here-and-now to process their interactions and perceptions as counseling continues to aid Nicole with obtaining her therapeutic goals she desires.

She continuously assesses Nicole. Communicates with her along with her family and physician (releases of information have been signed by Nicole) to determine if modifications may need to occur in the therapeutic process or if strategies in the home need to be altered to ensure effectiveness.

Summary

The B-Well model is a valuable resource alongside the evidence-based interventions clinicians use to support clients with a Christian worldview. This chapter has allowed individuals to examine how the model can be paired with a therapeutic approach, Reminiscence Therapy (RT), to operationalize Entwistle's (2015) Allies model to aid clients with achieving their therapeutic goals and wellness.

The case of Nicole requires one to explore how to infuse each facet of the B-Well model in case conceptualization and treatment planning. This is salient because it allows the mental health professional to integrate the Bible and spiritual disciplines in the treatment plan by assisting professionals with understanding how a Christian worldview is applied to a client's life. With the B-Well model, it is important to collect information on each of the six facets during intake and throughout the counseling process. Gathering data on each facet of the B-Well model aids in obtaining more insights into the thoughts, emotions, interpersonal relationships, and societal variables that impact a client's life. Obtaining this data by using the B-Well model allows one to learn how clients' perceptions of self, others, their environment, and God. As a mental health professional learns more about each domain in a client's life, case conceptualization and treatment plans are created to support the wellness the client desires. The B-Well model, along with evidence-based practices and ethical decision-making, aids mental health professionals in being competent scholar-practitioners.

References

Alzheimer's Association. (2022, May 2). *Research and progress.* https://www.alz.org/alzheimers-dementia/research_progress

Butler, R. N. (1963). The life review: An interpretation of reminiscence in the aged. *Psychiatry, 26*(1), 65–6. https://doi.org/10.1080/00332747.1963.11023339

Entwistle, D. N. (2015). *Integrative approaches to psychology and Christianity: An introduction to worldview issues, philosophical foundations, and models of integration* (3rd ed.). Cascade Books.

Jogsma, A. E., Peterson, L. M., & Bruce, T. J. (2021). *The complete adult psychotherapy treatment planner.* John Wiley & Sons, Inc.

New International Bible. (2011). The NIV Bible. https://www.thenivbible.com (Original work published 1978)

New King James Bible. (1982). Thomas Nelson. https://www.thomasnelsonbibles.com/nkjv-bible/

Redulla, R. (2020). Reminiscence therapy for Dementia. Issues in Mental Health Nursing, 41(3), 265-266. https://doi-org.ezproxy.liberty.edu/10.1080/01612840.2019.1654572

Shellman, J., Everol, E., & Bailey-Addison, K. (2011). A contextual examination of reminiscence functions in older African-Americans. *Journal of Aging Studies, 25*(4), 348-354. https://doi.org/10.1016/j.jaging.2011.01.001

West, C. M. (1995). Mammy, sapphire, and jezebel: Historical images of Black women and implications for psychotherapy. *Psychotherapy, 32*(3), 458-466. https://doi.org/10.1037/0033-3204.32.3.458

Westerhof, G. J., & Bohlmeijer, J. T. (2014). Celebrating fifty years of research and applications in reminiscence and life review: State of the art and directions. *Journal of Aging Studies, 29*, 107–114. https://doi.org/10.1016/j.jaging.2014.02.003

Index